TINY
HOUSE

DESIGNING, BUILDING, & LIVING

GABRIELLA & ANDREW MORRISON

Publisher Mike Sanders
Editorial Assistant Kylie McNutt
Art & Design Director William Thomas
Cover Designer William Thomas
Book Designer Ayanna Lacey
Proofreader Lisa Starnes
Indexer Johnna VanHoose Dinse

First American Edition, 2023
Published in the United States by DK Publishing
6081 E. 82nd Street, Indianapolis, IN 46250

24 25 26 27 10 9 8 7 6 5 4 3 2
002-334200-AUG2023

Published in the United States by Dorling Kindersley Limited.

Library of Congress Catalog Number: 2022950520
ISBN: 978-0-7440-7624-0

DK books are available at special discounts when purchased
in bulk for sales promotions, premiums, fundraising,
or educational use. For details, contact:
SpecialSales@dk.com

Printed and bound in China

Reprinted from *Idiot's Guides®: Tiny House Designing, Building, and Living*

For the curious
www.dk.com

We lovingly and humbly dedicate this book to three exceptional human beings:

Our two children: Paiute and Terra. We don't know too many teenagers who would have been as enthusiastic about shifting into a tiny house lifestyle as you two were. Thank you for your trust and support and for always inspiring us to be the very best versions of ourselves.

Eileen Betty Morrison, who always taught us that in life, the important piece is to be true to oneself. The rest? Well, those are just details ....

Contents

Appendixes

Introduction

The story of small and tiny shelters is as old as mankind. Save for royal and ultra-wealthy families, lives were typically born, lived, and lost within the walls of little, humble abodes for thousands of generations. Isn't it ironic that it's the story of the tiny house that has hit center stage when in fact, it's really the tale of the "modern-day house" that deserves our attention?

Today's *average* American residence is a heavyweight champ scaling in at an unprecedented 2,658 square feet. Never have we seen larger average homes on our soils. In a worldwide competition, we would stand on the gold podium.

But how did we get here? What are the implications? Where do we go from here? And is all this extra square footage making us happier?

The tiny house movement is a diverse collective of people from teenagers to octogenarians, including all walks of life from military personnel, teachers, artists, scientists, professional athletes, musicians, financial investors, and millionaires, to those recently escaping homelessness. Many of us simply grew tired of working hard to pay for a house that was larger than necessary and that we rarely spent time in because we were wasting so many hours commuting and working to pay for it.

We've been living in the tiny lifestyle since 2013 and are happier than ever. All our needs are met, we're out of debt, and our family is thriving. We have been able to live in pop-up tent trailers on white sand beaches, a sailboat, and the tiny house of our dreams, all because of the tiny house movement.

Our new life didn't begin in the blink of an eye though. Instead, it began over the course of a few years. At first, our path rarely seemed clear, but in time, the guideposts became brighter. Our hope is that our experiences help shed light on your own tiny house journey.

We encourage you to take the plunge into your own downsizing, minimalism, and tiny house living adventure. You'll never know what's on the other side unless you dare to begin.

How This Book Is Organized

We've arranged this book in distinct parts to clearly explain all aspects of tiny house living, from downsizing to the installation of the final finish detail:

Part 1, Gearing Up for Tiny House Living, walks you through the essential steps you must take to embrace a tiny house lifestyle. You learn basic definitions and how to prepare for the downsizing process. We cover topics such as insurance, financing, and the ever-changing face of legalities surrounding tiny house living. You learn how to safely tow a tiny house and the details surrounding road restrictions, permit requirements, and route-mapping strategies.

Part 2, Defining Your Style, takes you room by room through a tiny house and addresses important details in each area. We guide you through options for furniture, appliances, layouts, costs, and more. We teach you how to be honest in your assessment of what you *need* versus what you *want*. And where would a tiny house book be without an open conversation about toilets? Don't worry, we cover that, too.

Part 3, Custom Designing Your Tiny House, takes you into the process of tiny house design, whether you want to do it yourself, hire it out, or buy an existing set of plans. You learn what foundation option is best for your situation, as well as how to ensure that engineering principles keep the structure safe, especially while being towed. Lastly, we cover how to read construction drawings like a pro and get you on the path toward building the very best tiny house possible.

Part 4, Building Your Tiny House, covers the nitty-gritty of the construction process. We show you how to find a great builder, how to work with subcontractors, and how to be your own general contractor. We cover the best tools for tiny house construction and how to acquire them without breaking the bank. We teach you how to anchor your house to a trailer; how to frame floors, walls, and the roof; how to install windows and doors; and how to add all the finishing touches for a beautiful end result. We talk about utility installations, loft access options, and ventilation. Lastly, we cover living off-grid, how to create a tiny house–appropriate solar system, and how to bring water to your little abode.

The appendixes provide a glossary of terms as well as a list of resources that will help guide you through your own tiny housing evolution. By the time you're done with this book, you'll have a comprehensive understanding of all things related to tiny house living and construction. Enjoy!

Acknowledgments

"No man is an island, entire of itself; every man is a piece of the continent."
—John Donne (1624)

The tiny house movement would be a mere shadow of itself were it not for the tireless efforts invested by early pioneers. Though many helped pave the tiny house road to where it is today, two people, in particular, served as our personal inspirations, and we would like to formally thank them here: Jay Shafer and Kent Griswold.

To all our amazing friends in the tiny house community (you know who you are!), thank you for your courage, your sense of adventure, your care for the environment, and your commitment to joy. You inspire us and make our lives a better and happier place every single day.

A special thanks to Macy Miller for showing us what grace, generosity, and kindness look like … every step of the way.

We are grateful to our fantastic technical editors for reviewing the manuscript: Richard Brundt, Darrell Grenz, and Jeremy Weaver. Special thanks also to Martin Burlingame, Chris Keefe, and the good folks at Recology in the Rogue Valley for their willingness to share their expertise with us.

We are indebted to the contributions and feedback of our talented editors: Terra Morrison, Lucinda Weatherby, and Khaliqa Rogmans. Becky Brown, Maud Powell, Eva LaBonty, Michael Morrison, Penelope Boettiger, and Heather Morrison, your support and encouragement each step of the way served as fuel for those long midnight-oil nights.

This book would not be possible without the help and support of our original acquisitions editor at Alpha Books: Janette Lynn. Thank you for believing in us and for seeing the potential in the tiny house movement.

Last, but certainly not least, we want to personally acknowledge each one of you who's just starting to dip those toes into the tiny house movement. We're thrilled you're taking this step and wish you every success imaginable. We invite you to create the life you've been dreaming of and to jump in with all those toes when the time is right. Come on in, the water's fine!

Stay tiny, friends.

Gabriella and Andrew Morrison

About the Authors

Gabriella Morrison co-designed and co-built hOMe with her husband, Andrew, and has been involved in the construction trades for more than 20 years. She is a professional writer as well as the marketing director for tinyhousebuild.com, strawbale.com, and beyourowncontractortraining.com.

hOMe, along with Andrew and Gabriella's lifestyle, has been the subject of hundreds of articles and news stories around the world and has been featured on or in *World News Tonight with Diane Sawyer*, *The Today Show*, *Forbes*, playboy.com, dailymail.com, FOX News, *YES!* magazine, *House Beautiful*, and more. hOMe was also included in Fine Homebuilding's 2015 Awards Issue, *Houses*, and featured in Fine Homebuilding's *Small Homes* special edition, *The Best of Fine Homebuilding*. The YouTube tour of hOMe is the most watched tiny house video on record. You can visit tinyhousebuild.com to find out more about Andrew and Gabriella's workshops, how to build hOMe, and the tiny house lifestyle.

Andrew Morrison has been a leader within the tiny house movement since he and Gabriella designed and built hOMe—their modern 207-square-foot tiny house on wheels (THOW). They've been living and working in their tiny house full-time, off-grid, and debt-free since 2013.

Andrew has traveled around the world speaking about tiny houses and sharing his knowledge with others. His speaking engagements have included TEDx, USGBC's Greenbuild Expo 2016, the Tiny House Jamboree, the Tiny House Conference, Summit Immobiliario Sao Paulo, Brazil 2016, and more. Andrew is also coauthor of the national tiny house building code Appendix AQ, which provides legal framework for tiny houses.

With more than 20 years of professional construction experience, Andrew is the construction expert at tinyhousebuild.com, beyourowncontractortraining.com, and strawbale.com. Since 2006, he has taught more than 3,000 students at his workshops focusing on tiny house construction and straw bale construction.

Gearing Up for Tiny House Living

There's no question that our current housing trends aren't sustainable when it comes to affordability and environmental friendliness. Fortunately, a major shift away from the McMansion has begun, and a new kid has appeared on the block: the tiny house. Simply efficient, exquisitely designed, and beautifully built, these tiny homes can provide everything necessary for a fulfilling life without the traps that their larger cousins must bear.

In Part 1, we cover the benefits of tiny house living, how to have fun while downsizing, and raising the funds for your build. We also cover all those practical topics, such as insurance, legalities, and towing. Are you ready to get started? If so, let's take the first steps on the tiny house road. It's an amazing adventure, and we're excited to share it with you!

CHAPTER 1

A House with Benefits

If you've been feeling like things are harder than ever, you're certainly not alone. Houses are bigger and more expensive today than they've ever been in the history of this nation. Unfortunately, our household income hasn't kept pace and now is actually lower than it was in 2000.

Home ownership is at a 50-year low, and rental vacancies are so slim that even the dumpiest places are fetching top-shelf prices. It's no wonder that the tiny house movement has exploded with interest. For less than half the cost of the down payment on an average new home, you can build your own beautiful, sustainable, and fully furnished tiny house.

If you're tired, stressed, and frustrated by how unfulfilling your life currently feels, fret not and read on. In this chapter, we will cover the numerous benefits to living tiny, ranging from financial freedom, to improved relationships, quicker cleaning, smaller environmental footprints, increased joy, and much more. An exciting new life could be just a decision away for you!

Financial Freedom

In today's economic market, home ownership has become an increasingly distant dream for many. According to the U.S. Census Bureau, the average-size new house in the United States will set you back a record high of $360,000. In comparison, that same house in 2000 would have cost $200,000, reflecting a whopping $160,000 increase in just 16 years.

The housing market hasn't been kind to American home renters either. In 2000, a median rental went for $475 per month according to the U.S. Census Bureau. Today, you'll pay $875 (almost twice the cost) for the same house.

In the meantime, the median household income has actually dropped from $57,000 in 2000 to $54,000 in 2015, according to Federal Reserve Bank of St. Louis (FRED). The disparity between income and housing costs as well as other economic factors are contributing to the rate of homeownership being at a 50-year low.

In comparison, a comfortable, self-built tiny house costs an average of just $23,000, according to a survey conducted by thetinylife.com. We have seen tiny homes completed for as little as $8,000 with the builder using free and reclaimed materials whenever possible. A professionally built tiny house can be fetched for as little as $50,000.

Here's another way to punctuate the dramatic difference in cost between a tiny house and a conventionally sized residence. Using the average new-home cost of $360,000—and assuming you'll have a standard 20 percent down payment due at closing—you'll be staring down the barrel of a $72,000 down payment. Ouch. To add insult to injury, you'll then spend thousands of dollars furnishing and filling all those empty spaces. With a tiny house, though, you can build something wonderful for less than half the cost of that down payment.

We designed and built hOMe, our tiny house on wheels (THOW) in which we happily reside full-time, for just a hair over $33,000. This included all appliances and furnishings. It fulfills all our needs while allowing us to live a lifestyle that is well within our means. Assuming that we live here for the rest of our lives, we will never, ever have another housing payment. The sense of security that this brings is truly priceless.

By now, you might be wondering why we haven't mentioned the cost of land in these equations. After all, if a tiny house is on wheels, it will need a place to be parked. This is a very fair point, and one that must be addressed.

After connecting with hundreds of people who are building and living in their tiny houses, we have found again and again that those in significant financial hardship manage to find a low-cost/free place to park their tiny houses. Often, this is on a friend or family member's property or in a work-trade scenario.

Generally, the most expensive component of housing is the structure itself. While you can certainly buy your own land or pay rent for a place to park your tiny house, you can most likely find something at very low cost or even free in a pinch.

The financial benefits of living in a tiny house go well beyond the initial housing-cost savings. Take the issue of debt for example: getting out of debt is extremely challenging, if not impossible, when your mortgage/rental costs are high and your income is proportionally low. There's typically not enough money left over at the end of the month for anything other than minimum monthly payments.

The small size of tiny homes is generally viewed as a concern, but the size constraint can actually be an incredibly helpful tool in limiting overspending on nonessential items. Without the physical capacity to support the accumulation of unnecessary possessions, the planet and your pocketbook will find some relief. We saved thousands of dollars the first year we lived in our tiny house simply by not buying things we didn't truly need.

Once you've tamed your housing expenses, it becomes much easier to chip away at debt. According to a poll by thetinylife.com, 89 percent of tiny housers have less credit card debt than most Americans, and 65 percent don't have any debt at all. That's something to get excited about!

Another way of saving big in a tiny house is by not having the high utility expenses that those in larger houses must bear. The cost to condition and illuminate a tiny house is drastically lower than that of a conventional house. We often hear from full-time tiny housers paying just $20 per month for all their utilities. This isn't too surprising considering that the average-size house guzzles 12,500 kilowatt-hours (kWh) per year in electricity, while a tiny house sips less than 1,000 kWh.

Improve Your Relationship Dynamics

In 2009, we moved into our "dream" house, a large two-story with three bedrooms, two and a half baths, two living rooms, an entertainer's dream kitchen, a two-car garage, and an abundance of space. Previous to this move, our family of four had always lived in smaller homes that had fostered an environment of connection.

In our new house, we all disappeared into its various corners, and our day-to-day contact decreased significantly. We didn't think anything of it at first, but after about six months, we noticed the toll that our lack of interaction was taking. Awkwardness had set in, and conversations felt strained for the first time. It took a while, but eventually, we realized that the culprit was, in large part, the size of the house.

Our experience is certainly not unique. We hear again and again from families and couples who experienced a dramatic improvement in interpersonal dynamics after moving into a tiny home. Sure, there was an adjustment period, but in time, their relationships improved because close contact invites healthy communication and there just isn't the option of retreating into seclusion when things get tough. Ever see someone storm off down the hallway and slam the door to their bedroom? That's not an option in a tiny house.

Prior to owning our tiny home, we lived in a pop-up tent trailer in Baja, Mexico, for five months with our (at the time) 10-year-old daughter, Terra. One day, she was mad at us for something and stomped down the narrow corridor, jumped onto her bed, and "slammed" her curtain shut. Because a tent trailer is essentially just one open space with a couple curtains for visual privacy, we suggested that she open the curtain and talk about what she was feeling rather than staying on her bed fuming for hours. That one interaction set the stage for all future conversations. Later, when we lived in our tiny home, Terra talked to us rather than retreating to her room.

Terra sitting and reading in our pop-up tent trailer where we lived for nearly five months on the beaches of Baja, Mexico.

Honest and vulnerable communication is a major component of a happy and successful relationship. This way of interacting is fostered in a tiny space, and we would argue that a large one hampers it. A lot has been written on the topic of how to create a joyous life, and it all points to the same sentiment: a happy and fulfilling life is one in which a person prioritizes their relationships and focuses on the things they love. The way to achieve that level of closeness is through communication and connection.

Relationships suffer immensely when people are stressed about money, impending foreclosures, or long work hours and commutes. (Ours certainly did!) Living outside one's means is a sure-fire way to create unnecessary stress. At the end of the day, when people are tired and drained, that penned up tension is often taken out on those who are closest.

On the other hand, living in an affordable tiny house can have a positive effect on a strained family dynamic. When you live within your means, financial fear goes away, and you have time and energy to pursue the things that you are passionate about. Your sense of humor, joy, patience, and kindness increase, and you have a chance to thrive in a way that's not possible when you're buried under stress.

Cleaning Made Simple

There's something meditative about the ritual of organizing and tidying space, and sometimes, it's a really nice way to bring calm and order to a chaotic day. In contrast, cleaning a 2,200-square-foot house after a really long day at work can become a dreaded burden.

There's something rather enchanting about cleaning and maintaining a space where everything was placed with intention and given a home. When you value the things that surround you and they truly benefit your life, you'll likely want to take really good care of them. We've never enjoyed cleaning a house as much as we love taking care of hOMe. To thoroughly clean from top to bottom takes us only 30 minutes!

Studies show that a clean and tidy environment invites greater productivity and mental clarity. This allows you to be more effective at work and, thus, generate more money in the shortest period of time. Conversely, a lack of cleanliness fosters distraction and becomes a detriment to productivity.

Cleanliness even inspires people to make healthier food choices. A study published in *Psychological Science Journal* shows that people in tidy work environments are twice as likely to choose healthy food options over unhealthy ones than those in a cluttered space.

There are also the obvious health benefits of living in a clean house, especially for those that suffer from asthma and allergies. The accumulation of pollen, mold spores, pet dander, dust mites, and general dirt are all much easier to eliminate in a small space. Having a tiny house makes it much more likely that you'll keep things clean and that your indoor air quality will be as clean as possible.

Environmental Benefits

According to the National Association of Home Builders (NAHB), the average new residential house in the United States is about 2,600 square feet. In comparison, the average tiny house measures a diminutive 225 square feet. As you can imagine, the difference in resources it takes to build a conventionally sized house compared to a tiny house is staggering.

The national average cost per kWh of electricity is 15.4 cents. The owner of a conventionally sized house must pay $1,966 yearly for their electric bill. A tiny houser, on the other hand, spends a mere $140. That's a savings of more than $1,800 every year!

Laid end-to-end, the amount of lumber used to build a 3,000-square-foot house stretches more than 4 miles and requires more than seven logging trucks of material. Conversely, the average tiny house consumes just half of a logging truck worth of wood. Being that the construction industry accounts for 75 percent of the lumber used annually, this is a significant impact.

Furthermore, the average-size house consumes more than 12,500 kWh of electricity yearly for running appliances and lighting. This contributes a staggering 16,000 pounds of CO_2 to the atmosphere annually. A tiny house, on the other hand, uses just 914 kWh and generates just a little more than 1,000 pounds of CO_2. Heating and cooling combined in a conventional house generates 12,000 pounds of CO_2 yearly, while a tiny house generates only 780 pounds.

Mobility

Once upon a time, life was a bit simpler, and the path to a lifetime career was clear. One could go to college, get a job, work there for 40 years, retire, and then receive a pension in retirement. A hard-working employee was afforded the comfort of knowing where his next paycheck was coming from, and it was common for families to plant lifelong roots in the same community.

Today's job market looks quite different. The path to employment is uncertain, and even if one follows all the rules, there's no certainty of reward. Companies are less and less comprised of workers, but rather, of projects and tasks that must be completed. The digital age has enabled remote, offshore, freelance, part-time, contract, and less-expensive solutions to enter the equation. Generally, the cheapest offer takes the cake.

This impermanence in the job market has significantly influenced homeownership trends. It no longer makes a great deal of sense to lock into a 30-year mortgage when a job change could occur at any time. The value of flexibility is becoming synonymous with survival in the work force.

Tiny houses on wheels allow for the utmost flexibility and can provide the best of both worlds—the stability of a home coupled with the ability to move it to the next job or adventure. We often hear that people who serve in the military, as well as traveling nurses/caretakers, tech industry specialists, consultants, artists, entertainers, and so on, are tired of uprooting and finding a new home each time they must move. With a tiny house, you take your home wherever your career leads you.

Free Up Your Time

Assuming that you fall within the range of averages for Americans, you currently have a housing payment in the form of monthly rent or a mortgage, and you spend 27 percent of your income on housing. That means roughly 10.8 hours of each 40-hour work week go toward housing costs. When you add in utilities and maintenance, two of your five workdays are solely devoted to earning money to cover the costs of housing.

Then there's the issue of commuting. Consider that you not only need to work, but also need to get there and back, often in traffic. Census numbers reveal that you likely have a 1-hour round-trip commute for an 8.5-hour workday. Right off the bat, you're looking at 9.5 hours away from home. According to the Bureau of Labor Statistics, when you finally do get home, you spend another 9 hours sleeping, leaving you with just 5.5 hours of time to enjoy the house that you've worked so hard to pay for. Is it worth it?

We're not saying that spending money on housing is a bad thing. Rather, we're suggesting that the pattern of wasting money on things that we don't actually need and which don't actually benefit our lives ought to be reconsidered. Why spend more on your housing than you actually get out of it? Jose Mujica, former president of Uruguay, said it best: "When you buy something, the instrument is money, but in reality you are buying it with the hours of your life that you spent earning that money."

When we realized the real costs and sacrifices we were making in living in a house that was much bigger than we needed, we experienced a couple weeks of sadness and regret. It took us a little time to pick ourselves back up, brush the dirt off, and start taking active steps toward creating a life that allowed us to be our best selves.

It's rare for someone on their deathbed to say they wished they had worked harder, lived in a larger house, or made more money. Any regrets tend to revolve around not spending enough time with loved ones or not following passions. You don't need thousands of square feet to be joyful. In fact, we're suggesting you need less square footage to find your freedom and ultimately, your happiness.

Living Simply

Thousands upon thousands of others have realized that contentment has nothing to do with material possessions or large homes. Tiny home owners are learning that by living with the least, we are experiencing the most. In fact, we're finding that too much stuff stifles our ability to feel joy because material things, in excess, serve as a distraction.

A UCLA study titled "Life at Home in the Twenty-First Century," found that all the study subjects' stress hormones spiked when they were dealing with their belongings. Researchers at the Princeton University Neuroscience Institute found that productivity and efficiency are greatly hampered by clutter and an excess of material possessions.

Humans own more material possessions today than at any other time in the history of mankind. The average U.S. household hoards more than 300,000 items (from paper clips to large furniture), 1 in 10 people rent an offsite storage facility (there are five times more mini-storage facilities than there are Starbucks coffee houses), and it is estimated that there are between 5 and 14 million hoarders in the United States. To top things off, we waste more than $1 trillion per year on "nonessential" goods.

The worst part? Americans are unhappier today than they were 30 years ago, according to a study presented at the "Policies for Happiness" symposium. "The increase in hours worked by Americans over the last 30 years has heavily affected their happiness because people who are more absorbed by work have less time and energy for relationships," said one of the study's authors.

Interestingly, the study found that happiness had remained stable in Europe during the same time period. They attributed this to the fact that European workplaces had, for the most part, avoided some of the pitfalls seen here in the United States, such as longer hours, less vacation time, and more pressure to excel and succeed.

There are high costs associated with the acquisition of stuff: energy, money, and, most importantly, time. When we started calculating the "real" costs of all the nonessential stuff we had surrounded ourselves with, we were heartbroken. The sacrifices and choices we had made were painful to face, especially when it involved our kids. It took us seeing things from this perspective to commit to living a more mindful life.

Living the tiny house lifestyle has allowed us to share some wonderful values with our kids. We are raising them in an environment where happiness is not dependent on the acquisition of material possessions, and they are given the opportunity to learn positive communication skills as well. We all help to make each other the best versions of ourselves by focusing on balance, joy, and life experiences.

Living simply isn't about surviving with as little as possible, but rather, about removing the extraneous so that the important things have a chance to shine and be appreciated. When money and time are not spent on unnecessary items, resources free up for things that really do matter. Leonardo da Vinci knew it even back in 1452 when he said, "Simplicity is the ultimate sophistication."

Natural Disasters

The rate of natural disasters around the globe has increased significantly. In 1970, 78 natural disasters were reported; in 2019, there were 396. There has been an 80 percent increase in climate-related disasters between 1980 and 2009. Every year, an average of 25 million people are displaced by weather-related disasters (the equivalent of one person per second).

A study by RealtyTrac highlighted that 43 percent of U.S. homes are at risk of one or more weather-related natural disasters (wildfire, hurricanes, floods, tornados, and earthquakes). One distinct advantage of tiny houses on wheels is their mobility.

In times of imminent natural disasters, they can be moved out of harm's way (assuming there is enough warning time). This is especially helpful in hurricane- and wildfire-prone areas.

Unfortunately, certain weather disasters such as tornados and earthquakes appear without much warning at all. However, events such as hurricanes, floods, typhoons, tsunamis, and forest fires can often have minutes, hours, or even days of warning of their approach. This is often more than enough time for a tiny house on wheels to be packed up with its contents stowed for travel, and driven away to safe ground.

A community in coastal California recently approved tiny houses on wheels to be built in a flood zone where residential construction is normally restricted. Due to the nature of flooding in that area and how slowly water levels typically rise during large rainstorms, the property owner argued that, need be, he could evacuate the structures to safety in ample time. The local building and zoning departments agreed and granted him permission to build tiny houses on wheels on that lot.

Rebuilding Communities

Census reports show that the urban migration is continuing and that younger residents are leaving smaller rural areas for larger cities. About 60 percent of rural counties saw a reduction in population in 2016, representing an increase from 50 percent of counties in 2009 and 40 percent in the late 1990s.

The population decline is decreasing the tax base in rural areas, which is having a negative effect on public services such as schools, health care, roads, maintenance, libraries, and the like. The private sector is suffering as well because such a large portion of the work force is leaving for the city. To put it bluntly, many small communities are dying because of a population shortage.

Spur, Texas, a sleepy community set in the western quadrant of the state, was nearly crippled by this phenomenon. Shops were boarded up and beautiful historic buildings fell apart from long-term vacancies. There wasn't much hope for a renaissance in population until one of its residents came up with a brilliant idea: proclaim Spur as the first tiny house on wheels–friendly town in the United States. Spur welcomed the tiny homes and their owners into the struggling community.

Two years after the city adopted their tiny house–friendly policy, all their city lots have sold, as have several county-owned ones. By the year's end, they will have 20 full-time tiny house residents calling Spur home. Many more plan on arriving next year, and there are even talks of buying larger county lots and creating tiny house communities on them. These new residents are bringing a variety of skills, enthusiasm, and a desire to infuse this small community of 1,200 with new life.

There are many advantages to living in a small town, such as lower real estate costs. (City lots cost just $500 in Spur.) Also, small towns experience 80 percent less crime than typical large cities, suffer less pollution, and have a strong sense of community. Perhaps there aren't as many six-figure job opportunities as there are in the cities, but if you're living in a tiny house and practicing minimalism, then there's no need to make that much money anyway. Instead, you can sit back, enjoy life, get your needs met, and thrive in a lifestyle that supports your physical and emotional well-being.

Tiny Houses for the Houseless

As humans, our five basic needs for survival are air, water, food, clothing, and shelter. When people don't have a safe house in which to lay their heads down at night, big problems can arise. The National Law Center on Homelessness and Poverty states that more than 3.5 million people suffer houselessness yearly in the United States. Along those lines, three studies conducted by the National Alliance to End Homelessness showed that it costs communities less money to create housing for the houseless than it does to let them remain on the streets and rely on social services.

Tiny houses cost significantly less to build than conventional housing for the houseless. They are currently being used as a part of the solution for houselessness in several municipalities, including Fresno, California (Village of Hope); Ventura, California (River Haven); Eugene, Oregon (Opportunity Village); and Olympia, Washington (Quixote Village). More are also in development in Wisconsin, New York, Texas, and other areas.

To Summarize

Tiny houses are a cost-effective alternative to traditional housing; you can fully pay for a tiny home with less than half the required down payment for a conventionally sized house. The financial benefits of living tiny are significant, but the improvement of interpersonal dynamics can also reduce huge amounts of stress. Speaking of stress—less space means less cleaning and more time for enjoyable activities. Decluttering your external spaces brings internal relief, which is much easier when living tiny. As climate change worsens, tiny houses provide a low-impact housing alternative that can be moved away from natural disasters to safety.

CHAPTER 2

What Is a Tiny House?

The tiny house movement is a large, diverse, and vibrant collective of people coming from all walks of life. It's growing by leaps and bounds and shows no sign of slowing down. But where did it come from and what events launched it to where it is today? Further, what even is a tiny house? Are you tiny curious? If so, pour your favorite hot beverage, make yourself comfortable, and let's go down the rabbit hole together.

In this chapter, we define what a tiny house is, as well as the different kinds of tiny houses. Next, we look into the history of tiny homes and the leaders who shaped today's tiny house movement. Finally, we glimpse into the future and take a look at where it all goes from here.

How Big Is Tiny?

Until recently, there's been some debate about how small a home must be in order to qualify as a tiny house. Some argued that anything more than 200 square feet was frivolous, while others felt that anything under 1,000 square feet must surely be considered tiny. The definition we use—and the International Residential Code uses—is "a dwelling that's 400 square feet or less in floor area, excluding any lofts."

In terms of the minimum square footage, well, that has yet to be determined. Just when we think a tiny house can't get any smaller, someone builds one that's even more petite. For example, our friend Dee Williams, a well-known tiny houser, teacher, and author, is currently downsizing from her 84-square-foot tiny house into a 56-square-foot home. The reason? She felt her original tiny house, her home of more than 12 years, was just a tad bit *too* large.

The average tiny house on wheels (THOW) measures in at 225-square feet. This includes enough space for a bathroom, kitchen, sleeping loft, eating area, and adequate storage for basic personal items such as clothing, books, and food. Because these houses are smaller than some people's walk-in closets, it's hard for many to even imagine that so many things can fit in that kind of square footage.

Our own tiny house, affectionately named "hOMe" as an homage to the sacred "Om" mantra, is 207 square feet plus 110 square feet in lofts. Because it was meticulously designed, it contains everything we need: a full-size kitchen, comfortable stairs leading up to the main loft, space for a home office for both of us, a seating area for four, a comfortably sized bathroom, an abundance of storage, and two lofts complete with queen-size beds.

hOMe, our tiny house on wheels, is 28 feet long × 8 feet 6 inches wide × 13 feet 6 inches tall and contains everything we need to live a happy, peaceful, and productive life.

Tiny House Types

A tiny house can be mobile, known as a tiny house on wheels (THOW); stationary, known as a tiny house on foundation (THOF); or a hybrid of the two, a tiny house on skids (THOS). A tiny house is not considered a manufactured home, park model, or RV. Rather, it's considered a mini-scale house built with traditional residential construction materials.

Which option you choose depends on your needs and how often you'll be moving with your tiny home. A THOW, a house built on a mobile trailer, is ideal for those with plans of towing it with relative frequency. A THOF, a tiny house built onto a permanent foundation, is perfect for those who want the simplest path to legalization for their tiny homes and do not plan on moving the structure. It's also a great fit for those who already know the long-term spot for their dream tiny home. A THOS, a tiny house built on a skid system that can be hauled on a trailer or attached to a permanent foundation, is well suited for those who want the flexibility and potential for moving their tiny home in the future but don't have immediate plans to move it.

The Story of the Tiny House Movement

The tiny house movement is a social collective comprised of tens of thousands of people around the world who are redefining their relationships with house size, material consumption, and their impact on the planet. Those who live in tiny houses, referred to as tiny housers, come from all walks of life. We are a diverse group of professionals, parents, singles, couples, artists, active-duty servicemen and women, health-care providers, musicians, teenagers, newlyweds, college students, retirees, gamers, clerics, educators, athletes, DIYers, contractors, and everything in between.

Nobody knows exactly how many people currently live in tiny houses, but it is estimated to be in the thousands. Whatever the actual figure is, the tiny house movement is certainly growing exponentially with no signs of slowing down anytime soon. A recent survey by HomeAdvisor found that 86 percent of Americans say they would live in a tiny house, which suggests the tiny house network will only continue to grow.

Let's explore who inspired this exciting movement, what economic events fueled it, and where it's going next.

Early Leaders Set the Stage

In truth, the concept of humans living in tiny houses dates back to our earliest ancestors. Up until the last 100 years or so, the average house was small, modest, and didn't require a lot of resources to build and maintain. However, with the advent of new construction technologies and the ability to heat and cool a space with ease, house sizes began to burst at the seams.

According to the U.S. Census Bureau, the average size of a home in the United States has increased 61 percent since 1973. Meanwhile, the average household size has decreased in that same time period. This means that the average amount of square footage each person uses has nearly doubled since 1973. This is a significant increase in how many resources it takes to build a conventional residence, how much money one must pay to buy one, and how much energy it takes to condition it.

In 1999, a visionary named Jay Shafer designed and built his first tiny house on wheels (named "Tumbleweed") as a solution to his challenges and frustrations of living through two winters in a poorly insulated Airstream. He wanted the flexibility of mobility but also longed for the benefits of living in something that was better constructed and felt more like a home. The world's gaze landed upon his 96-square-foot cutie, and many people instantly fell in love with it. And with that, the modern tiny house movement was born.

Although Jay would argue that he's not the father of the movement, there's no doubt that his actions inspired countless individuals to follow suit and jump into this lifestyle. Jay suggests that the true visionaries were those who inspired him through their books written in the 1970s, including *Tiny Houses: Or How to Get Away From It All* by Lester Walker, *Rolling Homes: Handmade Houses on Wheels* by Jane Lidz, the *Not So Big* series by Sarah Susanka, and *Shelter* by Lloyd Kahn.

Housing Crash Builds a Tiny Community

The cost of housing increased at the same rate of inflation for more than 100 years in the United States until 1995. Between 1995 and 2007, home values, adjusted for inflation, jumped a whopping 70 percent. There was so much equity built up in real estate values that homeowners found themselves sitting on gold mines. People began to shift their loans around to liquidate this newfound wealth. Many took themselves on the shopping spree of their lives, forgetting to save money for a rainy day.

At the same time, banks jumped on the bandwagon and started handing out three-year adjustable-rate mortgage (ARM) loans with ultra-low interest rates like they were candy. The future looked so bright in real estate that millions of what should have been unqualified homeowners were approved for these seductive loans. However, trouble loomed on the horizon, and after the real estate bubble burst, millions of middle- to lower-class homeowners ended up in deep financial water without a life preserver.

In fact, more than 9.3 million people lost their homes to foreclosure or distress sales during an eight-year period. Today, the economy is improving, and the real estate market seems to be on the mend. However, industry experts project less than one-third of those who lost their homes will re-enter the mortgage market. For some, damaged credit will prevent them from receiving loans, while for others, the psychological trauma associated with foreclosure is not something they want to risk again. It can take a decade for a foreclosure to disappear from public record, and it can lower one's credit score by more than 200 points.

It's no wonder that fascination with tiny houses is at an all-time high. They offer comfortable, safe, beautiful housing at a fraction of the cost of a conventionally sized residence. The possibility of homeownership, which previously had been ripped away from many, is now within reach again.

Tiny Houses Gain Popularity

During the last 15 years, interest in tiny houses has risen significantly with a noteworthy spike starting in 2013, according to Google Trends. Every month, dozens of new tiny houses are built, with builders shifting their focus to micro-housing and new people starting on their tiny house journeys.

This graph from Google Trends highlights the sharp increase in interest for search term "tiny house" on Google since 2004.

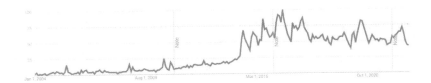

Tiny houses have become big business, and the housing sector and media have also joined in on the fun. Currently, television shows such as *Tiny House Nation, Tiny House Hunters, Tiny House Builders,* and *Tiny House: Big Living* are among some of the most popular programs on air. Scores of tiny house video tours can be found on YouTube, and thousands of images populate search engine pages. There truly is no shortage of tiny house inspiration out there.

The number of tiny house jamborees, expos, and fairs is also increasing quickly. The biggest of them all, the Tiny House Jamboree hosted by EcoCabins, Inc., drew in 40,000 participants in its first year and more than 50,000 the second. Whereas finding a tiny house to visit even just five years ago was a challenge, today there's a good chance you'll see one in your community simply by driving around.

All this begs the question, "Is the tiny house movement just a fad?" Only time will tell. However, we feel confident that as long as there are people who want to save on housing costs and are passionate about the environment, the tiny house movement will remain strong. With the massive strides recently made toward the legalization of tiny houses, we firmly believe that the number of tiny homes will steadily increase.

To Summarize

Tiny houses are defined as dwellings 400 square feet or less, excluding lofts, that can be built on wheels, a foundation, or skids (a hybrid of the two). The average tiny home is 225 square feet. Most are fully self-contained and house a kitchen, bathroom, eating area, sitting area, sleeping area, and storage space for basic items. Tiny houses create the possibility of homeownership for many individuals who would not otherwise be able to afford a traditional mortgage.

CHAPTER 3

Preparing for the Paring Down

The majority of future tiny housers must go through a significant downsizing process. For many, it's a rite of passage into the minimalist lifestyle and something they eagerly jump into. For others though, it's the part of the process they dread the most. Fortunately, there are some great strategies to make the process not only painless, but also fun.

In this chapter, we help you determine your ideal tiny house size. We show you how to deal with emotional attachments to personal belongings such as heirlooms, and we also discuss the joys and freedom of living a clutter-free life.

Finding the Perfect Fit for You

A tiny house on wheels (THOW) that's too big will cost more than necessary and force you to drag more weight around while towing. A house that's too small will leave you feeling claustrophobic and ready to abandon ship at the first opportunity. A house that's sized just right will leave you feeling happy, fulfilled, and balanced.

Nothing will better help you find your ideal home size than actually staying in a tiny house; fortunately, there are dozens, if not hundreds, of tiny houses just waiting for your visit. They can be found in every state, and range from tiny houses on wheels, to backyard cottages, to tricked out Airstreams, to lofty tree houses. There's even larger-scale tiny house lodging available, such as WeeCasa Tiny Home Hotel in Lyons, Colorado, and Mt. Hood Tiny House Village outside of Bend, Oregon.

Online resources, such as airbnb.com and vrbo.com, are excellent tools for finding tiny houses to rent. Because many owners are listing their tiny houses on these sites, a web search should yield numerous results. If renting a place isn't an option, look for a tiny house jamboree, fair, or festival in your area. There are several of these events happening in all regions of the United States. If you are interested in locating one of these events, Tiny Living's website keeps an up-to-date list of tiny house festivals in the United States. Visit tinyliving.com/festivals for more information and resources in regard to tiny house events.

There are other tools for discovering your ideal tiny house size. One of our favorites is the use of colored tape to layout a full-scale tiny house floor plan on a driveway, garage floor, living room floor, or any other large area. For as long as practically possible, move basic furniture into that space (including your mattress) and occupy only that area to get a sense of scale and space functionality.

The tape system is not practical for day-to-day kitchen and bathroom use, so in those areas, sort through your belongings, pick out only the vital items and tape off access to the drawers and cabinets with nonessentials. Experiment with adding and taking items away. What's vital? What can you live without? This exercise is a great opportunity to start getting into the tiny house mindset even while living in a large house.

Recreate your proposed floor plan on a large surface of your current home/garage/driveway to get a sense of what your tiny house layout will feel like. (Photo by Alek Lisefski, tiny-project.com.)

Living with Just the Basics

Determining what's vital in your life can pose an interesting challenge when you likely have spent a majority of your life in conventionally sized housing. Sorting, organizing, and thinning out all your possessions can feel overwhelming, so it's best to start this process with plenty of time to work through everything. Select only the items you believe to be essential, and put them somewhere accessible. Over the next month, use only those items, and see if you miss any of the other ones. If you miss an object more than a few times, consider moving it back into your essentials. Play around with paring down those items and see what you actually use and what you can live without.

We remember lying awake many sleepless nights during our tiny house design process, worrying that we would invest all this time and money into building a space that wasn't properly sized for us. After all, how were we to know what we really needed when we had spent most of our lives in conventionally sized homes? To answer that question, we decided to move with our (at the time) 10-year-old daughter to the beaches of Baja, Mexico, for five months while living in a used 16-foot pop-up tent trailer. We each went down with nothing but the absolute basics:

- One set of cutlery—one plate, bowl, and cup
- Basic spices

- Two pairs of shorts
- Three T-shirts
- One sweatshirt
- Two pairs of pants
- Seven sets of undergarments
- One bathing suit
- One jacket
- Two books
- Some board games and cards
- One guitar
- One laptop computer for us all to share
- Basic provisions, such as a flashlight, toiletries, one hairbrush, and other things of that nature

We turned off our social media accounts and kept our phone lines open only for talking with our son who was attending boarding school in Colorado.

Through that experience, we learned that in living with the least, we had the opportunity to experience the most. We enjoyed a sense of calm and joy that we had not felt before. As our attachments to material possessions and electronics weakened, and the stress of being constantly busy faded away, our love for life increased. We came back from that five-month adventure with a clear understanding of which material possessions were necessary (very few) and which ones were just frivolous (everything else).

When envisioning your ideal tiny house life, really take stock of the things that you value, and even more importantly, the things you can leave behind. Take notes on how often you cook at home, how much space you use in your refrigerator (without letting food items spoil), how many clothing items you actually wear, how many books you read, how much athletic equipment you use, how often you actually need all the space in your full-size oven, and so on. All this information will help you whittle away the items and spaces that are frivolous and taking up unnecessary space in your life.

Creating a tiny house life means so much more than just moving into a small space. It's about becoming mindful of your day-to-day habits and perhaps making some new choices. It's also an opportunity to surround yourself with the items that you truly love and that haven't had a chance to be appreciated amidst the clutter that surrounds them.

Declutter Your Life

Space is a vacuum—if you have it, it begs to be filled. This is why drawers are so rarely empty, and why garages fill up with who-knows-what. It's easy to accumulate clutter when we've been steeped in the values of consumerism from a young age.

Many people feel that tiny house living is unattainable because they're shackled by their relationship to material possessions. Committing to the decluttering process isn't for the faint of heart and requires a lot of honest introspection. You might be surprised (we were!) at how deeply your upbringing has patterned your relationship to stuff and how difficult that can make it to let go of nonessential items.

Though decluttering might seem overwhelming at first, the great news is the process gets easier with time, and the more you do it, the better you'll feel. Soon you'll be so fueled by how liberated you feel that the last legs of the journey will fly by with ease. Let's get you going with some great decluttering strategies that you can start applying today!

The 365-Day Rule

When we started our downsizing process in earnest, we felt completely overwhelmed. We were clueless as to where to begin, and the prospect of going through thousands of possessions nearly paralyzed us. We knew we would need a systematic approach, so we created the *365-day rule*.

The 365-day rule is incredibly simple to apply. It involves going through every item you own and asking one simple question: "Have I used this in the last year?" If not, it must go into a potential-discard pile—no matter how cheaply you bought it for, how much emotional attachment you have to it, or how valuable you perceive it to be.

This exercise will reveal your underlying attachments to material possessions. We learned more about our relationships to stuff here than at any other point in our tiny house journey. The key to success for the 365-day rule is that you must be merciless while sorting through everything. And when we say everything, we mean it, even down to the paperclips. Don't shortchange yourself by getting lazy in this process. The following photo shows just some of the items we identified as being unnecessary using the 365-day rule.

This photo shows just a portion of the useless stuff we got rid of when we applied the 365-day rule in our own house.

The process might seem exhausting at first, and, depending on how much stuff you own, you could feel drained. The average American household is filled to the gills with 300,000 items, so this process might take some time. Stick with it though. As you continue your decluttering journey, you'll start feeling better and better.

It took us about four weeks of decluttering for three hours per day to get through our house. By the time we were done, our two-car garage was covered two feet deep in a sea of stuff we hadn't used in the last year. We were shocked. We weren't even living in a huge house, and we certainly weren't shopaholics.

Our discard pile consisted of kitchen gadgets, books, sports equipment, knickknacks, toiletries, clothing, toys, CDs/DVDs, office supplies, instruments, camping equipment, and the like. We experienced quite a pang of sadness when we considered how much money, time, and resources had been sacrificed to purchase those items. We felt embarrassed when we saw that a lot of them hadn't even been used.

The next step in the 365-day rule involves living day to day without all those possessions. We highly recommend doing this stage for at least two weeks. (We did it for about eight.) If your experience is anything like ours, you won't miss any of the items in the potential-discard pile. You might even forget what's in that stash of nonessentials.

The final step involves sorting through the discard pile and deciding what to keep and what to get rid of. This part will likely be easy and fun because you'll already have gone through the emotional detachment process. Using the 365-day rule alone, we eliminated about 75 percent of our material belongings.

You can sell, give away, recycle, and/or trash the stuff you decide to discard. We hosted garage sales over two weekends and made enough money to pay for our entire five months in Baja, Mexico. Not bad for a bunch of stuff we didn't even need!

Managing Your Emotional Attachment to Stuff

Getting rid of stuff we didn't have an emotional attachment to was easy, but we sure were stumped when it came to things like heirlooms. Our collection of keepsakes had included the majority of our kids' early artwork, about 15,000 printed photos, large boxes filled to the brim with letters, clothes from our infancy, and a petting zoo worth of stuffed animals. Needless to say, we had accumulated way more than we wanted to bring into our tiny house.

We managed to get rid of 75 percent of our things in about three months, but it took more than three years to psyche ourselves up for the task of sorting through the heirlooms. We knew we had to come up with a game plan and some serious strategy to get through the job. We started by simply separating our keepsakes into three categories: photographs, letters, and personal effects (toys, clothing, medals, and so on).

In going through the letters, we realized that even though we had hundreds of them, they had all been written by a couple dozen people. We recognized that we didn't need to keep every single one, and that a few of the best letters did a better job of capturing the sentiment from each relationship.

In terms of what to do with the extra letters, we actually mailed a lot of them back to the authors. Most people don't keep diaries, so those letters served as wonderful time capsules into their pasts.

With our kids' artwork, we quickly realized we didn't need to keep all of it, just the pieces that really tugged at our heartstrings. It became easier to sort through them once we laid them side by side. Removing the pieces that weren't stellar allowed us to really appreciate the special ones. After this initial paring down, we decided which pieces to keep in hard copy and which ones to scan and digitize. By the end of this process, a large box of artwork had been whittled down to a small folder.

In terms of personal effects, we had saved everything from trophies, medals, and high school jackets to yearbooks, stuffed animals, and more. Combined, those items were taking up a lot of space. To solve the issue, we ended up snapping pictures of ourselves with several of them. Taking those photos actually brought the keepsakes to life and we had a ton of fun in the process. We realized we didn't need to hang on to most of the physical items anymore and were able to joyfully part with nearly all of them.

One of the best ways to encapsulate a memory with an heirloom is by taking a photo. Here, Gabriella is posing with her silver trophy from the Karate Junior Olympics. After she took the photo, she didn't feel the need to hang on to the trophy anymore.

Some people have the misconception that they must get rid of virtually all personal belongings and heirlooms to be a true tiny houser. This is simply not true. What's important is that you're clear and honest about what's truly important to *you*. If something from your childhood brings you incredible joy and you really want it in your life, create space for it in your tiny house.

Of the thousands of items that we sold and gave away, we don't have a single regret. Not even one! And if we're really being honest here, we actually don't remember

99 percent of what we used to own. It's hard to imagine a time when we were surrounded by so much stuff.

Defining Your Own Life

The topic of housing can be contentious, and some people have very strong opinions on what types of houses people should live in. As tiny houses have become increasingly popular, it's less and less common to hear criticism, but you could still run into some people who disapprove of your tiny house vision.

We personally experienced this after announcing our move to tiny back in 2009. Because most people hadn't heard of tiny houses back then, we had a lot of explaining to do. After a while, we felt disheartened, and eventually people's doubts heightened our own.

Fortunately, our experience living in Baja with essentially nothing but the basics and a roof over our heads brought such clarity that any negative comments from that point on simply rolled off our backs. We knew without a shadow of a doubt that we were on the right track, so other people's judgments simply couldn't hold a grip on us.

If you're met with cynicism after sharing your tiny news, remember that only you can know what's best for you. Though outside feedback can be helpful, no one can completely understand your needs and wants. And remember that even if your friends and family think you're nuts, there's a community of hundreds of thousands of people interested in tiny houses that will warmly welcome you with open arms.

Finding Fun and Freedom Through Decluttering

Growing up in Western society, we've been told that material possessions are the measure of success and that we'll be more beautiful, joyful, and popular once we purchase all the latest gadgets and gizmos. Fortunately, these myths are being debunked, and studies are showing that an excess of material consumption and possessions actually *creates* emotional distress.

Knox College Professor of Psychology Tim Kasser conducted a series of experiments analyzing the correlation between material possessions and happiness. Kasser's findings suggest that as subjects became more materialistic, they also became emotionally unstable and unhappy. Conversely, those who prioritized a reduction in materialism, became more joyful and relaxed.

A study conducted by The Checkout, an organization that analyzes the effects of shopping culture, found that the average American spends $200 each month on impulse purchases they later regret. Once a person stops the habit of spending money on nonessentials, their financial resources have a chance of improving. Money that would have been spent on housing now goes toward fun adventures, educational opportunities, and health. We have traveled more than ever since making the move to tiny. Because our housing costs used to represent a large burden in our monthly budget, we felt an immediate and positive impact after we moved into hOMe.

As we thinned our possessions, we felt exponentially lighter and freer. It was wonderful, and this new sense of buoyancy fueled our downsizing process, making it easier each step of the way. It's so easy that, toward the end of our downsizing process, we had to rein in our enthusiasm a tad and resist the urge to get rid of everything we owned.

Dare to radically declutter your life and see what the future has in store for you. Although the process is not without challenges, the rewards are extraordinary, and the implications potentially life altering. Even if you never move into a tiny house and you simply focus on decluttering, you might experience a remarkable expansion of your life's horizons. Living tiny is a mindset!

Thinning Out by Digitizing

Most people living in conventionally sized houses have amassed years of document clutter ranging from receipts to tax papers and everything in between. We were no exception as our document arsenal included more than 50,000 pieces of paper stored in large filing cabinets. There simply wasn't room in our tiny house for this stash so we had to employ a solution: create a paperless office by digitizing all our documents.

There is no shortage of scanning tools out there, and they make easy work of digitizing a home office. The most well-suited combo we have come across is the ScanSnap scanner partnered with evernote.com. The beauty of this marriage is that they create readable files from scanned documents, meaning that whenever you need to find something, all you have to do is enter the search term, and voilà, your file magically appears. No more sorting through thousands of pieces of paper wondering where the receipt for that pipe wrench ended up.

In terms of storing that data, we recommend you save everything in three places: on your computer, on a remote/exterior hard drive, and in a secure storage solution in the cloud. Having your documents in the cloud allows for remote searches when you're not with your computer (and provides a vital backup in case your hard drive fails, your computer is stolen, or if your computer is lost in a fire or natural disaster).

Knowing what documents to shred after scanning can be confusing, so be sure to do your due diligence when researching what to keep. Different industries have different expectations of what documents must be physically saved and for how long.

Although most documents don't need to be kept as hard copies, some absolutely do. Be sure to keep the following in their original form and, preferably, in a locked and fire-resistant location: Social Security cards; ID cards; last wills and testaments; power of attorney paperwork; insurance policies; loan paperwork; passports; pension and military documents; and birth, death, marriage, and divorce certificates.

Digitization was a saving grace for photo hoarders such as ourselves. We started out with about 15,000 prints, negatives, and slides. We organized the piles by sorting photos into separate events and then choosing our three or four favorite prints from each pile. We realized we didn't need 43 photos from the camping trip at Lake of the Woods with the kids; instead, we just wanted a few that told the story and kept the memory alive.

During the course of about five really fun sittings, we whittled our collection down to just 1,000 prints. Truly just the best of the best. We purchased a consumer grade photo scanner (ImageBox 9MP) rather than hiring out the digitization. We selected it because it accommodated slides, negatives, and prints.

The ImageBox 9MP does a reasonable job of scanning photographs without too much loss in quality. If you need them to be exceptionally high quality though, you might want to look more in the professional range instead. They cost quite a bit more but really produce excellent results for DIYers.

Scanning 1,000 images took about 12 hours in total. It was quick, easy, and something we could do while listening to the radio or talking on the phone. We backed up our images on CDs, an external hard drive, and in the cloud as well. The originals were either given away or thrown out. Years later, we still have no regrets about digitizing our photo collection.

Music and movie collections can also be digitized. Various options exist for transferring DVD and VHS files into digital formats. Which one you choose will be dictated by your computer's operating system and your budget. One nice perk about digitizing your music and video collection is that if you have a laptop or smart phone, you can take them with you everywhere you go.

To Summarize

It's incredibly important that you take the time to find out what the best tiny house size is for you; failing to do so could leave you living in a space that feels too big or too small and have you ready to abandon ship. Most people have emotional attachments to material possessions, which can make the process of downsizing feel overwhelming. With the right tools and strategies, though, it can be a cathartic experience! Using the 365-day rule to get rid of unused items can easily thin down more than half of your possessions. Digitizing documents, photos, and old letters is a fantastic way to not only save space but also safely archive those keepsakes.

CHAPTER 4

Financing a Tiny Home

In an ideal world, everyone could make a wish for a tiny house at bedtime and wake up with the cash under their pillow in the morning to make it all possible. If your version of the tooth fairy isn't that generous and you don't have that kind of cash on hand, you'll need to think about how to pay for your new home in more traditional ways.

In this chapter, we cover everything from estimating strategies, to effective ways of saving money, to financing options available on the market. With those pieces in mind, let's get you on your way to affording your tiny house!

Estimating 101

Estimating the cost of your house is not for the faint of heart. There are hundreds of moving parts and thousands of items that go into putting a home together, even a tiny one. Do it right and you'll fall within budget. Do it wrong and you could end up running out of money halfway through the build.

Set yourself up for a successful build by learning how to estimate not only how much the materials will cost, but also how long each task will take. Even if you plan on hiring someone to build your tiny house, it's beneficial to know how to estimate so you can be sure you are being charged a fair price.

Before any estimating can begin, you'll need a set of architectural plans and a materials list to work from. Whether you purchase a predesigned set, create one yourself, or hire someone to draft it for you, a materials list is essential. Several tiny house plans on the market come with such a list, which can save you hours of work and ensure that it is completely comprehensive.

Contractor-Built vs. Owner-Built Homes

The first question you'll need to answer when you're estimating costs is whether you'll build the house yourself, hire out specific aspects of the project, or hand the entire thing off to a professional. Each option has its own benefits and drawbacks. Weighing each one against the other is a great way to determine what the best scenario is for you.

For many tiny housers, the ultimate dream is to build their own home. Creating shelter with our own two hands is burned into our genetic code, and for many, it's a bucket list priority. Estimating time and materials as a first-time builder will prove to be quite challenging, though, because there's no way for you to know how long each task will take.

The good news is that there are several resources that can help you estimate not only the material costs but also the man hours each task should take. We highly recommend you pick up the most recent construction estimating book you can find. These publications are updated yearly, and the dollar values are adjusted by region. This is important because construction costs in Sonoma, California, are much higher than in Des Moines, Iowa, for example. With the drastic increase of the cost of construction materials during the COVID-19 pandemic, it's more vital than ever to secure updated dollar values for your resources prior to starting the build.

In terms of how long each task will take, we suggest you double the man-hour figures shown in estimating books since those are calculated for professional builders. This should give you a nice buffer while you learn how to build and also leave room for fixing any mistakes along the way.

You can also pay a contractor for an estimate on your architectural plans. If you intend on doing the whole build yourself, be up front with them and offer to pay them for their time. Ask them to break it up between time and materials rather than presenting it as a lump sum. Keep in mind that contractors not only work faster than you do, but often get special pricing on materials. This estimate will not be exact, but it will give you a general idea of how to budget for the project.

You can save big by being your own contractor and building your tiny house yourself. Although the fees charged by contractors are well within the scale of reason, you can avoid those fees if you take on the position of general contractor yourself. There are risks in this approach, such as potential lack of experience; however, if you run the job well, the savings will be worth it. If you choose to go this route, be sure to engage in a fair amount of research prior to starting your build.

If you hire someone to handle some of the tasks during your build, you're still considered the general contractor. That means the responsibility of having an accurate construction estimate falls on you. An advantage of having a professional builder on your team is that they can likely help you along the way and advise you with your cost estimates.

If you hire a general contractor to build your tiny house, the burden of cost accuracy falls on them. After you've agreed to a price and signed a contract, it's up to them to ensure that it all gets done within budget, barring any changes to the scope of the work.

Most general contractors charge upward of 15 to 20 percent of the total construction costs as their fee. On a project that costs roughly $30,000 in materials alone, eliminating that fee would save you $4,500 to $6,000 right off the bat. If you add the cost of labor into that equation, your savings will be substantially higher.

Count Every Nail

One common area in which new builders miss costly details in their estimation is on items such as glue, structural brackets, nails, screws, and other small items. To give you an idea, one box of framing gun nails can cost as much as $180. Imagine how quickly your costs will add up if you forget to add these items into your calculations!

Having a complete set of plans and a materials list to work off of is your best resource. Keep in mind that you need to budget for waste/excess in your calculations. A safe rule of thumb is anywhere from 10 to 15 percent waste. This number changes as the project gets more complicated in design and execution.

How Schedule Changes Can Make or Break a Project

Managing time on a jobsite can be one of the most important factors to staying on budget. Time is money. Changes to your schedule can come back to haunt you financially and emotionally. This is especially true if you are building the house yourself but hiring subcontractors for some portions of the build.

Imagine that your plumbing contractor calls on Monday morning to let you know that they can't make it to your jobsite on Wednesday as planned. Instead, they will be out there on Friday. No big deal, right? It's just a couple days. Besides, you could use that extra time to clean up some details in the framing.

You call the next subcontractor scheduled for the project, the electrician, and inform them that they won't be able to start work on Thursday after all but will need to come that following Monday. "Drat," they say, "My company is jumping on a big job that day and no one will be available for another three weeks." Your schedule has now been severely delayed because of a two-day change made by the plumber.

Not only can this schedule change be a major inconvenience, but it also can cost you money. If you're renting your shop space or need to move out of your current location by a certain date, you could end up going over budget. Do your best to keep your project on schedule, and you'll minimize headaches as well as potential costs. Also be sure everyone on your build team, including subcontractors and anyone else you're working with, understands all the scheduling constraints ahead of time.

The True Cost of the DIY Builder

Most DIY builders fall into one of two categories:

- The weekend warrior club, in which each member works tirelessly during the few hours they have off from their day job

- The full-timer club, where the member quits or pauses their day job while building their tiny house

Both of these options have costs associated with them, which should be factored into your overall estimate.

If you're a part of the weekend warrior club, anticipate significant fatigue and a potential decrease in productivity and mental clarity not only on the jobsite but also at your day job. Building a house, no matter how small, is hard work and requires a lot of focus. Budgeting downtime is essential for long-term success. Be sure to give yourself a minimum of several months to complete your build if this is your chosen path.

If you choose to work on your tiny house build full-time, you likely won't be earning income during that period (unless you have a business that generates passive income and can be left on autopilot). This loss in wages most definitely needs to be factored into your estimate. Depending on how much you make per hour, it sometimes makes more sense to hire someone to build the house for you, especially if your job will be at risk when you are ready to go back.

Simple Ways to Lower Costs

When it comes to building a house, most people are looking for money-saving strategies. After all, the costs associated with house construction, even a tiny one, are often larger than any other purchase you'll make in your lifetime. Fortunately, there are several opportunities for saving money before and during your build to help ease some of the stress. Here are our top three.

Lowering Tool Costs

Few things can deplete a savings account faster than a blind shopping spree at the local tool supply store. Fortunately, you don't have to spend a sizeable portion of your budget on tools if you get creative. Between bartering, borrowing, signing up for a local tool co-op, and/or buying used, you can save thousands of dollars.

Craigslist, pawnshops, and yard sales can be great places to start looking for inexpensive tools. Reselling your items into the community after your build is complete can help recoup costs. Ask your local hardware store if they know of any tool cooperatives in the area, and if there aren't any, consider starting one! Reaching out to friends and family to see if they are willing to loan out some of their tools is also a great place to start when getting everything ready to build your tiny home.

One important detail for you to consider as you're daydreaming about the tool collection you'll amass for your build is space. Unless you live on a piece of property with an extra tool shed, you'll likely be short on space in your newly built tiny house for all those tools you've just purchased. This means that it really might not make sense to buy new tools when you'll just end up selling them at the end of the job anyway, so be resourceful and try to borrow when you can.

Using Salvaged Materials

The use of nonstructural salvaged materials such as cabinets, sinks, and the like can bring your costs way down. On the other hand, there can be a lot of risk when dealing with structural materials because it could be impossible to tell if they're still safe for tasks like framing and carrying loads. We suggest you avoid using salvaged structural materials. If you do decide to use them, be sure to work with an engineer or other professional inspector who can verify the quality and strength of the materials. No amount of initial cost savings is worth risking the overall quality of your build and safety of your home.

Sinks, doors, windows, and more can all be salvaged. Places such as craigslist, Freecycle, and the Habitat for Humanity ReStore are all great places to look for bargains. You can also talk to local remodeling contractors to find out if they have projects underway that you'd be welcome to pull materials from. You might be surprised how many contractors are willing to let you pilfer their discard piles. When you take materials off their hands, it saves them on disposal fees.

Finally, you might be able to score some good deals at window/door retailers or lumber yards. It's not uncommon for contractors to place orders that are subsequently changed by the client. In those cases, brand-new materials are often sold as "seconds" at a great discount, so this can be an incredibly cost-effective alternative.

Corporate Sponsorship

This tit-for-tat idea might already have seen its best season. When tiny houses first exploded in popularity, many companies became interested in sponsoring high-profile projects as a way of getting their products in front of more people. Although less popular now, sponsorship could still be an option if you ask the right people and provide them with the right incentive.

The best way to gain sponsorship is by creating some buzz around your build early on. Media channels are still covering the tiny house movement, and there's a good chance that your local news stations will be interested in your project. We recommend approaching companies you're seeking sponsorship from after you have some press interest. To learn how to get corporate sponsorship for your build, we recommend Andrew Odom's book, *Gaining Corporate Sponsors for Your Tiny House*.

Be specific when asking for what you want, and be clear about what you can offer in return. Most companies are looking for positive reviews of their products in the form of a blog post and also exposure for their products in news stories. Be certain to only choose items that you're confident you'll like so you don't end up in an awkward position of having to say nice things about something you hate.

Using social media to document your tiny house journey can get you enough publicity to secure corporate sponsorships more easily. There is a huge amount of interest in tiny house living across platforms such as Instagram and TikTok, so this can be a great route to pursue. If you are building your tiny house from scratch, documenting the entire process on social media can be a win-win for the entire tiny house community—you receive publicity and sponsorships while sharing invaluable information.

Saving for Your Project

Even the humblest savings will add up if you stay focused and patient. If you find yourself tempted at the checkout line by something you don't ultimately need, consider that exercising patience in that moment might help you get closer to your tiny house dream.

Take the time to open a new savings account dedicated solely to your tiny house build. Set up a savings plan so that each week, a fixed dollar amount is automatically withdrawn from your checking account and deposited into your tiny house fund. Contribute what you can, and remember that the more aggressively you save now, the quicker you'll be living in your tiny house.

Can you put away $10 a week? $200 a week? More? Remember that you're supporting a life goal here, not a short-term gain. Putting aside $200 per week translates to an annual savings of $10,400. That is a significant amount of money. In fact, if you add those funds to your salvaging efforts, tool-sharing savings, and the decision to self-build, you might have enough to build your house in full in just one year.

Lowering Your Living Expenses

Most people spend hundreds of dollars per month on things they don't actually need or even want. Let's look at some areas where a routine change can make a significant impact and get you closer to your tiny house dream.

Reinvent Shopping

The average American spends $200 per month on impulse buys that are later regretted because they serve no real purpose. That's $2,400 annually!

Learn a new way to shop. Bring a list from home each time you go out. If you see something you like that's not on that list, don't buy it, even if it feels really important. You can always add the item to the next list.

We recommend you wait at least seven days to really consider whether it's worth spending your money on that item. Remember that you pay for items not only with money but with the time it took to earn it.

Cut the Cable

The average monthly cable bill is $100. Why not save $1,200 per year simply by cutting the TV habit? You can still watch movies through less-expensive online subscription services, and there's endless free content online as well. If you're a huge sports fan, buy an online season, like we do for ice hockey, for a fraction of cable costs.

Break Up with the Barista

The average adult spends $1,000 per year at coffee shops. Create a new routine in which you make a fantastic cup of coffee with all the trimmings at home, and easily save a cool grand each year.

Momma's Cooking

The convenience of eating out is expensive. Avoid it when you can. By not eating out for just *one* meal per week, a family of four can save $1,500 per year. If you're a terrible cook, buy a secondhand cookbook or pull some recipes from the web for free. Cooking for yourself is less expensive and also healthier, which also will save you money down the line with lower health-care costs.

Smoking and Drinking

We all know that smoking and excessive drinking are not good for our health. They are also expensive habits. A pack-a-day smoker spends $2,352 each year on cigarettes. The average beer drinker? A whopping $1,250 per year. Cutting back has huge physical and financial benefits.

Drive Less

Gas is expensive. Take a few minutes to calculate how much money you spend on gas yearly. (The national average is $2,000.)

Look at alternative transportation options to get you where you need to go. Can you work from home and eliminate a commute altogether? Perhaps you can do away with a car by using public transportation and renting a car for road trips. See what you can do, and put the excess money into your ever-growing savings account.

Skip the Hollywood Ending

The average American household spends more than $2,600 in entertainment yearly. This includes going out to movies, concerts, sporting events, and other activities. You might be able to save more money than you realize by renting videos to watch at home or going on hikes in nature when you feel like doing something. Look for free shows and events in your community.

Our little town in Southern Oregon offers amazing free shows in the park during the summer. We also have a monthly "First Friday Art Walk" involving dozens of galleries that offer free admission and often snacks and beverages to anyone that wants to attend. Ask around to see what events your community offers free of charge.

Stop Hoarding

There are more mini-storage facilities in the United States than there are Starbucks and McDonald's combined. The average cost for a small 5×5-foot unit is $50 per month for a total of $600 yearly. Some people pay twice that when renting a larger space. Imagine spending all that money on stuff that clearly isn't needed for daily life? If you have a mini-storage unit, this is the first place to start your downsizing process. You'll save money by cutting those monthly payments and make a profit when selling everything that's just been accumulating dust.

Chances are that when you calculate the savings from driving less, quitting smoking, drinking less, eating at home, curbing your shopping habits, and getting rid of your cable, you'll be close to that $200/week savings mark. Remember the goal of $10,400 per year? Suddenly it's within reach.

The best part is that none of those options require you to diminish your quality of life. You don't have to starve yourself or live without shelter; rather, you simply need to make some modifications in your spending habits.

Financing Your Home

There are several approaches for securing financing on a tiny house, and those options are expanding regularly. Some of them are conventional while others are outside the financing box. Let's go over each one and assess what your options are.

Banks and Credit Unions

Banks and credit unions are risk shy and as such, aren't keen on handing out loans for tiny houses on wheels. THOWs are seen as high flight risks. If the homeowner defaults on the payment, the collateral (the tiny house) could be in a completely different state by the time the bank realizes it. Tiny houses on foundations, though, are a completely different matter and are much more viable when it comes to securing standard bank loans.

Credit unions operate in much the same way banks do, but they're nonprofit and owned by their members. They can accept deposits, hand out loans, and provide various financial services. Any profits made by the credit union are returned to members by way of reduced fees, lower loan rates, and higher savings rates. Consider using a credit union to finance your house if your community has one.

This doesn't mean that banks will never fund a THOW build. The popularity of tiny houses has piqued the interest of some lending institutions, and it's likely just a matter of time before conventional loan options become more readily available.

The same thing happened in the insurance industry; no one was willing to insure a THOW until one broker stepped up and created a way to underwrite them. Now insurance options are available for nearly every tiny house type out there, including self-builds.

Most banks require a tiny house to have some type of certification to prove that it's well-built, safe, and investment worthy. This could be a Recreation Vehicle Industry Association (RVIA) certification, a certificate of occupancy, or a third-party inspection report. Because the loan process happens prior to construction, you'll know if you need to plan for certification before you start the build.

In general, local credit unions are more likely to lend on unusual projects than the larger banks are. Credit unions are a great place to start. You might only have one or two of them locally, so it's important to approach them with a clear plan of action. You'll want to present a professional and complete application that addresses all their concerns from the get-go.

Lines of Credit and Equity Lines

If you already own a home and are looking to downsize to a tiny house, you're in a great position. Banks are much more willing to lend when there is a low-risk asset (such as a home on a fixed foundation) that they can claim as collateral.

A lot of people are taking advantage of this scenario and building tiny houses in their backyards. They're renting out their large house while living in the smaller one and using that income to offset their living expenses. Some people with high equity in their homes live in areas where rent is so astronomically high that they're able to quit their day jobs and live a lovely life funded entirely by the rental income.

Another financing option with a bank (if you own a house) is a line of credit. This is slightly different than a home equity loan, but provides you with the necessary funding nonetheless. The great thing about this option is that you don't typically have to specify what the money is being used for, which can be helpful if your bank is nervous about funding tiny houses.

Finding Private Money

There are always investors interested in loaning money for unconventional projects; you just need to connect with the right people. This could be as simple as looking in your local newspaper.

To be crystal clear, I'm not suggesting you get involved with anything risky or dangerous. These are not "brown bag" loans where cash is handed out in the back of a diner. A legitimate investor will be professional and aboveboard with everything. A contract will bind you both to an agreement. It's a good idea to run the contract by an attorney in order to make sure you won't be presented with any surprises down the road.

To ensure that both parties are protected, never accept a loan from someone without sealing the deal with a contract. Repayment deadlines, fees, and terms should be clearly spelled out so there's no room for interpretation. Always have a lawyer review these types of loan contracts.

You also should look at angel investor websites, which connect you with people looking for interesting projects to invest their money in. These websites typically take a percentage of the loan as payment, increasing your interest rate; however, that cost hike may be worth it since your investor will have been professionally vetted.

Private money funding is more expensive than funding through bank loans because you're dealing with individuals who don't have the backing of a large corporation to protect them. They typically have higher interest rates to compensate for the risk. Just how much more you're willing to pay is up to you.

Tiny House Loans

LightStream, an online lending agency, provides loans up to $100,000 specifically for tiny homes. They offer competitive interest rates as low as 5.73 percent, and there are no appraisals or home equity requirements. There's no down payment, and you can receive funding the same day you apply or receive approval! Visit lightstream.com to learn more or apply.

SoFi Lending also offers tiny house–specific loans at impressively low interest rates, although they are a bit higher than LightStream's. The loan comparison tool and a variety of deferred payment options coupled with the high loan limit of $100,000 make SoFi a great option for tiny housers seeking funding.

Depending on the lender, there might be closing costs. Although loans might be available for up to $100,000, most fall under the $50,000 range, which is ample for the majority of tiny house builds.

Builder Financing

If you plan on hiring a builder or a company to build your tiny house, be sure to ask them if they have financing options. More and more companies are offering this to their clients, and builder financing can be an amazing resource for financing your tiny home.

Banks are often more comfortable writing up a loan on a professionally built home for two main reasons.

- The builder knows the trade and is more likely to complete the construction properly, on time, and on budget.
- The builder gets paid only once his or her work is complete, typically in scheduled draws against the loan. This provides an incentive for them to finish the project so that the bank isn't left with an unfinished home due to a defaulted loan.

The Importance of Contingency Funds

No matter how you fund your project, whether building it yourself or hiring it out, be sure to add a contingency fund to your financing portfolio. This is a "just in case" fund that can really come in handy if something goes unexpectedly wrong or last-minute changes are made that impact the project cost.

There are no fees for the contingency fund on a conventional loan, and you aren't even charged interest unless you use it. If you need it, it's available, but if not, it simply goes back to the bank.

If that option is not available through your lending source, you can opt to increase the value of your initial loan. The drawback is that you'll pay fees and interest on the money, even if you don't use it. It's better to have that option, though, than to get stuck mid-project without any contingency backup at all.

To Summarize

It can be challenging to accurately estimate all the resources necessary for your build; however, with the right tools in hand, you'll be able to anticipate the cost and minimize financial surprises down the road. Utilizing secondhand tools and tool cooperatives can save you thousands of dollars on construction costs. If you can save

$200 per week for one year by cutting back on purchasing nonessential items, you'll accumulate more than $10,000 for your tiny house build. If necessary, you can look for loans through conventional banks, credit unions, private lenders, and tiny house builders.

CHAPTER 5

Insuring Your Tiny House

Until recently, obtaining insurance for a tiny house on wheels (THOW) was virtually impossible; consequently, many tiny housers simply went without coverage and hoped for the best. Insurance companies seemed largely disinterested because they struggled to find answers to three important questions:

- Was there enough interest for THOW insurance to warrant the effort?

- What the heck was a tiny house anyway?

- How were they going to write a policy for something that hadn't even existed until a few years before?

However, with the explosion of new tiny houses came a surge in interest, motivating insurance companies to invest their resources toward finding solutions. It took some time and an impressive amount of effort, but thankfully, coverage options exist for nearly all types of tiny houses out there today.

In this chapter, we provide an insurance term primer, cover what options are best for each type of tiny house, and discuss how to find a great insurance agent.

Insurance 101

Insurance solutions for THOWs are complex and often involve the marriage of two or more standard types of coverage. For example, if a THOW is parked on a piece of property, then a normal homeowner's policy covers it. But as soon as that tiny house is hooked up to a tow vehicle, the homeowner's policy no longer applies, and you must have a THOW policy.

Add to this complexity the fact that not all THOW insurance solutions are available in every state, and you might soon begin to feel overwhelmed. Fortunately, there are a couple great insurance brokers out there dedicated to providing solutions for even the most unique tiny house builds. Finding insurance for tiny houses on foundations, on the other hand, is a breeze. They usually fall under normal homeowner's policies.

Homeowner's Insurance Policies

Homeowner's insurance is a standard policy that protects a house, its contents, and the property it sits on. It also provides liability coverage for any injuries incurred by other people visiting your place. Homeowner's policies are now available for THOWs through some insurance companies. This coverage can sometimes extend to tenant-occupied tiny houses as well.

The primary exclusions for THOWs in homeowner's policies are earth movement (damage incurred while in transit) and theft of the tiny house itself. Because houses on fixed foundations can't typically be stolen and taken off-site, no clauses exist for stolen structures in standard homeowner's policies.

A homeowner's policy is ideal for those individuals parking their tiny houses on their own property. If you plan on moving your tiny house from place to place, you'll need to add one of several available policies (more on this coming up) because any homeowner's policy becomes void the moment your tiny home is hooked to a tow vehicle.

Some insurance carriers are starting to include stationary THOWs under their park model/manufactured home programs. If your THOW qualifies, this is a viable and comprehensive option (without theft exclusion). Some programs even offer a trip endorsement for a one-time or limited-time frame. MAC Insurance, Inc., offers a comprehensive tiny home policy through which even self-built THOWs can find homeowner's coverage.

RV Insurance Policies

RV insurance options are bountiful. The policy you choose depends on a variety of factors, including how often you use your RV, if your RV is your full-time residence, and what type of RV you own (class A, travel trailer, tiny house RV, etc.). RV insurance is similar to automobile policies in that they offer collision, liability, and add-ons such as protection of personal belongings, roadside assistance, and the like.

RV insurance is required in every state, although the amount of coverage required varies. If you live in your RV full-time, you'll need to secure additional full-timers coverage. Not all companies offer this option, so be sure to ask around until you find one that does.

If you have an RVIA-certified tiny house and plan on towing it frequently, ensure that your policy has you listed as an RV and not a manufactured house. Manufactured housing policies only allow you to move once or twice per year. Also, be sure to verify that the RV insurance covers full-time residents because many policies don't.

A self-built tiny house isn't eligible for RV insurance; only RVIA-certified tiny houses bearing the RVIA seal qualify for this insurance. Some insurance companies are opening up to certification from other organizations as well. In your application process, you'll need to present proof of certification before your policy is approved.

Inland Marine Insurance Policies

Inland marine insurance covers property that's mobile in nature. This can include everything from a contractor's trailer and tools to a THOW. They're sometimes known as "floater" policies and have been on the market for many decades.

Inland marine insurance covers your tiny house but doesn't provide any liability coverage. That means if your actions while towing your THOW cause personal or bodily harm, you'll be on the hook for any bills. If you go with an inland marine policy, you'll need to get liability coverage from another source. Inland marine policies often exclude personal belongings, so renter's policies are often added to protect the contents of the tiny house.

Automobile Insurance Policies

Auto policies protect your car and provide liability coverage in the event of an accident caused by a mistake on your part. By law, all states except for New Hampshire and Virginia require a minimum of liability insurance on the policy. Other states require car owners to include add-ons, such as uninsured motorist and/ or personal injury protection policies in addition to the baseline liability coverage.

When it comes to towing a travel trailer or tiny house, many automobile insurance carriers will allow you to add an endorsement—a document amending the original policy—to your primary policy for this purpose. You must call your provider to be sure you have this option on your plan. This endorsement will provide you with liability coverage in case you accidentally damage another person's property or cause physical harm. However, it will not cover the tiny house itself or any of its contents. A renter's policy combined with an inland marine policy can make up for that shortcoming.

Renter's Insurance Policies

Renter's insurance provides many of the perks of a homeowner's policy, but it doesn't extend coverage to the actual structure itself. Instead, it offers liability protection as well as protection of personal belongings from events such as theft, fire, and vandalism.

One cool benefit of renter's insurance is that your belongings are covered no matter where you are in the world. If something is stolen from you while you're on a European vacation, your renter's policy will be there to help. It should also pay for temporary living expenses if your dwelling becomes uninhabitable due to a catastrophic event.

When selecting your policy, you'll have the option of choosing between actual cash value (ACV) coverage and replacement cost coverage (RCC). RCC covers your contents at current market value and doesn't take depreciation into consideration. That means if the two-year-old computer you paid $1,000 for is stolen, you'll receive $1,000 from your insurance company to replace it. ACV, on the other hand, values your property at what it's worth today. With this coverage, you might only receive $500 for that same computer because its current value is less than what you originally paid for it. The cost difference between these two policies is often insignificant, so go with the RCC option if you can afford it.

Insurance Options for Each Tiny House Type

Many tiny housers have no plans of ever moving their homes while others intend on living the nomadic lifestyle for years to come. Depending on where you fall on this spectrum, your insurance options will differ. Let's go over the potential scenarios and look at what choices are available in each.

RVIA-Certified Tiny Houses

The tiny housers who reside in RVIA-certified tiny houses have it the easiest when it comes to insurance. RV insurance companies have existed for decades, and they've mastered their domain. The application process is simple, coverage options are plentiful, and the premiums are affordable.

Many RVIA tiny house manufacturers have negotiated special deals with RV insurance companies. Also, many have done all the research so you can spend your hard-earned time kicking your feet up rather than shopping around.

There are a couple relatively new tiny house certification programs—Pacific West Associates, Inc. (PWA) and the National Organization of Alternative Housing, Inc. (NOAH)—that some insurance carriers are beginning to recognize in the same light as RVIA standards.

If you want standard RV insurance, you will need to purchase a RVIA-certified tiny house. There is also the possibility that an RV insurance company will recognize a tiny house certified by a third-party organization. At any rate, there will need to be some form of certification for standard RV insurance coverage.

Be sure your potential carrier offers full-timer's coverage if you intend on living year-round in your tiny house RV. Also, if you plan on moving it more than once or twice per year, be sure your insurance carrier doesn't list your tiny home as a manufactured home. A manufactured home policy requires endorsements each time you want to move the home, and the policy only protects the structure while it's parked in one place.

RV insurance policies are a complete solution that provide coverage for your tiny house structure, belongings, liability, uninsured/underinsured drivers, collision, medical, and even roadside assistance. The policy stays with your tiny house when you're parked at your favorite hidden beach cove, and it moves along with you when you're off to the next adventure. There is no need to notify your agent each time you pick up and move.

Professionally Built Non-RVIA-Certified Tiny Houses

Many folks don't want to build their own tiny house, but they also don't want to be confined to RV standards—the primary reason being that most areas that are constrained by zoning also have strict limits on how many days an RV may be parked in one spot (30 days on average). Instead, they want a THOW that abides by most (if not all) conventional construction building codes. In these situations, builders are often hired to complete the job.

Typically, finding insurance options in this scenario is not difficult, and policies are available in most states. If the THOW will be kept on your own property, the solution is as simple as a homeowner's policy from one of the many tiny house insurance providers. This coverage will extend protection for contents, the tiny house itself, the property it sits upon, and liability.

If you plan on living in your professionally built non-RVIA tiny house on rented property, you can get a homeowner's policy that includes coverage for the dwelling and personal property and also includes liability coverage.

With this policy, you don't need to remove the wheels/axles or place the THOW on a permanent foundation as far as the insurance coverage is concerned. The policy catalogs the tiny house as a primary residence and has no prejudice against it being on wheels, or that it is so small. Rates are quite reasonable, especially considering that the policy isn't a standard offering.

Most conventional insurance companies don't offer this plan, but it doesn't hurt to call and ask. If nothing else, asking for the policy tells your carrier that there is a demand for it. The more insurance companies hear about tiny houses and the need for coverage, the sooner those companies will get on board and start offering policies of their own.

If/when your professionally built tiny house is ready to be moved to its next location, other insurance policies will need to be employed because a homeowner's policy no longer applies once your tiny house is hooked up to a towing vehicle. In those situations, collaboration between an auto policy (for liability), an inland marine policy (for the tiny house itself), and a renter's insurance policy (for contents) is often used.

When your tiny house is settled into its new location, simply contact your broker and let them know the new address. Because premiums are based in large part on the distance of a residence from fire response services, it's important they know exactly where you're parked so that you get the appropriate coverage.

Fortunately, you don't need to contact individual providers to stitch this together. Currently, there are at least three tiny house insurance brokers providing this suite of solutions for most states. Professionally built tiny houses receive easier approval for coverage than self-built homes because insurance companies see them as a lower risk. Policies aren't available in every state, so be sure that your next place of residence has the coverage you want before making plans to move there.

DIY-Built Tiny Houses

Those of us who crafted our tiny houses with our own hands might have the hardest time finding coverage. Because insurers weren't there to see your construction practices, they really don't know if the home was built well or not. The most important advice we can give you on this matter is to take photos of your construction process and document every step of the procedure. This is especially important during installation of your plumbing, gas, and electrical systems.

Some insurance companies require a signed inspection report from a licensed electrician; be sure to inquire if that's necessary before you close off your wiring and electrical panel inside your walls. You'll need to go through an on-site inspection process and most likely show that your electrical was installed safely. We had to go through this process ourselves because hOMe was self-built. Thankfully, the process was all very reasonable and relatively straightforward.

Assuming everything checks out with the inspection, you should be eligible for coverage on your tiny house and its contents, and for liability.

Things become complicated when the DIY builder wants to move their THOW often. In this scenario, look for an inland marine and renter's combo. With that duo, you'll receive coverage for the structure, its contents, and liability.

If you want the freedom of the road as well as a simple insurance option, but you can't afford a professionally built tiny house, a tiny house shell might be the answer to your dreams. Several companies are now offering tiny house shells on trailers that are framed, sheathed, and roofed, which can save you months of labor. Chances are good that you'll gain easier approval, plus you'll have the benefit of being able to hit the road weeks or months earlier than if you were building the whole thing from scratch.

A newer product on the tiny house scene is builder's risk insurance. This option now allows the DIY market to insure their tiny house while it's in construction. Builder's risk insurance provides coverage in the case of loss, theft, or damage. It doesn't provide liability coverage, but rather, protection of the physical structure itself.

Builder's risk insurance might or might not include coverage for tools, so be sure to ask your agent to know exactly what you're getting. Also remember to ask if there are riders for special natural disasters if you're in a high-risk area. After your tiny house build is complete, your builder's risk insurance terminates, and you should move into whatever policy makes the most sense to you at that point based on the details previously discussed. This product is also available to professional THOW builders.

When filling out your insurance application, it's important to include all the labor it took to build your tiny house. That way, if there is total loss, you will get the true replacement value, which includes the materials as well as the number of labor hours it took for you to build it.

Finding an Agent

Luckily, it's becoming easier to find insurance agents who understand what THOWs are, what unique challenges they pose, and how to insure them. Currently, there are four we know of who deal specifically with tiny houses and can provide coverage in most states. We recommend that you reach out to them first because they've come up with viable solutions for nearly every type of tiny house out there and can ensure that you get the coverage you need.

Darrell Grenz Insurance

The first tiny house–specific broker is Darrell Grenz of Darrell Grenz Insurance in Portland, Oregon (InsureMyTinyHome.com). Darrell has been an insurance agent since 2004 and has specialized in tiny house insurance for the last 10 years. He interfaces with several major insurance companies and can offer tiny house insurance for THOWs, THOFs, THOSs, self-builds, RVIA (and other certification programs), builder's risk, rental/Airbnb/owner occupied, tiny house communities, earthquakes (in California), and much more.

Strategic Insurance Agency

The second insurance agency is Strategic Insurance Agency, a unit of Burlingame Insurance Agency. Martin Burlingame has a passion for helping the THOW community. His 12-year-old agency is located in Colorado Springs, Colorado, and focuses on providing affordable solutions for tiny homebuyers. His custom-built insurance program handles tiny homes that move across the country. He's also able to quote DIY, travel trailers, secondary dwellings, rentals, Airbnb locations, and tiny businesses.

MAC Insurance, Inc.

The third insurance agency is MAC Insurance, Inc., based in Portland, Oregon, which provides comprehensive policies for RVIA certified and self-built THOWs, THOFs, and THOSs. MAC Insurance currently can write policy in more than 40 states, making it a great option for many tiny housers.

Foremost Insurance Group

Lastly, Foremost Insurance Group, which is operated by Farmers Insurance, offers tiny house–specific and travel trailer coverage options. The USAA works directly with Foremost to develop specialized coverage options for USAA members. Foremost provides coverage for RVIA- and NOAH-certified tiny houses in every state except Hawaii and Washington, D.C. Personal property coverage, diminishing deductible, full-timer coverage, and additional living expense coverage are all offered and can be used to insure up to $150,000 of home value.

Questions to Ask Prospective Agents

It's worth stressing the importance of being up front with your insurance broker. Don't hide the fact that you're insuring a tiny house. If you submit a claim, and the insurance company finds out they weren't covering what they thought they were, they'll likely deny the claim. You'll be out all those premium payments and be stuck with all the repair, legal costs, and medical bills associated with the claim.

If you'd like to work with a non–tiny house–specific agent, there are some questions you'll want to ask to be sure you're getting the right coverage. If they don't fully understand what they're dealing with, you could be the one that bears the consequences if anything goes wrong.

Start your conversation by asking if the agent has ever heard of tiny houses or "custom travel trailers." If you aren't completely convinced, ask tough questions. You'll be armed with a fair amount of insurance lingo after reading this chapter, so apply all you've learned and put the agent to the test. The intention, of course, isn't to make the agent feel badly about themselves, but rather, to be sure the agent understands your needs so that you actually get compensated in case you file a claim.

Be certain to ask the broker what states they are insured in (this is especially important if you plan on moving your tiny house quite a bit), if they have provided coverage for THOWs before, if they require RVIA certification, if they will insure self-built tiny houses, and what insurance companies they represent. Be sure you're not pushed into a product that doesn't suit your specific needs.

You'll be asked specifics about your tiny house including its dimensions, its value, if it's a full-time residence, if it's RVIA-certified, if it's on wheels, and whether it's self-built. You'll also be asked where your THOW is parked, how old it is, how often you'll be towing it, and what vehicle will be doing the hauling. You'll get a pretty good sense by the time you're done with this phone call or meeting about how much the agent understands your needs. If the agent and policy are a fit, and the premium matches your budget, you'll be all set to go.

Keep in mind, too, that if you decide to hire a professional hauler to tow your tiny house, ask them how much "on-hook" or "moto-cargo" insurance they have per vehicle. It's not unheard of for a hauler to have insurance that doesn't fully cover the value of your tiny house, or to have enough total coverage but spread out among all their towing vehicles. Asking these questions up front can lower the risk of you paying out of pocket if something were to go awry during transport.

To Summarize

A variety of insurance options are available for THOWs nowadays, with more and more alternatives showing up every few years. The insurance package you get for your THOW depends on whether it's RVIA certified, whether it's professionally or self-built, and how often you plan on moving it. It's important that you work with an insurance broker who fully understands your coverage needs so you don't end up with any surprises if you have to file a claim.

CHAPTER 6

The Legalities of Tiny Houses on Wheels

Figuratively speaking, tiny houses on wheels (THOWs) are the new kids on the block. Even though THOWs are increasing in popularity by leaps and bounds, current building codes and zoning laws still need some work, especially at the state level. Thankfully, the U.S. housing industry is taking notice and changes are starting to happen.

In this chapter, we cover various details regarding the legalities of living in a THOW, ranging from general building codes and zoning to Accessory Dwelling Unit (ADUs), variances, tiny house communities, and RV parking.

Understanding Certification Options

A huge amount of progress has been made in the past few years toward legalizing tiny houses; however, large discrepancies between states still exist, so it is important to have a basic understanding of the roles each policy-making entity has in your tiny house journey. The primary players are the International Code Council (ICC), the Recreational Vehicle Industry Association (RVIA), and the Department of Transportation (DOT).

Which agency you approach depends upon your needs. If touring the country with a THOW is your dream, you should look at the RVIA route. If sitting on your tiny house porch watching the vegetables grow in your garden is your goal, you'll want to look into ICC codes. If you want the minimal amount of oversight but want to ensure your tiny house trailer is legal for hauling your home, you'll want to connect with your local DOT. If breaking away from any oversight is the vision, you'll want to look for areas with no zoning ordinances or building codes.

International Residential Code and THOWs

The International Residential Code (IRC) is a nationally recognized construction code used for one- and two-family dwelling unit construction in the United States. Even though it's called the *International* Residential Code, it's used primarily in the United States.

According to the International Code Council (ICC), which oversees the IRC's development, the code is currently adopted in 49 states (not enforced in Wisconsin) plus the District of Columbia, Guam, Puerto Rico, and the U.S. Virgin Islands. Building departments and inspectors at the local level enforce IRC codes and provisions.

One- and two-family dwelling units built to IRC requirements and inspected by building officials are eligible to receive a Certificate of Occupancy (COO). A COO is what gives a homeowner the green light to live in their new residence full-time. Without a COO, a structure isn't considered a legal dwelling unit or permanent residence. COOs are awarded to both professionally built and owner-built houses.

The ICC meets every three years to revise and update the code; however, some communities in the United States are still using IRC codes dating back to the early 2000s. Just because the ICC approves a code change at the national level doesn't necessarily mean your local building department has adopted the most current version. The building codes applicable to tiny houses change quite quickly relative to traditional construction, so it's important to thoroughly research the current developments on legalities.

Since the original publication of this book, some drastic changes have been made to the IRC's understanding of tiny homes. With the adoption of Appendix Q in 2018, there is now a clear framework laid out for the path to permanent residence status, although some challenges still remain for THOWs. Note that in the updated versions (post-2018) of the IRC, this appendix is now known as Appendix AQ.

The ICC also recently announced that it is working toward a consolidated document—the International Tiny House Provisions (ITHP)—that outlines the building codes applicable to tiny houses and enables building officials to certify THOWs for full-time residence status. The ITHP will simply provide a clear outline for state and local officials to follow when it comes to tiny house legalities; however, there is still some confusion regarding what will be considered a foundation under this code.

The ICC's decision to dedicate resources, time, and money toward the legalization of tiny houses—particularly those on wheels—is truly remarkable considering how little the council cared about THOWs just a few years ago. We were quite literally laughed at by the committee when we originally presented to the ICC on tiny houses, so these provisions represent a historic shift in the movement. And it wouldn't have been possible without the dedication and passion of tiny housers across the country coming together.

IRC for Tiny Houses on Wheels

According to the recently added Appendix AQ, the IRC considers dwellings under 400 square feet to be tiny houses. The changes to the code that Appendix AQ provides make the process of building a legal tiny house much easier. The primary requirements for THOWs to comply with IRC codes are outlined in the following sections.

Ceiling Heights

Tiny houses on wheels towed on public roads are subject to state and national highway regulations. Most states limit the height of a moving vehicle to 13'6". This maximum is set to protect tall vehicles from hitting bridges and overpasses as they drive underneath.

Prior to the recent amendments, the IRC had required a minimum ceiling height of 7 feet on every story—largely inhibiting the ability to include lofts. The new standards in Appendix AQ allow for ceiling heights of 6'8" for general-use areas of the home and 6'4" for bathrooms and kitchens; additionally, loft ceilings are permitted to be less than 6'8". This simple reduction in ceiling heights has a significant impact on tiny house design, construction, and use.

Foundations

In the eyes of code inspectors, there's no such thing as a permanent residence on wheels. All houses they oversee and permit are set on permanent foundations. Even manufactured houses, which are delivered on wheels to their location site, are set on permanent foundations before receiving COOs.

That said, options do exist to satisfy the need for a foundation. The type of foundation you use is determined by local soils, topography, and other factors. Let's go over the foundation options that can be applied to THOWs:

- Concrete slab on grade with adequate anchoring
- Concrete pad and pier
- Perimeter concrete foundation
- Certified manufactured housing system
- Permanent wood foundation

Foundation systems and trailers were not directly addressed in the code change of 2015. People can design foundation systems that meet the intent of the code, as described in the 2021 IRC under Section R101.3: "Intent," and submit them under Section R104.11 of the 2021 IRC: "Alternative materials, design and methods of construction and equipment." Until the IRC completes the ITHP document and there is specific verbiage for THOWs, RVIA certification will continue to be your most straightforward option for legalizing your THOW.

As long as the proposed foundation system satisfies the building official in regard to the intent of the code and, therefore, the health and safety of both the inhabitants and any emergency crew that might service the home, you should be able to receive a building permit—assuming the rest of the design meets the required standards. To be sure, there's a lot to know about foundations and properly attaching your home to them. For more detailed information, check out Chapter 11.

Emergency Escape Access

The intention of building codes is not only to keep a home's occupants safe, but also to protect emergency crew members. One area of particular interest for building inspectors is fire safety. Emergency egress is an opening that provides direct access to a structure's interior and addresses both the points of escape should your home catch fire and the emergency rescue routes for emergency crews.

A tiny house loft could prove dangerous in a fire without a means of egress. An emergency roof access escape window is an ideal solution and meets code requirements when installed within a maximum of 44 inches off the floor. We have officially added this standard to the IRC appendix. As a secondary safety measure, we recommend you install a folding escape ladder to get you safely to the ground in the case of emergency.

Sleeping Lofts

It's common for people to build sleeping lofts in their THOW. With the adoption of Appendix AQ, lofts can be legally constructed in tiny homes, as long as they meet the minimum area and dimensions of sections AQ104.1.1 through AQ104.1.3.

In addition to the emergency egress and rescue requirements previously mentioned, there are now standards for minimum loft ceiling heights as well as loft area square footage requirements. With these two provisions in place, you can design a sleeping loft that is both comfortable and within the code. For a loft to be considered legal by the IRC, it must have a floor area of no less than 35 square feet, a width of no less than 5 feet, and a ceiling height of at least 3 feet at its highest point.

If you don't want to build your house with a code-compliant sleeping loft, you have three other options for dealing with potential loft constraints.

- The first, and easiest, is to build your THOW without a loft and place your bedroom downstairs.

- The second option is to design your THOW with a freestanding loft, or bunk bed system. Because the loft is freestanding, it's considered furniture, not structural. That means the loft isn't subject to ceiling height provisions and restrictions.

- The third approach isn't one we recommend, but we need to mention it because it's done so often. Many people simply label lofts on architectural plans as *storage*. Because building officials can't require emergency egress, minimum ceiling heights, or stair access for storage areas, it removes any oversight from the code official. Once the COO is issued, the occupants then use these storage lofts as bedrooms.

Loft Access

The IRC has detailed specifics for the construction of stairs in conventional residential housing. Unfortunately, building a code-compliant set of stairs to those standards in a THOW is very difficult, if not impossible, to achieve. There are specifications on ceiling heights above each stair tread (which can't be met as you approach the top of the stairs). Also, there is a minimum 36-inch stair width (which can't easily be met because these homes are so narrow). Lastly, the dimensions of the stair treads and risers themselves can't be met due to limited space.

The issue of loft access was a big one in the newly approved code appendix. All the requirements have changed in a way that makes building stairs viable in a THOW. Required stair width has been reduced. Ceiling-height requirements above stairs have been lowered. Stair riser and tread dimensions have been altered to simplify the construction in tight spaces. In other words, we now have our own set of standards for stairways in tiny houses.

An example of stairs using alternating tread devices in a tiny house built by Chad Smith of StructuralSpaces .com. (Photo by Jenn Walton/Digiwerx Studios.)

The new appendix also allows for the use of ladders for loft access as well as alternating tread devices and ships ladders. The issue had been that these loft access devices previously permitted in the code were *not* allowed to be the primary means of egress. That provision has been successfully changed so that you can choose which type of loft access best suits your design: stairways, ladders, ships ladders, or alternating tread devices. They're all legal to use under Appendix AQ.

IRC for Tiny Houses on Foundations and Skids

When building a tiny house on a fixed foundation, you get back all the things you wanted: when you remove the trailer and its width and height restrictions, you have a clear path to approval within the current IRC for most tiny houses.

A code change in the 2015 IRC modified a semantic contradiction in the previous versions, which stipulated that a habitable room needed to be at least 120 square feet. This clarification now permits a habitable room to be as small as 70 square feet. It's a big deal for tiny houses as this new minimum standard allows for a much smaller tiny house, around 93 square feet, which includes a bathroom.

The provisions of the 2018 Appendix AQ improve the design and construction of tiny houses on foundations (THOFs), too. The same provisions that help a THOW find a path to legality also help keep the scale of THOFs in check. After all, a 200-square-foot tiny house with two stories, each 7 feet tall, would look weird. Under the new code, the design details will all make better sense and, as a result, help create more aesthetically pleasing tiny houses.

We should note that according to the IRC, a dwelling unit, which is an official name for a home, is required to have specific elements within it in order to qualify for a COO. For example, you need permanent areas for eating, sleeping, cooking, sanitation, and living. All these requirements can be met in one room, similar to a studio apartment, except for the sanitation area, which is required to be separate.

Tiny houses on skids (THOSs) are an interesting hybrid when it comes to IRC requirements. On one hand, they can be built on permanent foundations, yet on the other, they can be moved by being detached from those foundations. Because a THOS can be moved, you need to consider road restrictions and requirements.

The good news is that codes do evolve, but it takes time. The approval of Appendix AQ into the 2018 IRC shows that the topic of tiny houses has truly landed on the ear of building departments across the country, and they are looking for help in the approval/disapproval process. Several building officials at the ICC hearings told us that most code changes of this scale take two or three code cycles to approve. That's 6 to 9 years! We got ours approved the first time around.

RVIA-Certified Homes

There's another option for legalizing tiny houses on wheels: by obtaining a Recreational Vehicle Industry Association (RVIA) certification. At this juncture, RVIA accreditation is only available to professional builders that have gone through the certification process. Unlike the IRC, the RVIA certification is not available for the DIY builder.

The advantage of purchasing a premade RVIA-certified tiny house or working with an RVIA builder while building the home yourself is that you'll get a certified home in the end. It's then easier to secure insurance and financing and may even be required at some RV parks. It also offers peace of mind knowing that your THOW was built to meet safety standards.

The RVIA requires that homes built under its umbrella meet the provisions of the American National Standards Institute (ANSI) code, specifically sections A1192 and/or A119.5. These code provisions are more lenient than those in the IRC and allow for more flexibility when it comes to building a THOW. For example, it recognizes a movable trailer as a legitimate foundation option, something not currently allowed in the IRC.

The downside of RVIA certification is that it doesn't provide you with a certificate of occupancy. In other words, you're no closer to owning a permanent residence at the end of the day in the eyes of local zoning and building departments. To them, your tiny home is still considered an RV.

This distinction is critical depending on what your needs and wants are. If you plan on traveling more than once per month in your THOW or renting space in an RV park, then an RVIA certification is your best option, especially because many RV parks won't accept noncertified units on their property for liability reasons.

If you intend on parking your tiny house legally in one location for several months or more, a COO is what you'll need. Because zoning regulations in most municipalities have strict rules against long-term parking for RVs (typically a maximum of 30 days), an RVIA certification won't be of much help.

If you want to move your tiny house from time to time and still have a COO, you'll need to ensure your house meets the local code requirements for each new location. Just as full-scale homes can be moved from location to location, you can also move your tiny house and its COO. During the move itself, your house will be considered a *load on a trailer*, not a residence. Once situated in its new location and attached to a foundation, a new COO will be issued, which voids the previous one.

Although there are unincorporated communities around the country that don't impose zoning/code rules, and more and more municipalities are changing their zoning laws to accept THOWs, such communities are still few and far between. These areas are mostly rural and take some research to find, but they are out there and can be a viable option if you don't plan to seek certification for your THOW.

Additionally, there's significant confusion about the Office of Housing and Urban Development's (HUD) role in the tiny house movement. This is because of misinformation found on the internet. HUD doesn't currently oversee tiny houses in any form. HUD is only in charge of manufactured housing and certifies only the facilities that produce said housing.

DOT-Certified Trailers

You can get your tiny house certified as a load-on-a-trailer through the Department of Transportation (DOT). This option is typically the easiest and the one with the least amount of oversight. At the end of the DOT employee's inspection, you're granted the right to transfer a load (your THOW) onto a DOT-registered trailer.

The primary focus of these inspections is the connection between the trailer and the load it's carrying. A DOT inspector might or might not look at your construction plans. They might not even be concerned with the construction progress of your home.

This certification only represents a right to transport a load on your trailer. You should not consider this an endorsement of your home or a COO. If you want something more than a trailer certification, then the DOT route isn't for you.

Zoning and Where to Park

Now that you have a clear understanding of which agencies govern what in the world of tiny house construction, you need to consider where you're going to park your THOW. Once again, you'll need to contemplate the kind of life you want to live within your house. Will you be skipping with it state to state, or will you be keeping it parked in one place for quite some time?

Your local zoning department is the entity that dictates where you can park your THOW. As much as they might love tiny houses and want to help, they're bound by local zoning ordinances and must act accordingly. These laws are complex, so let's look at how the system operates.

How Zoning Works

Zoning departments are charged with regulating the use of land in a municipality. In very simplistic terms, they decide who gets to be neighbors with whom. If you get a knock on your tiny house door by an official citing a complaint from a neighbor saying that you're parked illegally, that's your friendly zoning enforcement officer paying a visit. Building codes tell you *how* to build your tiny house while zoning codes tell you *where* you can park your THOW.

The motives for zoning regulations in a community are inherently good. Without these policies, an industrial chemical salvage company could set up operations next to your house.

The challenge for the tiny house community is that because tiny houses are on wheels, zoning officers often lump them into the same category as RVs. There has long been a stigma against year-round RV living in residential communities, so most municipalities in the country have set a time limit of 30 days for inhabiting a location in an RV.

It won't matter if you have an RVIA-certified tiny home now or not. What matters is that your tiny home is considered an RV by local zoning departments. Knowing how to approach a zoning department to gain permission to live full-time in a THOW is essential. For starters, you'll need to know which zoning department to contact.

There are multiple layers of zoning control, from national oversight all the way down to the land parcel itself:

- *Federal zoning* laws oversee land use in areas such as national parks and other federally owned lands.

- Below federal oversight is *state zoning*, which manages areas such as state parks, restricted wetlands, and so forth.

- Next comes *county zoning*, which is typically the first office you'll contact regarding your zoning questions. Even though federal and state guidelines might be in place on your property, private landowners rarely deal with those agencies directly because the local zoning offices are charged with ensuring that the larger requirements are met.

- If the property in question is located within city limits, you'll deal directly with the *city zoning* office rather than the county zoning office. This varies from location to location, so it's a good idea to make a few phones calls before visiting any of the offices.

There can be more layers of zoning control, such as plat requirements or setbacks from property lines. *Plat* refers to the specific piece of property in question as defined by public records and land surveys. Another layer of zoning control can be homeowners associations (HOA), which can prohibit RVs from being parked on the property. Sometimes, regulations at this level are the strictest and most challenging to appeal. For example, a piece of land on the market might be saddled with a new construction minimum square footage requirement of 2,000, which would eliminate any hopes of putting a tiny home on that land.

Each level of control can present a challenge, whether you're parking on someone else's property or buying your own land. We recommend you search for any zoning restrictions on the property in question before making any decisions. You can do this yourself through the office of public records or through your zoning department.

Some zoning records are complicated and difficult to interpret. If you're unsure how to interpret what you've found, we highly recommend hiring a title company to do the research for you. It'll cost some money, but in the end, you'll receive a detailed and comprehensive report explaining everything in laymen's terms.

How to Approach Zoning

Now that you've done your research on the property in question, it's time to contact zoning directly. The best advice we can give is to always be friendly, professional, and appreciative. Keep in mind that people working in building departments frequently must deal with disgruntled applicants. A warm smile and a sincere thank you can go a long way.

Here are some action steps to take when approaching officials:

Anonymous contact. If you call the zoning department and say, "Hi. I own the property at 123 Main Street, and I want to build a tiny house on wheels on it," you've put all your cards on the table before knowing their position on THOWs. Instead, tell them you're considering purchasing a property on Main Street and that you're interested in building a residence no larger than 400 square feet. If they say it's not a possibility, take notes on the reasons provided. Ask them to be as specific as possible so you can address each issue when you eventually fill out your application.

Learn the details. Do your research and ensure you have at least a reasonable understanding of the codes and zoning in your area. If the RR2 zoning you hope to build on allows for only one house per two acres, don't show up and ask for a permit to build three. Be smart in your approach, and know what you can and can't do before making your application.

Preparation. When you're ready to officially present your application, be sure it's complete and addresses the issues the zoning officers initially specified. Your application should demonstrate that you have a thorough grasp of your project and that you understand the zoning process.

Keep in mind that zoning officials are often swamped with applications. They typically prefer conventional projects because anything out of the ordinary represents more work for them. If you present them with not only an unconventional project but also a poorly prepared application, you've likely stepped off on the wrong foot from the get go. Few things irritate a building official more than receiving an incomplete application.

Present your project in terms of benefits to your community. For example, the city or county might be required to provide a certain number of affordable housing units to their jurisdiction. Meeting that quota can be difficult, so you should suggest that perhaps your THOW can be counted as one of these units. Maybe you live in an area in which there are more residents moving out than in. In that case, highlight other communities that have welcomed tiny houses and have seen a population boom. The more you can show that your build will be an asset, the more likely they are to approve it.

Professionalism. This might seem obvious, but showing up to the zoning office or a meeting wearing sweatpants and a ripped T-shirt doesn't exude professionalism. Do yourself a favor and show up looking professional and acting politely and respectfully.

Land use consultants. Although expensive, hiring a land use consultant can be a very smart decision, especially if your project has several unusual aspects to it. These consultants will ensure that you don't overlook important details in your application. They'll also know who you should and should not speak with at your zoning office. They will steer you to the right people, so you don't end up potentially compromising your project by approaching someone who can make it very difficult for you.

Avoiding Common Pitfalls

We all want our projects to run smoothly, and we certainly don't want to make a careless mistake and create unnecessary hardships. There are several pitfalls that can easily be avoided if you know what they look like. Here are the top ones:

Don't demand anything. As soon as you start expressing that something is your right, you'll lose the building official's attention. Communicate, don't dictate.

Be strong but not rigid. It's important to be passionate and enthusiastic when presenting your project. At the same time, you need to be flexible on any changes that won't cause a *huge* impact on your project. Give a little when you can.

Respect. If you disrespect a building official, you might have lost them for good. Show them that you value their opinion, even if you disagree with it. A civil conversation is always more effective than a shouting match.

Don't rush them. Your lack of planning does not constitute an emergency to anyone on the zoning staff. Provide yourself with plenty of time when dealing with this office.

Smile in the face of adversity. If an official is rude, continue to be polite and even friendly. You may find that it disarms the situation and changes the entire tone of the conversation.

It can be difficult to remember these points when faced with an uncompromising building or zoning official. If you can manage to apply these tools when needed, you could turn a bad situation into a good one. In the end, it's better to have your project approved than to simply win an argument.

Your Primary Residence

If you plan on making your tiny house your primary residence, you'll need a COO to do so legally. As you might recall, it's the building department (not zoning) that issues those certificates. COOs are important in zoning because residential areas are zoned only for residential homes. That's why you won't find industrial chemical salvage yards next to houses. It's also why you're not allowed to live full-time in RVs in residential neighborhoods.

Currently, unless you have a COO, you won't be allowed to inhabit your tiny house legally in most jurisdictions. While there are some exceptions, and many positive changes are happening around the country, non-COO-approved THOWs simply are not allowed in the vast majority of residential areas at this time.

Parking in RV Parks

RV parks can be a great option for a THOW. Many of them are very nicely developed, situated in pretty locations, and foster a tight-knit community. They can offer amenities such as community gathering spaces, swimming pools, playgrounds, Wi-Fi, and more.

Most RV parks have opened their gates for THOWs with enthusiasm, but others have unfortunately taken a stance against them simply because they're different. Knowing whether you'll be welcome or not is something you can find out ahead of time by simply placing a phone call. Do the research beforehand.

In most cases, RV parks have time limits for how long someone can stay there. This is because zoning regulations have earmarked RV parks for recreational, not permanent housing. These time constraints are almost always enforced by the park owner (not by zoning officers). That means if they're comfortable with you staying permanently, there shouldn't be any issues.

If you have a house on a trailer that was certified by the DOT or a self-built tiny house, it might be hard to place it in an RV park. Many RV parks require RVs to be RVIA certified and meet basic safety standards. If an unsafe RV or tiny house were to catch on fire, it could be devastating for all the neighbors and the property.

Accessory Dwelling Units (ADUs)

The frequency of THOWs being used as Accessory Dwelling Units (ADUs) has increased dramatically in a short time. Several towns, including Fresno and Ojai, California; Nantucket, Massachusetts; Rockledge, Florida; and others across the country, have changed their zoning ordinances to allow THOWs to be placed as backyard cottages. Although not considered primary residences, ADUs offer another option for those looking to park their homes in residential neighborhoods.

In general, ADUs or backyard cottages are allowed on properties that have already developed a primary residence. The size of the ADU typically can't be larger than a specific percentage of the main house. In most cases, the ADU must share a utility meter with the main house and can't have its own. The main downside of this approach is that ADUs typically must be owned by the property owners themselves and their rental may not be allowed.

To improve your chances of being allowed to place your THOW as an ADU in your community, be sure to highlight the quality design and construction of your home. You want to showcase the value it brings as a backyard cottage when approaching the zoning department.

Finding Creative Solutions

You might find yourself in a position in which normal routes to home approval just won't work for you. This could be due to local ordinances, your home's design, or some other combination of issues. No matter what the cause, the solution might take some creativity. Persistence is a great quality in times like this. There are always options available if you look hard enough.

How Variances Work

The most commonly used alternative approach for home approval is the use of a variance. A variance is simply an official request to deviate from the standards of current zoning requirements. An approved variance does not change the zoning in which the home is located. Instead, it provides the property owner with a waiver from the specific requirements of the zoning ordinance.

Each application process is slightly different, so you'll need to contact your local zoning department and ask what specific steps you need to take. One certainty is that there will be a fee involved with the application process. The amount of that fee varies from place to place.

Variance applications can be challenging and require a lot of forethought and planning. Since you're asking for an exemption to a zoning law, you'll need to assemble evidence explaining why they should give it to you. How hard it is to get a variance depends largely on the community you live in. Some make it super challenging, while others gladly hand them out.

An example of where a variance could be approved is in the case of caring for an elderly family member. Perhaps the caregiver wants to live on the land, close to the elderly person but not in the same house. A THOW is a great solution for such a scenario. The home can be in close proximity to the main house, yet everyone's privacy is maintained.

Developing a Tiny House Community

Many people in the tiny house movement are excited about the idea of living in a tiny house community. Several tiny house communities are emerging around the country and more are in the planning stages every day.

If you're interested in starting your own, look for land zoned for RV parks and/or recreational use. Research the likelihood of a variance to allow for full-time residency. These proposals are best framed from the perspective of affordable housing. Because so many communities are experiencing significant hardships with real estate costs at all-time highs, they're often happy about projects that can ease this burden, especially when it comes with no hard costs to them.

Another option is to look for property zoned for multi-family use. In those situations, there's little you need to do in terms of zoning because it's already designated for this type of use. You might, however, need to make some modifications on how many homes are allowed on the property. Once again, present your project from the perspective of mutual benefits.

To Summarize

THOWs currently fall into a gray area in terms of codes and zoning, although much of that is changing as tiny houses gain popularity. The primary players are the International Code Council (ICC), the International Residential Code (IRC), the Recreational Vehicle Industry Association (RVIA), and the Department of Transportation (DOT). There are options for people who want to live in their THOW legally; knowing which route to take depends on your goals. Zoning plays a big part in tiny house living, so knowing the basics of how zoning works is essential. Variances are the most commonly used approach when looking for an exemption from current zoning laws and can work well for many tiny housers.

CHAPTER 7

Tiny Houses on the Move

Road trips with tiny housers are unlike any other. Being mobile is one of the key perks that draw people into the tiny house movement. The freedom of the road and promise of beautiful sunsets in new destinations inspire people to choose a mobile lifestyle.

Understanding the rules of the towing world is something you'll need to invest time in while designing your THOW. There are restrictions for width and height, and sometimes for weight and length as well, and they all vary not only state by state but also road by road. Fortunately, there are some excellent resources to help you make informed decisions. Let's take a look at various factors you'll need to consider from size restrictions, to special travel permits, hiring out the move, and mapping out a safe journey.

Size Restrictions

Hopping into your car and driving into town is no big deal. You know your vehicle's going to fit under bridges, be narrow enough for road widths, and be easy to maneuver. Hook up a tiny house to a trailer hitch though, and suddenly your driving experience becomes quite a bit more complicated.

Vehicle size restrictions are in place to keep drivers safe. They are also there to ensure that vehicles on public roads don't hit low bridges or cause accidents because they're too wide. Even though these limits vary state to state, there are some general guidelines to help you.

Maximum vehicle heights range from 13'6" to 14'6", depending on the state you're traveling through. If you intend to tow your tiny house through more than just your home state at any point, we recommend you not exceed 13'6" on your design. That way, you won't confine yourself to traveling only in states that allow vehicles with heights over 13'6".

As is the case with vehicle height, vehicle width is also a big deal when designing your THOW. The national limit is 8'6", so that's a number you can commit to memory as you consider how wide to design your tiny house.

One often missed, but essential, point is that measurements are taken at the widest and tallest portions of a trailer. In other words, if your THOW, from roof edge to roof edge, measures 8'6" wide, but you have an entry light or vent shroud that extends beyond that dimension, your house is now considered wider than 8'6" and will require a wide-load permit.

If you want to extend venting or other features beyond the road limits, be sure to install them in such a way that you can easily remove them before hitting the road. Highway safety officers don't often pull over THOWs, but when they do, they could choose to measure the height from top to bottom, so it's important to be within the legal limits.

Length isn't quite as much of an issue for THOWs being towed on highways. You can haul a trailer up to nearly 60 feet long, which is much larger than a typical tiny house. We doubt you'll run into a situation where your tiny house is too long from a highway restriction standpoint.

Where length does become a design consideration, though, is when you plan on towing your THOW in areas with larger than normal grade changes and when you need to maneuver through small towns and roads. Hauling a long trailer is a lot more challenging than a short one. They are more prone to issues with sway, which can lead to fishtailing and loss of control. If you tow something 30 feet or longer, you should consider using a gooseneck trailer, fifth-wheel trailer, or a pintle hitch, all of which require a special hitch attachment on a pickup truck (ideally a 1-ton dual-wheel truck).

Weight restrictions typically aren't a significant issue for THOWs. Generally, roads are established with much larger loads in mind. That said, if you need to cross a very small bridge or someplace with a strict weight limit, you'll need to heed those warnings.

Weight restrictions are often described per vehicular axle. For example, rather than saying a 17,000-pound vehicle is not permitted, the sign could read, "Road restricted to vehicles over 17,000 pounds with less than three axles" or "Road restricted to vehicles carrying over 5,000 pounds per axle." This is because spreading the weight over a series of axles lessens the individual impact of the load through each tire. In other words, the same load is spread out over more surface area, thus reducing the potential impact per square inch on the road surface.

Knowing how your trailer and tow vehicle's weight is distributed is important. Just because your trailer has three axles and your truck has two doesn't mean you can simply divide 17,000 pounds by five and get an accurate answer.

For example, a 17,000-pound home being hauled by a bumper pull trailer hitch might only have 10 percent of the total weight on the tongue of the tow vehicle. This means that two of the five axles are only carrying 1,700 pounds. The remaining 15,300 pounds are distributed across the three trailer axles, or 5,100 pounds per axle. As you can see, you are thus restricted from the 5,000-pound-per-axle road, not because of your overall house weight, but because of the per-axle weight.

Special Travel Permits

If your THOW's dimensions exceed the size restrictions mentioned previously, you can most likely still tow it, but you'll need to obtain special permits. These permits aren't issued at the national level but rather state by state. That means if you plan on cruising through 30 states in your wide-load tiny house, you'll need to go through the application process in each state and pay all the individual permit fees. You can research vehicle size restrictions state by state on the Department of Transportation's website, transportation.gov.

Some roads are wider than others and do a better job accommodating wide loads.

Generally speaking, a vehicle wider than 8'6" but narrower than 12 feet requires a simple wide-load permit. The fee usually costs less than $50 per state line crossed. Those wider than 12 feet and narrower than 16 feet require a wide-load permit, a DOT number, and an escort/pilot car. Wide-load vehicles might also be subject to restrictions on hours of travel. A great resource for specifics is heavyhaul.net.

Hiring Out the Move

Regardless of whether you build wider than 8'6" or not, hiring a professional hauler can bring peace of mind when moving your house. Always be sure the hauler is licensed, bonded, and insured. If the unthinkable happens and something goes wrong during your house move, the burden of responsibility falls on them and their insurance company. In addition, haulers are responsible for acquiring all pertinent permits and planning out appropriate travel routes.

It can be relatively expensive to hire someone to haul your tiny house, but hiring a professional could start looking quite affordable in these situations:

- You don't plan to move your tiny house often.

- You don't want to learn how to tow a large trailer.

- You don't want to deal with the white-knuckle drive.

- You don't want to spend tens of thousands of dollars on a vehicle strong enough to tow your house.

As is true with any contract, be sure to read your agreement carefully and identify what is and what is not covered. It's quite unfortunate when a towing company doesn't have comprehensive insurance or enough coverage to compensate their client.

Mapping Your Route

If you've ever driven into a parking garage or fast-food joint with those low-hanging yellow tubes and wondered if your car would clear it, you know the feeling of approaching a low clearance landmark. It's an unsettling feeling, even as you approach it at just 2 miles per hour (mph). Imagine what hitting a low bridge while cruising at 50 mph is like! Unfortunately, this happens regularly, even in places with clearly marked signs and flashing warning lights.

If you decide to move the house yourself, it's not just a good idea to map out your route, it's imperative. Some roads have tight restrictions on width, height, length, and weight due to obstructions or special circumstances such as tunnels, narrow roads, tight corners, or bridges. Know your THOW's dimensions as you begin the trip-planning process, and make the appropriate decisions regarding routing.

Be sure to pay special attention to signs that include "cars only," "oversized vehicles," or "truck routes," especially on the east coast of the United States. Many of their overpasses were built long before trucks reached current sizes. Virtually every public road that restricts travel for certain vehicles will have clear signs marking the dangers.

A great (and free if you're a member) resource for planning all your THOW journeys is goodsam.com. Simply type in your point of origin, destination, and vehicle details, and it will calculate an appropriate route for your trailer based on its size. You can also contact the highway departments in the states you intend to travel through and ask for their guidance.

RV and trucking GPS units are also available and are probably the easiest travel solutions. However, be aware that they are not always accurate—especially in rural areas. Always pay close attention to local signs, and don't trust GPS units 100 percent.

Lastly, another excellent resource used by the pros is the Rand McNally *Motor Carrier's Road Atlas Deluxe Edition*. This is a great option for those who prefer physical maps over virtual options.

Learning to Drive Your House

Our guess is that you never expected to need lessons on how to tow a house. If you're not a professional driver, you'll definitely want to put in the time to learn how to haul a THOW. It's not the same thing as driving a car or pickup truck. It's not even the same thing as towing a large RV because THOWs are typically heavier than conventional RVs. Here are some important safety tips and considerations to keep in mind.

Backing Up

If you've never backed up a trailer before, you'll need to practice this skill before hauling your house around. Getting a trailer to respond to turns while reversing is backward compared to backing a car without a trailer. The steering wheel needs to be turned the opposite way from the direction you want the trailer to go. It may sound simple, but it's counterintuitive, so takes some time to master.

I suggest you rent a moderately sized trailer, say a 4×8-foot box trailer, and practice in an empty parking lot for starters. Set up some cones as obstacles and practice reversing until you're very comfortable with the process. Every trailer backs up differently, so mastering one doesn't necessarily mean you'll be a pro with a THOW. Luckily, the longer a trailer is, the easier it is to maneuver in reverse. If you're skilled with an 8-foot trailer, you'll be poised to do well with its 28-foot cousin.

You'll also want to practice backing up while using just your mirrors as guides. If you turn your head and body to reverse, you're locked into seeing just one side of the trailer, whereas with mirrors, you can see both sides with a quick swivel of your head. This is an important skill that'll allow you to adjust the path of your trailer quickly if needed.

Backing up can be dangerous because you can't see what's directly behind you unless you have a camera on your THOW. Always have a person outside the vehicle to assist you and let you know if there is a hazard behind you. Purchasing an inexpensive pair of handheld radio transceivers (i.e., walkie talkies) can make this process quite a bit easier for everyone involved.

Know the Road

Understanding the significance of the size and weight of your THOW is important. Even though it's called *tiny*, the reality is that it's most likely the biggest thing you'll ever tow. This will take some getting used to.

You may be surprised to see just how big your house is after you complete the build, so don't plan on taking a cross-country road trip right after it's done. Instead, drive your house locally for a few weeks. Perhaps set up a mini road trip and go to a couple RV parks to get used to driving, parking, hooking up, unhooking, and so on.

Keep in mind that you'll need to swing out to the left when turning right so that you don't clip the curb or anything on the road edge. There are a lot of things to get used to when pulling a THOW, but stick with it and you'll be a pro in little time.

Driving Downhill

THOWs are significantly heavier than regular vehicles and often more so than RVs, so you'll need to learn how to manage that weight when driving downhill. Brakes aren't designed for long-term application, so if you ride them down a long, steep grade, you'll likely burn them out. Instead, you'll need to learn how to "engine brake" (or "Jake Brake"). When engine braking, you downshift to lower gears to limit the velocity of your vehicle. This eliminates the risk of burning out your brakes and losing the ability to slow the vehicle entirely.

Speed is always a factor when discussing braking, so be sure to reduce your velocity. We suggest drivers not exceed 45 mph when traveling with their tiny house, even on highways. Patience may just be the virtue that gets you to your destination without incident. We also recommend that you triple (at least) your normal braking distance while towing a THOW, especially when you are first learning.

Trailer brakes are a non-negotiable requirement for all THOWs. They're installed on the trailer itself and hooked up to the tow vehicle electronically. When the brakes are applied in the tow vehicle, a signal is sent to the trailer brakes to engage, placing a stopping force on the trailer instead of relying on the towing vehicle's brakes to do all the work.

Most trailer brakes are adjustable based on the weight of the trailer. Be sure to read the installation instructions and adjust them accordingly. Setting them too aggressively or too weakly can have unpleasant consequences when you need them most.

A runaway truck ramp is not something you want to experience firsthand for several reasons. First of all, it would be terrifying to be so out of control that you actually have to use one to save your life. Secondly, if you use a runaway truck ramp, you'll be required to pay for the towing vehicle that pulls you out. Thirdly, you'll likely incur an expensive reckless driving ticket to top it all off.

Weighing In

The best way to determine the exact weight of your THOW is by taking it to a public or private weigh station. They're relatively easy to use and provide a lot of useful information, including the Gross Vehicle Weight Rating (GVWR) and Gross Trailer Weight Rating (GTWR), tongue weight, trailer weight per axle, and tow vehicle weight per axle.

GVWR is used to identify the total weight of a vehicle when loaded to capacity and as specified by the vehicle manufacturer. This includes the weight of the vehicle plus any loads carried upon but does not include any information related to trailers or their cargo. GTWR, conversely, is used to identify the total weight of a trailer when loaded to capacity but does not include any information related to the tow vehicle.

The general guidelines for knowing when it's required to stop at a weigh station are as follows:

- Your vehicle is a commercial vehicle.
- Your GVWR exceeds posted weight limits for the specific road you're traveling on.

You're most likely not a commercial vehicle (you would know if you were), so that part's easy. The second guideline refers to both your GVWR and GTWR numbers. If either exceeds the stated limits, you'll need to stop.

Depending on the station location and requirements, you might not be able to avoid stopping at weigh stations along your route. You can visit AAA's website (aaa.com) to learn more about these laws across the United States and Canada.

In some states, a commercial driver's license is required if the weight of your towing vehicle and THOW exceeds a certain number. In most cases, the weight threshold is 26,000 pounds, which is more than most tiny houses and tow vehicles weigh combined. As THOWs become larger, however, this is a factor that could come into play with greater frequency. You can find out what your state requirements are by visiting your local DOT as well as by contacting the DOTs in the states you plan on towing through.

Commercial drivers are subject to stricter regulations. They must pass yearly physicals and drug tests, stop at all weigh stations (unless specifically told otherwise), and keep daily travel logs. Whether you're a commercial driver or not, we recommend daily inspections on your tow vehicle and THOW before hitting the road. By ensuring all lights are working properly and fluids are topped off, you'll reduce a lot of risks while towing your beloved tiny house.

Some states and specific routes might require recreational vehicles to stop. In the eyes of weigh station authorities, your THOW is an RV, even if it's your primary residence. Be sure to pay attention to these directional signs.

To Summarize

Designing your THOW to comply with the rules of the road will save you a lot of money and headaches down the line. Special permits can be issued/purchased for larger-than-normal trailers. Hiring out the move is often a great option for peace of mind, ease, and overall cost. In most cases, you don't need to stop at weigh stations with your THOW, but it's vital to know when you are required to do so. Always check the road restrictions and requirements of each state that you plan on driving your THOW through because the laws often vary.

PART 2

Defining Your Style

One of the best parts about designing and building your own tiny house is playing with style and creating something that truly represents you. That said, if you haven't spent much time considering your specific needs and wants in a tiny house, you might feel challenged without some guidelines and suggestions.

In Part 2, we cover the main areas of a tiny house: the kitchen, bedrooms, living area, and bathroom. We list various considerations as well as options and solutions for each. We consider aesthetics, function, safety, budget, and layouts. By the end of this part, you'll have a strong understanding of what your needs are and how to meet them in your dream tiny house.

CHAPTER 8

Kitchen Necessities

For some people, the kitchen is the focal point of the home and the priority of their tiny house design. It was for us! On the other hand, some folks love nothing more than going out to eat or are simply atrocious cooks. Knowing what type of chef you are is the best information you can have when going into your design process.

In this chapter, we'll cover all the factors you'll need to consider when creating your dream tiny house kitchen. We'll look at fun exercises to help you identify your needs, as well as a list of questions to ask yourself before you even begin the design process. We'll go over the major necessary appliances and offer suggestions on how to find the right ones for you. We'll even cover three tried-and-true tiny house kitchen layouts to help inspire you. Let's get cooking!

How Important Is Your Kitchen?

We loved everything we saw when we first started looking at tiny houses except for one thing: the miniscule kitchens. We are an active family of four, both of our kids have celiac disease (an autoimmune disease aggravated by the ingestion of gluten), and we rarely eat out. Food is a centerpiece of our lives, so the prospect of having a dorm-size fridge and a two-burner stove wasn't appealing in the least.

This was back in 2009 when tiny house kitchens were impossibly small for a family like ours. We knew we were going to have to break some design boundaries and find a way to create a custom kitchen, even if it meant sacrificing space in our living area.

Not everyone needs a kitchen quite as large and well stocked as ours, though. Many tiny housers work outside the home, are gone most of the day, and enjoy their meals at restaurants. Their kitchen serves as a place for breakfast food and storage for restaurant leftovers.

Perhaps you fall somewhere between these two extremes. What size kitchen you need is a question that only you can answer. It's important to be crystal clear on what your priorities are when it comes to food and cooking. Following are some questions to ask in your initial design process.

How Often Do You Cook?

Do you record cooking shows on your DVR and subscribe to culinary magazines? If so, it's safe to say that you have a passion for cooking. A reasonably sized kitchen with ample storage for the freshest ingredients is likely something you'll want to prioritize.

You'll want to budget ample space for countertops as well as a four-burner range with a built-in oven. In lieu of that oven/range unit, you could purchase a high-quality convection oven/microwave unit. Your refrigerator should be large enough to store your fresh ingredients, but not so big that you can't see what's in the back. A lot of space isn't a requirement for cooking a fantastic meal, but it helps to have enough so that you can perform all the necessary tasks without feeling cramped.

How Many Live with You Full-Time?

How much food you need to store is largely based on how many people live in your household. Because there are four of us in hOMe, we need quite a lot of space. As omnivores, we utilize an equal amount of storage for dry goods, frozen foods, and refrigerated items.

The best way to get a sense of how much space you'll need is by taking stock of your current refrigerator and cabinets. Take out every food item from your cabinets, refrigerator, and freezer. Remove all foods that have expired, not been used for at least two months, and realistically will never be eaten. Take your time with this exercise, especially in the condiment and spice shelves. We used to have at least a couple dozen condiments that we never consumed. Today, we have about seven, and all are used regularly.

Be fearless in this exercise, and keep in mind that the less food you need to store, the smaller your kitchen will need to be, leaving you more space in other areas of your home. Use a measuring tape and calculate how much space you'll need to budget in your tiny house kitchen.

Keeping your fridge and stocking space limited also can save you money in the long run by reducing food waste. According to the National Resources Defense Council, the average family of four in America throws out about 25 percent of their food and beverage purchases. This waste costs anywhere from $1,365 to $2,275 per year. Protect yourself from doing the same by creating an appropriately sized kitchen that prevents the blind accumulation of excess food.

What Are Your Cooking Habits?

If you're a bit of a tornado while preparing your culinary masterpieces, you might want to consider more counter space and a larger sink to handle the volume of dirty dishes. However, if you're a clean-as-you-go kind of chef, a smaller sink will be ample for you to prepare your food. You also won't need quite as much counter space to store the stacks of dirty dishes.

What Is the Power Source in Your Tiny House?

Appliance options for tiny houses are largely dependent on the source of power available. Because it takes so much electricity for an appliance to generate heat, those of us living off the power grid use propane for our cooking and space-heating needs. Those connected to grid-tied power, though, can choose between standard electric appliances and gas.

Natural gas is only available for houses on fixed foundations connected to a municipal system, so if you plan on being on a trailer, your option is propane.

Filling those containers can be a bit tedious, so you'll want to factor in how often you'll need to do that.

If you are lucky enough to have both propane and grid-tied power options available, your appliance choices come down to preference. We know avid cooks that refuse to cook on electric, while others wouldn't dream of cooking on gas. Be sure to factor the initial costs of the appliances as well as any long-term operating expenses.

What Is Your Budget?

Although tiny house kitchens are small, they can get expensive quickly. Knowing how much money you have available to invest will help when deciding which appliances and cabinets to install. If saving money is a priority, look for lightly used appliances, cabinets, and countertops.

Search for resell stores such as Habitat for Humanity, and always check craigslist and Freecycle. With time and effort, you can save a lot of money and outfit your entire kitchen with reclaimed materials for $1,000 or less.

What Are Your Culinary Needs?

Striking the right balance between dry-goods storage and refrigerated space depends on the types of food you eat. Omnivores generally need a balanced combination of storage for dry and refrigerated goods. Raw foodists tend to need proportionally more refrigerator space and less cabinet storage. Meat enthusiasts might want considerably more freezer space for long-term storage. Factor this piece in so that you don't end up with a kitchen larger than what you actually need.

Getting Ready to Design Your Kitchen

If you've been gadget heavy in your cooking habits for some time, it may be hard to remember which utensils and appliances are vital and which you can do without. We used to own about a dozen wooden spoons, and for some reason, we really believed that each one was necessary. We are now a one-wooden-spoon family, and we've had no need to get another one even after eight years of cooking large meals for friends and guests.

Before you sit down to design your kitchen, we highly recommend you pare down all your unnecessary gadgets, appliances, pots, pans, and cutlery. If you can go into your design process with a clear idea of what you'll be moving into your new kitchen and how much space those things take up, you'll have a much easier time.

To help determine what's vital, we recommend you move all items that aren't 100 percent necessary into separate drawers and cabinets, preferably away from the main kitchen area. Keep the doors shut and access to the contents limited by adhering blue tape (a nonmarring, gentle, painter's tape) to their fronts. This applies to utensils, small appliances, gadgets, and also spices and canned, dried, and refrigerated foods.

For as long as practically possible (minimum of two weeks), use only the items that you didn't store. Challenge yourself to thin things out even more and see if you miss the items when they're gone. You'll likely be surprised at how unnecessary the majority of those gadgets really are. Your goals are to end this challenge with two things:

- A detailed list of all the items you'll be bringing into your new tiny house kitchen

- A clear understanding of how much space those items require

Appliances and Equipment

Even though appliances are some of the last components to be installed in a build, you'll need to know which ones you're going to use way before you start the construction process. The dimensions and weights of your units will play a significant role in your design, so it's important you start your research early.

The RV industry is a fantastic place to shop for space-efficient and lightweight appliances. There are a wide variety of options when it comes to aesthetics, size, and price in RV units, and you can also find just about everything in either propane or electric.

Another exciting place to search for tiny house appliances is in the marine industry. Most live-aboard boats are superbly designed and incredibly space efficient, so they know a thing or two about compact, high-performance appliances. The downside to marine specific units is the premium costs charged for most items.

Ranges, Cooktops, and Ovens

Ranges typically come in two sizes: 30 inches (standard) and 20 to 27 inches (for apartment units). What size you choose will depend on how much space you've budgeted and how many pots and pans you'll use simultaneously while cooking. Also consider how large those pots and pans are and how much space they take up on the range.

Here at hOMe, we have a standard 30-inch combination range/oven with four top burners and a center grill between them. Despite us cooking large quantities as frequently as we do, we have never used the center grill, so this full-size range is overkill. In hindsight, we would have preferred a smaller unit, which would have given us more counter space and used less propane to heat the oven.

Our hOMe kitchen has a standard 30-inch range/ oven combo with a center grill that has never once been used.

Apartment-size oven/range combinations are perfect for those that want more of a traditional cooking appliance but don't want the wasted space. You can find them as narrow as 20 inches with four burners, which is large enough for full-time cooking for two or three people. If you're a Thanksgiving meal fan, you'll be pleased to know that their ovens are even spacious enough for a small turkey.

Rather than installing a combination range/oven, a lot of tiny housers opt for a countertop-cooking surface. This is only an option for those with grid-tied power because they come only in electric, which would place too great a burden on an alternative energy system. Unless you are a true gourmand, a three-burner cooktop should do the trick.

Induction countertop units are small, lightweight, and plug into a standard wall outlet. They are the sophisticated cousins to traditional coil-top electric burners. They provide a source of steady heat and are highly coveted for their performance by even the most discerning chefs.

Induction countertop units are easy to wipe down and keep clean. When cooking is done, they can be stored out of view, opening up coveted countertop space. One potential disadvantage is that they only work with cookware containing iron so if you have an aluminum set, you'll need to invest in new pots and pans.

The need for an oven is often solved in a tiny house with a convection/microwave combination unit. Again, this option is only available for those with grid-tied electricity. Convection ovens do a superb job of distributing heat evenly and efficiently in the baking process. They come in various sizes and are small enough to be stored out of sight when not in use. No special electrical wiring is required, and the plug simply inserts into a standard wall receptacle.

No matter how small your tiny house is going to be, we highly recommend a venting hood over your cooktop to push excess vapor to the outside. This is true even if your bathroom and kitchen will be next to each other and your bathroom will have its own fan. If you have just one and it's over your cooking surface, it will pull the vapor and smells from your bathroom into the kitchen each time you turn it on. Be sure to install a unit that vents to the outside rather than one that just circulates air through a filter.

If you plan on using gas appliances, a kitchen vent is not optional, but rather, required. This is because carbon monoxide is produced during the combustion process and must be removed from the home.

Refrigerators

Refrigerator options are just as numerous as cooktops, ranges, and ovens, so knowing what to consider for your tiny house is important. Once again, you'll need to establish if you'll be getting your electricity from the sun (or another alternative source) or from the grid. Though refrigerators have become much more efficient, they still represent a significant power draw in an off-grid setup. An 18-cubic-foot unit demands about 1 kilowatt-hour (kWh) of electricity daily, which is not easy for a smaller solar set up.

If you can't spare that amount of power, you can look into residential propane units. These work well in areas where freezing temperatures are rare and propane costs are low. (An 18-cubic-foot unit uses only 0.35 gallons per 24 hours.) Propane refrigerators are among the heavyweights of the tiny house appliance world (300+ pounds) and aren't for the budget conscious ($1,500 and up).

Propane units require venting to the exterior, so be sure your wall framing can accommodate said opening requirements. Propane refrigerators can also be found in the RV industry, which might be a better solution for a tiny house because they are designed to take up as little space as possible.

Hyperefficient electric models, such as Sun Frost, are an option as well. They require only half the power of a conventional unit, but they come at a premium price and an exceptional weight. If these models appeal to you, search for one of the smaller ones, as they are a better fit for a tiny house.

Knowing what size refrigerator to invest in can be confusing. We are bombarded with commercials of people drooling over gargantuan units, but in reality, large refrigerators are often plagued with rotten food hidden in the back corners. Our favorite refrigerator ever was the dorm-size one in our pop-up tent trailer. During the five months we spent living on the beaches of Baja, we never had a single food item spoil because we always knew what was in our fridge. Granted, this wasn't a long-term solution for a family of four living 30 minutes from town, but it was great to see that bigger is not necessarily better.

The weight of refrigerators ranges substantially from just 60 pounds for a 4-cubic-foot electric unit to 300 pounds for a 16-cubic-foot electric unit. It is especially important that you consider the weight of your desired refrigerator if you plan on towing your tiny house because this can be the heaviest appliance you'll install. For reference, we use an 18-cubic-foot unit, and if we were to remodel our kitchen at some point, we would downsize to a 15-cubic-foot model without missing the extra space.

Finding the appropriately sized unit for you is a function of how many people will use it, how often you'll restock it, and how often you'll eat at home. For a family of four, a 15- to 18-cubic-foot model will easily do the job. If you're single and don't eat at home much, something in the 4- to 7-cubic-foot range will suffice and allow you to save hundreds of dollars and a significant amount of space.

Deciding to use a conventional electric refrigerator was a tough choice for us because we produce our electricity with solar panels. We knew we were going to add a significant burden to our power load, so we decided to invest in a larger solar system to handle the extra burden rather than to pay $1,000 more for a propane refrigerator as well as a year-round $50 monthly propane bill to run it.

Sinks

When we consider how often a kitchen sink is used day to day, we realize that they deserve our undivided attention when making tiny house design decisions. There might be a temptation to save space with your sink, but we highly encourage you to splurge in this arena. Choose one that is about 6 inches larger than your largest pot or pan, and you should have a pleasant experience doing your daily dishwashing. If you don't cook very much and don't produce a lot of dishes, look for the smallest sink that you can get away with and save yourself extra counter space.

Look to the RV industry for options as well. They have sinks of all sizes and shapes and even lightweight ceramic alternatives. Whichever one you choose, be sure it's sized for your long-term needs.

Laundry

Most tiny houses aren't large enough for a traditional side-by-side washer and dryer combination set, so the tiny house community has gotten creative in solving their laundry needs. In deciding the best option for you, you'll once again need to consider your power source as well as the abundance of water you have access to. Furthermore, you'll need to ensure you can install both electrical and plumbing lines where you plan to house the washer and dryer.

One of the most popular laundry solutions for tiny houses is a washer/dryer combination unit. Their effectiveness and efficiency have improved over time, and many are now using them with good results. One of their great advantages is that you can toss your laundry into the machine and not need to pull anything out until everything is dry.

Combination washer/dryer sets come available in vented or nonvented options. The vented units work by pushing waste moisture to the exterior through a vent line, while nonvented ones use an internal condenser, preventing excess vapor from escaping into your tiny house.

Generally, vented dryers cost less, dry faster, and are more energy efficient. Unless you truly can't vent your dryer to the exterior, we always recommend vented units over nonvented ones. One important consideration when choosing a vented unit is that a venting cap may protrude from your exterior siding, adding width to your

THOW, which may push you over the 8'6" standard width limit. If this is the case, consider not permanently attaching the vent cap so you can remove it while towing your home.

Most compact laundry units need 220-volt power, which requires a special wiring circuit in your tiny house. If that is not possible because of electrical service limitations, look into drying with propane or a 110-volt unit.

Some combination units are pretty small (24 inches wide × 22 inches deep) and can be stored underneath a standard-height countertop. Choose a model with higher-speed spin cycles—the more water you squeeze out during the wash cycle, the quicker your laundry will dry, and the more time, power, and money you'll save.

Stackable washers and dryers (available in electric or gas) are sometimes used in tiny houses and are most often placed in the bathroom. You can find units that measure about 24 inches wide × 26 inches deep × 70 inches tall. Given that head height underneath most lofts is at least 6'2" (74 inches), they generally fit nicely in a THOW bathroom. They do require venting, so consideration must be given to its placement.

Let's not forget about good old hand-washing and low-tech options, too. The WonderWash is 100 percent human powered, costs just $40, and provides washing room for two or three pairs of pants, several undergarments, and a few shirts. The best part is that when you're done with it, the small unit can be stored out of sight. In a pinch, you can always use a 5-gallon bucket, too.

Lastly, there are always Laundromats. We have certainly put in our fair share of Laundromat years, and to this day, when we have a lot of laundry after a camping trip, we prefer to go there. Everything gets put in at the same time, which makes quick work out of what would be hours of loading and unloading.

Countertops

Countertop space should be a top priority in your tiny house design because when you don't have enough of it, chances are high that you won't be super excited about cooking. You can start figuring out how much space you'll need by experimenting with your current setup. For at least two weeks, play with how much counter space you need, blocking off the areas not to be used. See at what point the space starts to feel like too little and at what point it's more than needed.

If you're limited in how much counter space you can spare for your kitchen, you can install an extra fold-down countertop that hinges off the main one. Open it when needed and fold it out of the way when not. You can also create some extra counter space by cutting a custom top that sits flush atop your sink and is easily removed when it's time to do dishes. In fact, some sinks come with this option "off the shelf."

Various countertop materials exist, and the one you select will be largely dictated by functionality, weight, aesthetics, and your budget. A primary factor you should consider carefully is the weight of your countertop material, especially if you plan on hitting the road with your tiny house. Some options are beautiful but much too heavy for a mobile house.

Cabinetry

Cabinetry can make or break the aesthetics of a space, so take your time when making a selection. Fortunately, there are nearly endless options out there, so you won't struggle to find something that makes your heart go a-flutter.

Weight is probably the biggest consideration when choosing cabinets for a THOW. Prefabricated ones are often made out of heavy pressboard material and can add more weight to a load than the trailer can bear, so it's important to know their weight before ordering a trailer.

You can save a lot of weight by looking at RV cabinets or having them custom made out of lighter materials. If you are pretty handy, you can even make them yourself and save a lot of money in the process.

Tiny House Kitchen Layouts and Shapes

Options in tiny house kitchen layouts are more limited than in conventionally sized houses, but with good creative design, you can make all your culinary dreams come true. The following are several tried-and-true tiny house layouts that can serve as great springboards for your own design.

U-Shape Kitchens

Gourmands rejoice, a highly functioning kitchen with full-size appliances is possible in a tiny house, but it comes at a cost—a loss of square footage in other parts of the abode. Because of this, you might want to consider a tiny house 28 feet or longer. Although a 24-foot length can work, your living space will be greatly impacted.

Placing a full-size kitchen at either end of your house will allow you to create a super versatile U-shape cooking area. This configuration is often touted as the most efficient layout as it naturally creates a work triangle, allowing for easy flow between the sink, range, and refrigerator. It's ideal for those who cook daily and need a good amount of counter space.

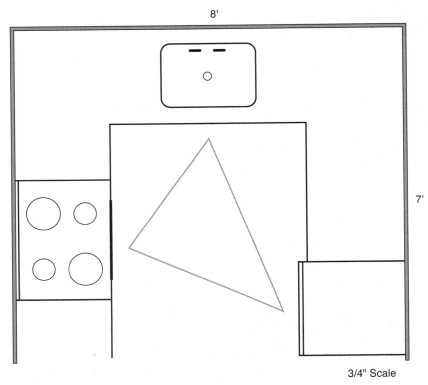

U-shape kitchens create a highly functional space with an ideal work triangle.

Our kitchen is 8 feet wide × 9 feet 6 inches deep and is large enough for a U-shape layout, full-size appliances, food storage for four adults (plus a one-month supply of emergency dried goods), place settings for eight people, and plenty of counter surface area for three people to simultaneously prepare a meal. It's amazing how often we've heard visitors share that our kitchen is larger than the ones in their conventionally sized homes.

Be sure to consider the weight of the kitchen when placed at either end of the trailer because it will impact the overall balance of the home. As a result, this effect on balance can impact the drivability of the trailer and the maneuverability of the tow vehicle.

Galley Kitchens

Galley kitchens installed in the middle of a tiny house create interesting opportunities by freeing up both ends of the house.

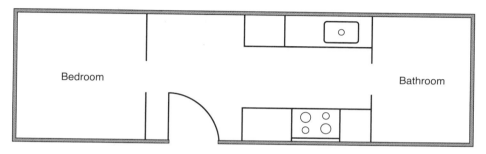

1/4" Scale

Galley kitchens installed toward the center of a tiny house keep both ends of the home open for a downstairs bedroom and a comfortable bathroom.

This layout in a 28-foot tiny house is large enough to accommodate a downstairs bedroom with a queen-size bed and a standard bathtub in the bathroom. It also creates three sleeping areas between two lofts and a downstairs bedroom.

You can leave the wall opposite your kitchen cabinets either open for a dining room table and chairs, or line it with more cabinets for a larger cooking area. This layout is large enough for two adults living full-time in a tiny house and perhaps one or two children.

If you leave the side of the house opposite your kitchen empty, relative to the kitchen itself, there might be effects on the weight balance within the home that affect towing. Be sure to consider this when choosing your design.

Smaller Tiny House Kitchens

Having a small kitchen that meets all your needs is still possible with a 20-foot or smaller tiny house. The best way we've seen people accomplish this is by combining the kitchen and bathroom in one end of the tiny house, freeing up a lot of space for the living area.

In this configuration, there's enough space for a reasonably sized refrigerator, two-burner cooktop, microwave, small pantry, sink, and counter space. The key to making all this fit is to use custom 20-inch deep cabinets and countertops. Because standard cabinets are so deep and things in the back are often hidden from sight, you might not miss the extra depth anyway.

We've heard concerns from people that odors from the bathroom may be noticed in the kitchen. However, if you have a good toilet, a strong bathroom fan, and a sliding door to divide the two spaces, you shouldn't have any issues at all.

The most efficient use of space in a tiny house is a shared kitchen and bathroom/entry vestibule layout.

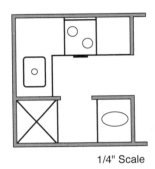

1/4" Scale

These smaller kitchens are ideal for one or two people who plan on moving their tiny house quite a bit. They're also a great configuration in a larger tiny house where the dweller rarely cooks, allowing for more square footage in the living areas.

Fun Storage Ideas

The key to a successful tiny house kitchen is ample storage for the things you really need. This sometimes requires clever solutions and unique design features. By providing a place for each of your belongings, you'll minimize clutter and have the best-functioning kitchen possible. Let's look at some creative solutions for space-conscious kitchens.

Toe kicks (the recessed area between the bottom of a base cabinet and the floor) can work double duty in a tiny house by not only providing comfort for everyone who uses the kitchen, but also creating enough space for slide-out drawers. Normally that space would remain empty, but with custom drawers, you can create enough storage for canned goods, baking trays, spices, and so on.

A lot of tiny houses have exposed framing underneath the loft above the kitchen. Consider sheathing off the surface and installing recessed drop-down storage bins to store your spices, canned goods, and other small items. You can create just one or several of these, potentially adding quite a lot of extra square footage in storage to your kitchen.

One great food storage solution for tiny houses is a mini wall pantry. It creates a lot of extra storage for dried food products without competing for space with upper cabinets or counter space. This wall pantry can be custom built to fit into any tiny house kitchen configuration.

The mini wall pantry found in the Toybox Tiny Home of Paul Schultz from Humble Homes illustrates a great use of space. (Photo by Mieke Zuiderweg.)

Lastly, we want to touch on the idea of a junk drawer. The concept of a place specifically designed to be filled with nonessentials is totally contrary to living an efficient and organized life. We invite you to avoid the temptation of creating a junk drawer and to instead create a highly organized place to store important items such as small hand tools, rubber bands, extra pens, and the like. Using small, labeled bins within a drawer can make it easier to keep the space organized.

To Summarize

You'll need to develop a clear picture of your cooking habits and kitchen needs before starting your tiny house kitchen design. Knowing what to look for while appliance shopping for a tiny house kitchen, especially in terms of the weights of your power sources, will save you time and money. Some kitchen layouts are better than others for tiny houses, so check out the tried-and-true ones first, and add your own adjustments as necessary. Numerous inexpensive and clever storage solutions exist for tiny house kitchens, and looking into them now can save you headaches later.

CHAPTER 9

Bedrooms and Living Areas

Having a comfortable place to kick up our feet at the end of the day, and a bedroom that welcomes us into a deep slumber, are two of the greatest joys that life has to offer. Whether a house is large or small, ornate or plain, the important part is that it should invite peace, calm, and above all, relaxation. With good design, your tiny house can become an oasis that you long to get back to each time you leave.

In this chapter, we cover bedroom options for singles all the way to families with multiple children, how to access lofts, and how to design them for the highest efficiency. Also, we talk about living areas, home offices, closets, home storage, and entertainment solutions.

How Many Are Home?

It used to be that singles were occupying tiny houses more than any other demographic, but today, more people are realizing this lifestyle is a great option for families, too. Creating an appropriate design for the number of people living in the house is the best place to start. Let's go over various scenarios and look at options and solutions for each.

Single Person

Creating a comfortable sleeping place for just one person is pretty easy. If it's just you, you can choose to build a relatively standard-size loft (7 feet 6 inches × 10 feet) with a single or full mattress (rather than a queen), and you're still left with an abundance of open space for clothes storage and anything else. Another option is to make the loft much smaller, which will actually make your downstairs feel taller and more expansive.

You can place your bedroom downstairs, either as a studio configuration with your bed in the main living area or in a separate room. You can create a comfortable bedroom with a twin-size mattress, clothes storage, and shelving for as little as the size of a queen-size mattress (60×80 inches).

If you truly want to economize sleeping space, you can always use a twin-size mattress as the base cushion for your seating area. Come nighttime, simply remove your bedding from a cabinet and make your bed. With this configuration, you take up no extra space for a bedroom, freeing up loads of square footage for everything else you want in your tiny house.

Couples

Unless you prefer sleeping in a sardine can with your partner, you'll likely want a queen-size mattress. Queens are 60×80 inches, and thus quite a bit larger than a twin-size mattress. In a loft bedroom under a shed roof, we recommend a space that's 7 feet 6 inches wide (full width of the interior trailer) and 10 feet deep. This is enough room for a queen mattress, dressers, laundry bin, dog bed, and space to move around and access clothes.

You can use a queen mattress in a gabled tiny house loft, too, but headroom is limited because the ceiling walls come down steeply on both sides. There also isn't much space left over for storing clothes or moving around. One solution is to install a dormer (a window that projects vertically from a roof creating a bump-out) in the loft to open things up dramatically.

A dormer bump-out in a gable-roofed tiny house is a nice way to create more space in a loft. (Copyright Tumbleweed Tiny House Company. Photo by Theresa Lee.)

Downstairs bedrooms are an option for couples, too. You can design the sleeping room so it's literally just a few inches larger than a queen mattress and takes up very little floor space while creating a comfortable and cozy place to lie down. Add some curtains to the windows, close the door, and you've got yourself a bedroom conducive to deep sleep. Incorporate shelves, and perhaps raise the bed frame about 3 feet off the ground to create storage for your belongings and clothes.

Families

The days of THOWs being just for singles or couples are long over. More and more families are choosing the tiny house lifestyle and finding creative ways of crafting comfortable and happy lives for everyone. How one deals with the challenges depends on how many children are living in the household and how old they are.

Living tiny with one young child is quite easy, especially if there's ample outdoor space for overflow when the youngster needs to run off excess energy. With infant children, parents often just sleep in the same bedroom with the baby, eliminating the need for an extra sleeping space for a while. A loft 7 feet 6 inches wide × 10 feet deep is certainly large enough for a queen-size bed, toddler-size mattress, and some clothes storage. Create tall safety walls, gates, and rails along the loft and stairs so the child stays safe when they begin to explore their world.

When a child gets to be a little older and can safely access a loft via stairs or a ladder, it might be time for them to have their own bedroom. There are various ways of closing off a loft so that the child runs no risk of falling out. Kids love lofts and climbing up and down to get to them, so they'll likely be thrilled to have one to call their own.

We recommend a tiny house 24 feet or longer to accommodate two lofts comfortably. Anything smaller will make it challenging to fit both lofts while keeping a sense of openness below.

Some families have created catwalks with safety rails between their loft and the child's loft, allowing a fun travel path for kids. An advantage to a catwalk is that everyone can access the same set of stairs, rather than needing a separate ladder on the other end, which eats up valuable floor space in the design.

Dual loft configurations are the most common design option we've seen for families with up to two children. This setup frees up the entire downstairs for cooking, eating, bathing, hanging out, and so on. Young children often enjoy sharing their sleeping spaces with a sibling, and a tiny house loft, when designed well, is large enough for two toddler-size mattresses, toys, books, and clothing for two young kids.

This setup generally works well with children who are up to about 12 years old. After that point, the need for privacy begins to increase. In even the closest of families, it's common for a child to want to individuate and spend more time with friends and the world around them. Whereas most young children thrive in tiny houses because the limited square footage invites a lot of contact among family members, it's possible that the preteen won't want to live in such close quarters anymore.

The tiny house lifestyle becomes more complex as children age. Tiny living with older children is quite possible, but the solutions for doing so comfortably need to be a bit more creative.

For families with three or more children, a larger tiny house (30 feet or longer) makes the most sense. In a bigger setup, a family can have two loft bedrooms that can accommodate four people as well as a downstairs bedroom for two people. Increase your living area proportionally to how many people live under the same roof.

A family needs space to move around comfortably without people bumping into each other, especially if there's sibling conflict. Keep in mind that lofts create overflow space when things become a little busy downstairs. It's likely rare (other than at mealtime) that everyone in the household will be downstairs at the same time. Make the lofts roomy and practical, and people will naturally gravitate to those spaces.

You may want to extend your tiny house to 10 feet wide if there'll be four or more people living in it full-time. That extra 18 inches of width makes a dramatic difference. In addition, you can build outdoor seating areas for dining and hanging out in. You'll be amazed how often you use those spaces.

Note that it's not unusual for well-meaning friends and family members to second-guess people with children moving into a tiny house. These concerns are typically based on a lack of information.

One discovery we've made in living in our tiny house for more than six years is that kids and teens love it. Most children thrive living in a tiny house because it means more contact and attention from their parents. And there's something about the scale that seems to appeal to the younger generations. Tiny houses are, after all, essentially glamorized playhouses, and most kids dreamed of having their own at one stage or another. It's nice that our house is considered one of the "cool" ones among our kids' friends and that both our son and daughter are proud of our tiny house lifestyle.

Multiuse Furniture

As the tiny house industry has grown, so have clever space-saving solutions. In today's market, you can find everything from beds that fold into walls, disappear under raised floors, and even drop down from the ceiling. Let's look over each option to help spark your imagination.

Beds that fold into walls, also referred to as *Murphy beds*, have come a long way, and you can now find them with incorporated desks and even sofas that hide from view once the bed drops down. A Murphy bed can now serve not only as a bedroom but also as a seating area or workstation. You can purchase these units premade, but you can also buy the hardware and build them yourself, saving hundreds of dollars.

On the nonlofted end of a tiny house, you can build a raised floor just tall enough for a mattress on a rolling platform. Pull this bed out at night before going to sleep, and slide it back after waking up.

On top of this platform, you can install a kitchen, living area, dance space, or anything your heart desires. This is an efficient way of creating a downstairs bedroom that takes up no additional space. You can even pull the bed out partially from underneath, place some throw pillows against the platform, and create a comfortable seating area during the day on the bed itself. The key to this setup is leaving enough floor space open in the main living area so you can pull your bed open at night.

One of the really neat design features we've seen incorporated into tiny houses are ceiling beds. A mechanical system lifts the bed all the way to the ceiling and out of sight during the day and lowers it at bedtime. These systems can be programmed to stop at a specified height, enabling you to keep a sofa, work area, or anything else beneath the bed without needing to move it daily.

This amazing bed design mechanically lifts up to the ceiling during the day and lowers down before bedtime. (Photo from The Tiny House Company. Photographed by Andrew Carter.)

Sleeping Lofts

Lofts are a wonderful asset in a tiny house. Because a THOW can be quite tall, it makes sense to maximize internal square footage by creating rooms out of what would normally be empty space. Depending on your tiny home's size, you can potentially add 50 percent or more of usable square feet by incorporating one or two lofts. There are some important considerations to bear in mind when you're designing a tiny house loft, so let's review them.

Accessing the Loft

Getting up and down from the loft shouldn't be a struggle. In fact, accessing a loft ought to be easy, so we suggest you always go with the safest option possible. Our preference is a set of stairs. When designed well, stairs provide safe access to a lofted bedroom. The downside is that they take up significant floor space on the main floor.

If you do opt to build stairs, make sure to incorporate storage so that they work double-duty for you. The stairs in hOMe provide an extra 25 square feet of space, enabling us to store our jackets, shoes, gloves, hats, scarves, dog leashes and collars, keys, purses, shopping bags, sunglasses, and so on. It's quite amazing how much we can put in there.

Creating code-compliant stairs in a tiny house is challenging for areas that have not adopted the provisions of Appendix AQ of the 2021 IRC, but you can get them reasonably close. Aim for stairs with a 9-inch riser and 10-inch tread. The riser is the vertical portion of each step on a set of stairs—it's the part of each step that actually *rises* the stairs from one tread to the next—while the tread is the horizontal step on a set of stairs. This configuration is comfortable enough for easy and daily access to a loft, even though it doesn't meet general IRC standards. If your building department is using Appendix AQ, then code-compliant stairs are easy to build.

We recommend eliminating the last step at the top of the run and creating a landing platform instead. Removing the step enables for an easier transition from the stairs to the loft area, both when going up and coming back down. The landing platform should be twice as deep as your standard treads and twice as tall as your standard risers for best results. Place a padded rug at the top of the stairs so that your knees are protected as you kneel onto the loft.

You can build alternating tread devices (stairs in which each step is staggered from the next one) to save some space in a tiny house. They're a bit odd at first, but after using them a few times, you'll get the hang of it. Alternating tread devices add a unique visual aesthetic to a tiny house design.

Most tiny housers just use loft ladders to get up and down. Typically, they're stored out of the way when not in use. Choose a lightweight option to make it as easy as possible to move. The hOMe ladder is simply a converted drop-down attic ladder from which we removed all the extra framing. Even though it's quite sturdy, it's so light that we can move it with just one hand.

This image illustrates the hOMe stairs' top tread and riser detail. Note that the tread as well as the riser are twice as large as those on the other steps. This allows for an easier and safer transition to and from the loft space to the stairs.

We don't recommend ladders that hang entirely perpendicular to the floor. Instead, design or buy one that provides a comfortable angle to go up and down on. Completely vertical ladders, although space efficient, are awkward and scary, especially when transitioning in and out of the loft.

Ceiling Heights and Roof Layout

How much ceiling height you'll have in your tiny house loft depends on your roof type, how tall your ceiling height is below the loft floor, and what kind of trailer you order. Nearly every tiny houser wants to maximize headroom, so here are some simple ways to accomplish that.

Use Drop Axles on Your Trailer

Using drop axles on your trailer maximizes your tiny house ceiling height by about 4 or 5 inches because the trailer deck can be lower to the ground. Drop axles aren't a great option for people that plan on driving their tiny houses considerable distances or plan on driving their tiny houses through anything more than average grade changes.

Lower Your Loft Heights as Much as Possible

We weren't sure how much additional headroom we should incorporate into our tiny house design for our bathroom and kitchen. We were worried that if we lowered it too much, we would feel like the ceiling was caving in on us. We also didn't want to add too much ceiling height to the main floor because we knew it would mean a reduction in ceiling height in our loft.

We opted to add 4 inches of headroom above Andrew's 6-foot height, which has been perfect. Even our 6'2" friends are surprised that they don't feel a sense of confinement when under the loft. The point is that you might need less headroom than you think to feel comfortable. Perhaps this is because our lofts aren't very deep and because they open into a living room with very tall ceilings.

Frame your ceiling/roof assembly with the smallest dimensional lumber possible. The hOMe architectural plans call for 4×4-foot rafters on the shed roof (plus rigid insulation on top). In our snow zone in southern Oregon, this meets engineering requirements. If you frame your roof with larger lumber (such as 2×10-inch lumber), you'll lose 6 inches of headroom right off the bat. Instead, consider shrinking the space between the rafters from 24 inches on-center (o.c.) to 12 inches o.c., and keeping the same low profile rafter material. As always, run this idea past an engineer to be sure you're safe.

Of course, the most important consideration is that your rafters must be able to safely carry any potential loads so there's no risk of roof collapse. Snow is extremely heavy and can add thousands of pounds to a roof system. Be safe. Use either engineered plans in which these variables have been factored in, or work with a professional who can help you determine the framing dimensions required for your climate zone and roof span.

Design a Shed Roof

A shed roof maximizes loft head heights. Shed roofs don't have a peak at the center like a gable roof does, rather they just have a single slope. A shed roof maximizes head space in a loft when compared to a gabled option. This is because the highest point in a roof structure is reached only at the peak of a gable, whereas the entire uphill side of a shed roof maintains the highest level for the entire length of the wall.

Emergency Escape and Rescue

Lofts can become dangerous traps in a fire, so it's vital you consider an escape path in case your primary means of access to the front door is cut off. Think about not only how you'll get out, but also how emergency rescuers will reach you in case you are unconscious. Keep in mind that firefighters carry large tanks on their backs and wear cumbersome equipment. Squeezing in through a tiny window won't be an option for them. A bedroom loft should have windows large enough to escape from and accommodate a firefighter with gear entering through them.

The best means of escape from a loft is with an emergency roof access escape window. Similar to a skylight in look and function, this system meets code requirements of emergency egress when installed with no more than 44 inches from the ground to the bottom sill.

We always recommend you have a folding fire escape ladder that easily attaches to the windowsill in case access to the front door is ever cut off.

Defining the Living Areas

When you move into your dream tiny house, you'll want a super relaxing place to kick up your feet and enjoy the fruits of your labor. What kind of lounger are you? Do you like a deep seating area to fall into? Do you like to play board games with others? Is watching movies your favorite way to decompress? Do you like to entertain a lot? Answering these types of questions will help you in your quest of creating the perfect tiny house living area.

Living Rooms

Tiny house living rooms range from bare bones all the way to spaces large enough to host six to eight adults at a party. If you like having people over regularly and want room to spread out, you should consider a tiny house that's 28 feet or longer. Seating areas take up a significant amount of space, so a smaller tiny house simply won't do the trick.

One of the best ways we've seen to create a larger living room is a galley kitchen installed in the middle of a tiny house with the bathroom on one end and the living room on the other. Assuming the living room is underneath a 7-foot 6-inch × 10-foot loft, this configuration creates 80 square feet for entertaining enjoyment.

This area is large enough for a sofa that comfortably seats six. Maximize this efficiency even more by building a custom seating area with embedded storage below the cushions, and suddenly you've got space for all kinds of things that are needed in a home.

If your friend circle is quite close and you don't mind getting cozy, you could certainly use one of your lofts as your entertaining area. We've held several small gatherings where we've all ended up in the loft hanging out and telling stories.

If you prefer to meet friends in other locations, you don't need something quite as large as a living room. Perhaps you'd rather have a larger kitchen or home office. In that case, look at a small sofa or custom-built option to fit your space perfectly. If you do buy one, look for a model that incorporates extra storage or some other added feature. You want all your furniture to serve at least one purpose other than simply being furniture.

Dining Areas

Eating around a table with people you love is one of the finer things life offers. Make mealtime count by designing a dining area into your dream tiny house. The challenge though, as usual, is space.

Tables, when combined with chairs, take up a significant amount of floor space. That means creativity is a requirement when it comes to carving out a comfortable eating area. Tiny housers most often use a folding dining set to solve this issue.

A table can be as simple as a card table stowed underneath sofa cushions when not in use or as elaborate as a folding table and chair combo set that all get stored away into a small portable cart when done. You can also hinge a table off a wall and open it as needed. Folding chairs can be hung from the wall or stowed in a cabinet. Weatherproof chairs can be kept outside the front door, and brought in for mealtime. The key is to be as creative as you can within your budget.

Give consideration to how often you'll host others for dinner. Since making the move to tiny, we entertain seasonally and have people over when the weather is conducive to sitting outside. During the cold winter months, we meet people in town for get-togethers. We actually enjoy the break from entertaining and then get excited when the weather warms to a point that we can have dinner parties again.

This tiny house boasts a large eating table and rolling benches that stow away underneath a raised floor when not in use. When open, this setup can accommodate eight people. (Designed and built by New Frontier Tiny Homes. Photograph by StudioBuell Photography.)

If you opt for a tiny house with a larger living area and a U-shaped sofa on one of the ends, you can incorporate your dining area into that space. Look at the RV industry for special floor brackets that allow you to insert table legs easily. Attach your tabletop to the legs and voilà, you've got seating for several people around a large dining room table. When done, fold and stow your tabletop and legs.

Home Office Spaces

More and more people are working from home these days, and we're here to tell you, creating a functional office in a small space is no problem at all.

The key to creating a tiny house office is digitization. Typically, there isn't enough room for excess documents, which can end up consuming a lot of space. Instead, you'll need to invest in a scanner and digitize documents as they come in. You'll also need to ensure you move into your tiny home with nothing but the basic documents.

It helps to know what type of worker you are when designing your tiny house office. For example, Gabriella feels most productive and relaxed while sitting on her bed in the loft. Andrew, on the other hand, gets a little *too* relaxed when sitting up there, so he needs a desk. Do you require a designated work desk, or can you use a laptop and move it when done, freeing up the work area for other uses?

Laptops are highly recommended because they free up valuable desk space and can easily be put away at the end of the work day. They also use significantly less power than desktops, which makes them a must for off-grid tiny housers. In fact, you can even charge them in your car when running errands!

An entire office can fit into a 13-inch-wide × 5-foot-tall cabinet. That's enough space for two shelves for loose documents not ready to be scanned and other miscellaneous items. It's also enough room for basic supplies such as a stapler, envelopes, tape, a slide out drawer with a small printer and scanner, and a box for recycling. That's what we personally use, and we are 100 percent self-employed and both work from home.

Entertainment Areas

If you're a television viewer, you can incorporate your lounge area into one of your lofts and use the mattress as the seating area. A queen-size bed is large enough for three or four people to enjoy a movie together. You can, of course, place your TV downstairs if you prefer. TVs are so light and thin these days that they can easily be mounted to a wall or to a telescoping bracket. With the option of hooking up the internet to a TV, one hardly even needs to store DVDs anymore.

If you're more of a puzzle and game fan, be sure to design a space that accommodates that. We've seen some creative solutions to the challenge of incorporating large tables into small spaces. One such example is a pair of slide-out benches and a large table that stow away under a raised kitchen platform. If you want something badly enough in your tiny house, think outside the box and make it happen.

Closets and Storage

Storage and closet space are limited in a tiny house when compared to a conventionally sized home, so you'll likely need to downsize your personal belongings before making the move to tiny. If you own a lot of clothes, pare down your closet significantly. You may find you actually prefer having fewer choices because you won't have to waste any time wondering what to wear.

If you're unsure of what to keep and what to part with in your closet, you may want to check out what's called a capsule wardrobe. The theory behind this system is that with just a few basic and complimentary pieces, you can combine items and create a lot of diversity with what you wear. Typically, a capsule wardrobe includes the following items: nine tops, five bottoms, and five pairs of shoes. A few key accessories are encouraged as well.

How much clothing storage you can have in your tiny house is largely a function of how highly you'll prioritize a place for those items. It's also dependent on what size house you move into. If you end up creating your own capsule wardrobe, you'll hardly need any space at all.

As a general rule of thumb, in a 20-foot or shorter tiny house, you'll typically have enough clothing storage for two people with a basic wardrobe and about three to four pairs of shoes each. You can of course create more space, but it will likely result in a sacrifice of square footage from somewhere else in the home.

In a larger tiny house, you should be able to build enough storage for a complete, year-round wardrobe for two people, several pairs of shoes, and some hanging space. If you've thinned out your closet to a set of functional basics, you'll have more than enough room for all the clothes you need. Lofts typically provide enough space for a dresser or two or some type of shelving system. We have two sets of dressers in our 7-foot 6-inch × 10-foot loft.

Consider creating storage in your loft floor. By cutting openings and creating lids in your loft floor between the floor joists, you can create a significant amount of room for various items.

In terms of general storage solutions, you can use prebuilt cabinetry or create custom units. Always aim to incorporate dual-use furniture and cabinetry in your tiny house. For example, create a base cabinet and use the top as a seating area.

By cutting cubbies into your loft floor like the folks at TinyHouseBasics.com did, you can create a lot of extra storage. (Copyright Joshua Engberg.)

To Summarize

Tiny houses used to be just for singles or couples, but more families are creating happy and fulfilled lives in them, too. All furniture in a tiny house should serve more than just one function and incorporate a few useful benefits—get creative! How much headroom you have available in a loft is a factor of your roof style, trailer type, and the height of the space under your loft. With good design, you can create a tiny house with seating for a party of up to eight people.

CHAPTER 10

Bathrooms

Designing a highly functional tiny house bathroom is perhaps the biggest challenge you'll have to solve. So many components need to fit into a miniscule space that it might take every bit of your creativity to make it all come together. You'll need to consider appearance, storage capacity, fixtures, cost, and—most importantly—function.

In this chapter, we cover all the components you'll need to consider for your tiny house bathroom, ranging from design to toilet options, wastewater management, and appropriate venting solutions for protecting your house from potential mold issues. With that in mind, let's get started!

Design Considerations

Design is one of the keys to a well-functioning tiny house bathroom. Do it well and you'll be rewarded with years of enjoyment; do it wrong and you'll be plotting your remodel just weeks after moving in. As in all situations related to tiny houses, you'll need to fully understand your actual needs. Maybe you love the idea of a bathtub (which requires a lot of space), but in reality, you only use one a few times each year. Perhaps you believe that you need six kinds of shampoos in your shower, but in actuality, just one will keep your flowing locks looking gorgeous.

Bathrooms are typically used for only a small portion of time in day-to-day life, so some tiny housers aren't willing to sacrifice too much extra space for them. Quite a few tiny houses don't even have bathroom sinks because the occupants opt to use the kitchen one instead. Your bathroom's design will depend on your specific needs and wants.

The bathroom in hOMe is plenty big for full-time use by four adults.

A common misconception plaguing our generation is that a family of four (especially one with teens) *needs* at least two bathrooms. Well, that's simply not true. Our family shared just one 8 × 5-foot bathroom and a mutiny never occurred. Our 20-year-old son and our 16-year-old daughter both lead active lives, showered daily at home, and had a collection of primping products. Between the medicine cabinet, sink vanity, and floor-to-ceiling storage, there was plenty of space for it all.

There are design tricks you should use to your advantage if you're trying to make your space look larger. Pocket and sliding doors provide visual and sound protection without all the square footage that a swinging door consumes. A large mirror works magic in opening up a space, though don't add more than one in a tiny bathroom or you'll feel like you're in a carnival fun house.

To further expand the feel of the space, use neutral- and light-colored finishes to make your tiny bathroom feel bright and roomy. Only keep things out in view that serve a specific function. Nothing visually closes up a space more than a bunch of knickknacks scattered about. Lastly, a glass shower door really opens up a bathroom dramatically.

One important factor that's often overlooked in tiny design is weight distribution on the trailer. Often, bathrooms are placed on the tongue side of a tiny house trailer. They can be heavy, so this can put an undue burden on the weight ratio, which can lead to dangerous trailer sway while towing. To be clear, we're not saying that you shouldn't put a bathroom there. After all, this is where the bathroom is in hOMe. But you need to consider this important factor when creating your design and ensure the weight is balanced across your tiny house.

If you plan on towing your tiny house more than once or twice in its lifetime, the materials you choose need to be lightweight and able to withstand road rattle. Tile might not be a great option for those reasons. Solid surface materials such as granite are also not ideal because of their weight. Look instead for lightweight products that can handle a little bit of flex.

Bathroom Layouts

An 8×5-foot dimension is the most common bathroom size in conventional construction. This is good news for us in the tiny house movement because the vast majority of tiny homes on wheels are about 8 feet wide in interior dimension. As such, a lot of the same design principles, solutions, and products that work in a standard house will work in a tiny home, too.

There are typically two places where you'll find the bathroom located in THOWs:

- On the end of the tiny house running along the 8-foot interior width
- Sharing the end of a tiny house with a kitchen or entryway vestibule

Let's go over design options for each situation.

An 8×5-foot configuration is the Rolls Royce of tiny house bathroom luxury. In that space, you can fit a full-size bathtub, a washer/dryer combo, toilet, and large sink. There's ample storage for toiletries, towels, and cleaning supplies. If you're not much of a soaker, install a corner shower instead of a tub to create even more space for storing bathroom items. All fixtures and appliances can be standard, saving you time and money.

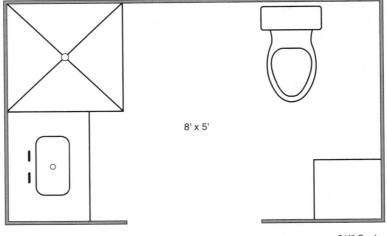

An 8×5-foot bathroom is the most common size in a small conventionally sized house. A space this big will provide a very comfortable bathroom for a family of four.

8' x 5'

3/4" Scale

If that bathroom layout seems unnecessarily large, you can certainly shrink it down to an 8-foot × 30-inch width. If you intend on building your tiny house to meet IRC code, be sure this configuration accommodates those specifications. A 30×30-inch fiberglass shower stall is about the smallest you'll find off the rack at your building supply store. Anything smaller will generally need to be found at an RV supply store or be custom made.

A conventionally sized sink will be hard to install in such a narrow space, so look for really small freestanding units (14 inches wide × 9 inches deep). You can increase your storage capacity in this configuration by maximizing cabinetry around your toilet. If you create a custom cabinet, it's quite likely you'll have all the storage space you need on that end of the wall.

An 8-foot × 30-inch bathroom is large enough for a toilet, a small free-standing sink (not pictured), and a standard 30×30-inch shower stall.

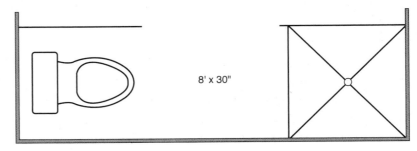

8' x 30"

3/4" Scale

Some people opt to keep their bathroom at the same end of their house as the kitchen or entry vestibule. There are a couple advantages to this layout, including the consolidation of plumbing/drain lines (thus minimizing material use) and a huge savings in space. If odor cross-contamination is a concern, proper ventilation and a solid door separating the spaces will eliminate any issues.

As we mentioned previously, proper weight distribution over the trailer axles is important for a safe towing experience. Coupling the kitchen and bathroom on one end presents a challenge in this regard. It's very important that you counterweight that side of the house by installing heavier items (such as a loft, furniture, personal belongings, and so on) on the other end.

This bathroom configuration enables you to place your bathroom next to your kitchen and consolidate your plumbing.

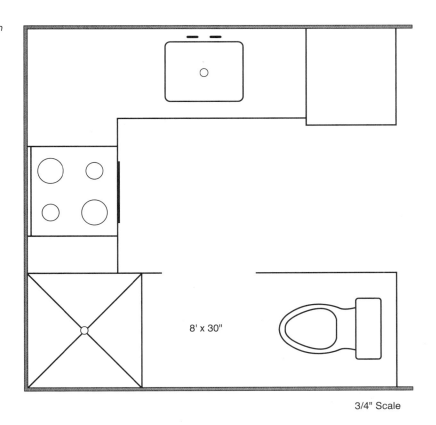

8' x 30"

3/4" Scale

The bathroom layout shown here provides room for a standard 30×30-inch shower stall, standard toilet, and a small sink (not pictured). The same storage opportunities are offered in this design as the bathroom pictured previously.

If you're willing to part with the bathroom sink, which is too small for anything more than brushing teeth in anyway, you can shorten the bathroom by about two feet and create a storage closet that backs to the wall with the toilet and opens to the living area.

Another way to save space in a tiny house bathroom is by building what's called a wet bath. In this design, the entire floor is lined with a custom shower pan and drain, and when it comes time to bathe, the entire room turns into a shower. You can use a curtain to separate your actual shower space from your toilet so that not everything gets wet. With this configuration, you can make your bathroom really small and save space for other areas that you use a lot more in your daily living.

Everyone's Favorite Topic—Toilets

As soon as the subject of toilets comes up at our tiny house workshops, the room gets animated. The topic of going to the bathroom never gets old, no matter how many adults are in a room!

Surprisingly, various options exist when it comes to toilets and tiny houses— everything from a simple $20 bucket system to $2,000+ composting toilets. You can choose a standard flush unit, an RV toilet, and even one that incinerates waste. Which one you choose depends on your budget, usage requirements, frequency of moving, electricity access or limitations, and access to a waste disposal facility.

Composting Toilets

By far, the most popular waste systems found in THOWs are composting toilets. They can range from super-simple buckets to imported high-tech units. Composting toilets are great solutions because they don't require septic systems or black water storage tanks—used to store wastewater from toilets that has come into contact with fecal matter and, therefore, is a biohazard. They also don't use any plumbing hookup, and you don't have to make frequent trips to RV dump stations to discard waste.

One important thing to mention is that, in reality, there are very few composting toilets that actually compost human waste within the unit itself. Usually, the units are used too frequently for true decomposition of the waste to occur, so the term *composting toilet* is a misnomer. It would be more appropriate to call them *holding toilets* or something along those lines.

Not all building departments allow for composting toilets. The departments that do will sometimes require a National Sanitation Foundation (NSF) or extract/transform/load (ETL) certified unit. That said, just because you buy a certified composting toilet doesn't mean you'll receive approval from your local building department. It really all depends on local codes.

Your most economical and simple composting toilet is going to be a 5-gallon bucket system. Yes, you read that right. Take a standard bucket, build a wooden box with a hinged lid around it, cut a hole in the box top to fit the bucket, attach a standard toilet seat to the hinged lid, and you've got yourself a bona fide toilet.

The bucket system is low cost and simple, has a small footprint, and is off-grid friendly. That said, you'll need to keep wood shavings or some other covering material on hand to sprinkle atop your waste each time you use the toilet. There are also issues with odor since urine combined with fecal matter creates a strong and unpleasant smell.

To mitigate smell, many have modified their bucket system by attaching a funnel to the front in which the urine bypasses the solids. Urine itself is sterile (although it's recommended that it be diluted at a 10:1 ratio with water before being placed on the soil surface), so it can be diverted from the toilet into a gravel-filled hole or holding tank outside the house. Further, you can install a venting stack at the back of the toilet frame and direct odors to the exterior with a small, low-voltage fan.

Another challenge with this system is that unless you own acreage and have a safe space to dump your waste, you'll need to find a way to compost it. One option is to close the buckets (or some other large storage drum) with lids and place them in a sunny spot for about 18 to 24 months. During that time, the pathogens will die off and leave you with compost that is safe to dispose of. At no point should you use this waste, or any composted human waste, to fertilize edibles.

If the idea of using a bucket for your toilet is more than you signed up for, you might be interested in some of the high-tech composting toilets on the market, which include the Separett, Nature's Head, Envirolet, Biolet, and SunMar. None of these units require an expensive septic system or RV holding tanks, but their benefits do vary significantly.

If you're terrified of the prospect of smelling waste-related odors in your house, you'll want to get a unit with a fan, which will require a small but steady stream of electricity. You'll also want to look at models that separate the urine from the solids. Anytime you isolate those two, you'll minimize the amount of waste that you have to deal with as well as any associated odors.

High-tech composting toilets can be quite expensive ($900 to $2,000+) and represent a major financial investment, so be sure you get the right one for your needs. Unfortunately, it took us two failed investments before we found the right one for us (the Separett). You don't know just how important a sanitary and odor-free toilet is until you don't have one! Take your time to read online reviews before sinking that kind of money into this important purchase.

We recommend you ask yourself the following questions before making any purchasing decisions:

- Are you squeamish about looking at human waste?
- Are you willing to turn a crank on the toilet after each use?
- Do you have enough electricity to power a small fan 24/7?
- Do you want your liquids and solids to be segregated?
- Would you prefer your waste to be composted inside the unit or someplace outside the unit?
- Do you have a place to easily compost the waste?
- Would you prefer the waste go into a composting bag or into a holding tank?

The following table compares composting toilet features found in some high-tech models.

High-Tech Composting Toilet Feature Comparison

	Separett	Nature's Head	Envirolet	Biolet	SunMar NE
Urine separation	Yes	Yes	No	No	No
Turn arm	No	Yes	Yes	Yes	Yes
NSF/ETL certified	Yes	No	Yes	Yes	Yes
Electric	Yes	Yes	Optional	Optional	Optional
Bagged	Yes	No	No	No	No
Visual barrier	Yes	Yes	Yes	Yes	No

When it comes to disposing human waste in municipal trash systems, there are contradictory pieces of information out there. Many argue that because it's okay to dump baby diapers, disposing composting toilet waste must be acceptable as well. Others say that it's not a viable option. Federal laws are unclear, so we recommend you contact your local trash service company and ask them directly. Do not dispose of human waste into the municipal trash system unless you have gotten permission directly from your local waste management company.

RV Toilet Systems

RV toilet options are bountiful, economical, generally odor neutral, and work well. They use only a small amount of water during the flushing process and are socially acceptable because all the contents discreetly disappear into either a black water holding tank or a dump line at an RV site.

If you plan on living in your THOW at an RV park, these toilets are a great option and require very little maintenance. They cost $100 and up. Even the most expensive ones cap out at $600, which is a lot less than most composting toilets out there.

Both liquid and solid waste go into a black water holding tank where chemicals help abate odor buildup. These tanks range in size from 8 to 40 gallons, and when they're full, they need to be emptied. A 40-gallon tank holds about 10 days' worth of waste for two people, so you'll need to plan your trip accordingly.

For comparison, we emptied our Separett, which was used full-time by four adults, every three weeks or so. If there were four of us using an RV toilet, we would have to drive our tiny house down our windy mountain road and empty our 40-gallon tank every 5 days. You can see pretty quickly how this becomes a major consideration when designing a toilet system for your THOW.

Water weighs 8.35 pounds per gallon, so an 8-gallon tank weighs 70 pounds when full, which isn't too bad. A 40-gallon tank, on the other hand, will add 325 pounds to your tiny house, which doesn't even include the weight of the tank itself. If you go with the RV toilet and black water holding tank combo, you'll need to factor those weights into your trailer design to ensure you end up with one that can handle those weight loads.

Flush Toilets

Flush toilets don't smell, are socially acceptable, and can be quite inexpensive, especially when compared to a high-tech composting toilet. The main challenge for THOWs is that flush toilets require a septic system or municipal waste line to tie into, making standard flush toilets only available for tiny houses on foundations or those that can tie into an approved waste system.

There's nothing different to consider when you're shopping for a flush toilet for a tiny house versus one for a conventionally sized home. Of course, we would recommend you go with the highest-efficiency unit you can afford to save water. On average, each person in the United States uses about 4,757 gallons of drinking water to flush their waste down the toilet each year. A low-flush toilet reduces that consumption to 1,850 gallons annually.

Incinerating Toilets

Incinerating toilets employ controlled combustion within the unit to eliminate solids and liquids. They vent the fumes to the exterior and catch the waste ash in a pan below the burn chamber. No water or plumbing is required to operate them. These toilets can be powered by electricity (Incinolet) or propane (Storburn and Scanlet). If you're off-grid, the electric versions are typically not an option because they draw too much power.

Incinerating toilets are pretty pricey at $1,500+ and require a new bowl liner after each use. The cost of the liners adds up over time, and they don't smell very good when they're being burned. Lastly, some of the mechanical components are susceptible to breakage over time. Not a lot of tiny housers use these toilets, but they are certainly a good option for some.

Dry Toilets

Dry toilets on the market such as Laveo Dry Flush seal up both solid and liquid waste in a disposable liner after each use. They are reasonably priced ($400 to $500), battery operated, and lightweight. Unfortunately, the waste from this toilet isn't biodegradable, and the cost of the liners is high.

With this system, you never have to look at any of the waste as it all gets wrapped up in a foil liner. The only way to dispose of these liners is through a municipal trash system, so you must ensure this is allowed in your area.

Gray Water Management

Gray water is wastewater from your showers/tubs, sinks, and washing machines. It's not tainted water that's come into contact with feces, but rather water that's gently used and still a beneficial source of irrigation for landscaping. When applied to plants, gray water is a valuable fertilizer and not only reduces the burden to our fresh water supplies, but also keeps excess wastewater out of sewers and septic systems.

To ensure the gray water is safe before being used on landscaping, avoid using any cleaning products that contain chlorine or bleach, whiteners, softeners, enzymatic components, borax, peroxygen, sodium perborate, sodium trypochlorite, boron, petroleum distillate, and alkylbenzene. Instead, use fully biodegradable options.

Some jurisdictions allow for the disposal of gray water, but unfortunately, they're few and far between. Despite an active collective of gray water activism, change at the legislative level has been slow to come. Before you use gray water from your tiny house to irrigate, you'll need to check with your local building department to learn what the regulations are. In some jurisdictions, surface use of gray water isn't allowed.

Gray water solutions can operate as simply as diverting wastewater outside from your shower, sinks, and washing machine to a vegetated area where the upper layer of soil and plants can absorb all the water. It's important that you not allow gray water to pool up and that it all is absorbed into the ground. You should also not allow gray water into any body of water because the oils and fats contained therein can be toxic to aquatic species. Ensure that your gray water waste is an adequate distance from any water sources, as leeching through the soil (especially if it is well draining) is a concern.

More complex gray water systems exist and include constructed wetlands, filtration systems, underground seep systems, buckets or barrels, and design-specific gravel beds. Installation ranges from easy to complex, and the costs vary from minimal to thousands of dollars.

You can certainly collect your gray water in an RV holding tank (as you would with black water). This option is practical if you plan on living close to an RV dump or at an RV park. Whichever option you choose depends on your needs, what your soils are like, what's allowed in your area, and your budget.

From an environmental standpoint, gray water systems make a lot of sense. After all, it doesn't seem wise or responsible to discard our gray water while using perfectly clean drinking water to irrigate landscaping with.

Ventilation

Tiny houses are more prone to moisture issues than conventionally sized houses because they're so small. Excess moisture in large houses tends to easily dissipate into all the square footage, but it builds up really quickly in a well-insulated and sealed tiny house. This accumulation of moisture is problematic because in time, mold issues will develop.

Ventilation refers to any system that helps mitigate excess air moisture and helps prevent condensation issues. A good solution to this moisture buildup can be as simple as installing a bathroom fan. A good one will easily remove excess moisture from the air while you're showering and, in a tiny house, can even mitigate moisture from the entire structure.

The challenge with bathroom fans is that most people don't leave them on for nearly long enough. Fortunately, there is an inexpensive apparatus called a moisture sensor switch that can be programmed to turn your fan on and off depending on the humidity level you choose inside your tiny house. These switches are sold separately from most fan units and cost ranges from $25 to $60.

As soon as the relative moisture in your tiny house reaches your programmed level, the sensor switch activates the fan and keeps it on until the moisture level goes below the programed target level. Target humidity levels do change relative to the exterior temperature. As winter sets in and cold temperatures begin to take hold, special attention needs to be placed on maintaining low moisture levels so that condensation can't build up inside. The most common locations for condensation are windows, walls, and dark hidden areas where mold breeds, so be sure to check these spots regularly for signs of excess moisture accumulation.

To Summarize

Creating an appealing tiny house bathroom design is possible; however, it can be very challenging because so much has to fit into a small space. Stick with it, and you'll be rewarded with a bathroom that meets all your needs and doesn't limit your space in other areas of your tiny home. Deciding which toilet option is best for your tiny house can be tough because there are so many entirely different choices.

Understand what your needs and limitations are, and choose the one that best fits the bill. Moisture buildup can pose a significant issue for tiny houses, which leads to mold growth and a host of health issues. A moisture switch may be all that's needed to rid the air of excess moisture.

Custom Designing Your Tiny House

Break out the pencil and paper; it's time to get down to the nitty-gritty. That's right, in Part 3, you learn how to design your own home! It doesn't matter if you don't consider yourself creative; we teach you what you need to do to design your dream tiny house.

We help you choose the best foundation option for your lifestyle and needs. We discuss whether you should buy existing plans or design the house yourself and which design programs to use for that purpose. We delve into important engineering considerations and show you how to hire the right design professional if you don't plan on designing the house yourself. We also teach you how to read construction plans like a pro.

CHAPTER 11

Choosing Your Foundation

Foundation options are not typically considered a tantalizing topic of conversation. Gather a few tiny housers at a cocktail party, though, and the lively exchange on trailers, skids, and fixed-foundation systems can easily continue into the wee hours of the morning. Determining the best foundation option for your build will take some time and research.

In this chapter, we cover the pros and cons of the various tiny house–appropriate foundations. We look at trailer options and how much each can tow. Lastly, we go over fixed-foundation options best suited for tiny houses on foundations.

Understanding Your Options

When designing a tiny house, the type of foundation you choose will be one of the most important decisions you'll make. It will have resounding impacts on nearly every aspect of your build, from design all the way to final construction details. There are advantages and disadvantages to each scenario, so let's go over each option.

Pros of Building on a Trailer

Even though people have lived in small houses for eons, the tiny house movement itself began with a simple concept: build an affordable house that's easy to move. Today, THOWs have garnered the imagination of thousands of others, and subsequently, trailer options have increased dramatically. Following are the pros of building a tiny house on a trailer.

Location Flexibility

Today's work environment is very different than it was in the past. The opportunities for finding secure, long-term positions in companies are far fewer than they once were. Long-term employment has been replaced by high-turnover jobs that force many to move more often than they'd like. Therefore, buying a home no longer makes sense for many people. Tiny houses on wheels are excellent home solutions in these cases; simply hook up and tow them to a new destination. There's no need for new furniture, high deposits, or the pandemonium of fighting for a decent rental.

Ease of Tax Burden

Tiny houses on wheels are not considered permanent real estate because they're not connected to the ground. As such, they're not currently assessed for property taxes. THOWs are often considered RVs and only require sales tax at time of purchase or construction. Some states do charge annual motor vehicle fees or taxes, but these fees are relatively low, especially compared to property tax.

No Building Codes

Because these tiny houses are relatively new in the construction industry, the government has yet to create residential building codes to oversee the building process. This lack of permits and inspections simplifies a build. A simple trailer registration with your local department of motor vehicles may be all that's needed to make your THOW road legal. Of course, this likely will change when the IRC officially adopts the International Tiny House Provisions (ITHP), so be sure to do your own research when it's time to choose your foundation.

Cons of Building on a Trailer

There are also some drawbacks to building a THOW on a trailer. These drawbacks might not be significant enough to deter you from choosing this option, but only you can determine that. Let's take a look at the most common challenges associated with tiny houses on trailers.

No Building Codes

The lack of inspections and codes for tiny houses on wheels is a mixed blessing. Many who build their own tiny houses have limited construction experience, so technical building errors are very common. Even though you'll save money by avoiding permit fees and save time by skipping inspections, you may very well find yourself ultimately paying more down the road. This is because mistakes that would have been caught by building inspectors may go unnoticed until a problem emerges. As previously mentioned, the ITHP document likely will eliminate this lack of clarity.

Greater Risk in High-Wind Zones

Tornadoes and other high-wind events often wreak havoc in mobile home and RV parks. Damage is usually higher there because these structures are extremely vulnerable to high winds because they aren't attached to the ground like permanent housing. However, with enough advanced warning, a THOW might be able to be evacuated to a safe area until the threat passes.

Greater Vulnerability to Earthquakes

A house improperly anchored to the ground has very little chance of faring well in an earthquake, which poses a serious threat to its inhabitants. Although there are ways to properly anchor a THOW, owners who frequently move their homes don't generally apply those systems because they can be tedious to install.

Increased Potential of Freezing Water Lines

Water service and wastewater lines must be protected from freezing temperatures in a THOW, which can prove to be a challenge. Insulating plumbing within walls is generally not the issue. Rather, the risk comes from the locations in which utilities are exposed to the elements (for example, waste lines and water service lines leading into a THOW).

Design Limitations

Both state and national highway transportation departments impose safety limits, which create significant design limitations for THOWs:

- Vehicular width (typically 8'6")
- Vehicular height (typically 13'6")
- Vehicular weight (varies with road)

Anything beyond those limits requires special permits and extra fees.

Need for a Large Towing Vehicle

If you intend on towing your THOW more than a few times, it probably makes sense to purchase a truck and tow it yourself. This might mean a financial investment of $30,000 or more for a rig that can adequately do the job. Considering that many owner-built tiny homes cost $20,000 to $30,000 total, it could be a stretch to also spend more for a capable towing rig. Furthermore, this truck typically becomes the only household vehicle, and it consumes significantly more fuel during day-to-day driving than a smaller car would.

Pros of Building on a Foundation

As more people join the tiny house movement, many have realized that being mobile is *not* their priority. Rather, their chief priority is living simply and within their means, and they're perfectly happy to stay in one place. For these folks, a tiny house on a foundation (THOF) is the best approach. There are numerous foundation options available: concrete slabs, stem walls, pad and pier, and more. Following are the pros of staying put.

Construction Code Compliance

The biggest advantage of building tiny houses on foundations is that they're considered legal homes in the current International Residential Code (IRC)—the model code for the majority of residential construction in the United States. In fact, you can build a code-approved house smaller than 100 square feet and still receive a certificate of occupancy (COO), assuming that local zoning permits it. This is a huge advantage when you consider that there aren't any national residential construction standards allowing for a tiny house to be built on a trailer.

Ease of Design Process

Designing a THOF is relatively easy compared to a THOW because there aren't as many restrictions in terms of maximum width and height. Details such as stairs, head heights, emergency egress, and so on become significantly easier to mitigate without the highway standard restrictions.

You can save a lot of time and money on any construction project when you opt to use conventional materials and techniques. Any time you do something outside the norm, your challenges (and often costs) will increase.

Structural Integrity

A fixed foundation creates a permanent point of attachment to the ground, enabling a THOF to resist high winds and seismic activity much better than a THOW. It also provides much better protection for incoming and exiting water service lines from freezing temperatures.

More Builder/Contractor Options

Choosing a THOF also means more options when it comes to builders. Although any experienced contractor can build a THOW, many are uncomfortable taking on projects with which they don't have experience. Constructing a THOF, on the other hand, is a simple process for any qualified builder.

Easier Resale

The resale value of a THOF is typically higher than that of a THOW because a THOF is considered real estate, having been issued an official certificate of occupancy, while a THOW is typically considered a recreational vehicle. Generally speaking, real estate grows in value over time, while RVs depreciate.

Cons of Building on a Foundation

There are a few challenges associated with foundation-built tiny homes that you need to consider as well.

Planning and Zoning Oversight

Because THOWs aren't currently considered permanent housing, it's become fairly common for people to live in them under the radar of local building officials. If a THOW's owner is turned in to local authorities, they generally just pick up and move. With a THOF though, that's clearly not an option. All planning and zoning oversight must be addressed from the very beginning to ensure compliance with all local and national regulations.

Incurring Taxes

Any residence with a COO is subject to taxes, no matter how small it is. How much you'll pay depends on where you live. Generally, it will be a small fraction of the taxes incurred by living in a large house.

Lack of Mobility

If flexibility and the option of taking your home with you is top priority, building a THOF is not your ideal approach. Although it's possible to move a house on a foundation, this option is not simple or inexpensive.

Pros of Building on Skids

Skids are large wooden beams structurally attached to not only the floor joists in a house, but also a concrete pad-and-pier foundation with steel connectors. Skids can be detached from a foundation, if necessary, enabling a house to be moved to a new location. Using skids for a foundation creates somewhat of a hybrid of a trailer and permanent foundation. It's this best-of-both-worlds approach that makes skids so appealing. Here are the top three advantages of tiny houses on skids (THOSs).

Code Compliance

Once you've received a COO for your THOS, you just apply for a new foundation permit and a new COO each time you move. Because building codes vary regionally due to climactic and natural disaster differences, you'll need to meet the provisions of the codes in the area to which you're moving.

Flexibility

Although skids are considered permanently attached to a foundation, they can be removed with relative ease. Once freed from the concrete pad and piers, your home can be moved to a new spot close by or placed on a trailer and moved across the country if necessary. This provides you with great location flexibility coupled with the perk of a COO.

Design Options

It's common for professionals, not individual owners, to move homes built on skids. Those haulers can easily acquire any special permits and have the appropriate rigs to move larger houses, saving you the stress of needing to tow your tiny house. This also enables you to design your tiny house without adhering to the strict road regulations THOWs are subjected to.

Cons of Building on Skids

When considering the cons of building on skids, be sure to compare them with foundation-bound and trailer-built tiny houses. Because skids are considered a hybrid between those two, they'll have some of the cons I've mentioned previously.

Design Limitations

Even though a THOS provides more design options than a THOW, fewer options exist than those found on a THOF. Road restrictions, which place limitations on the width and height of a home, must be considered.

Foundation Skirting

A THOS is built on a raised foundation system, which requires skirting to enclose the space underneath. Although several options exist, none are as good as a permanent foundation wall. If you're not careful when choosing skirting, your house may look temporary and low quality.

Limited Foundation Options

The most common foundation type for a home built on skids is a pad-and-pier foundation. This system type provides relatively easy access to any plumbing lines below your house and meets building code requirements. If, however, your location site's soils or topography aren't conducive to a pad-and-pier foundation, an expensive engineered alternative may be your only option available.

Associated Costs

A THOS requires hiring a professional hauler because it must be pulled onto a trailer bed with heavy-duty equipment. This increases your costs significantly, so if you plan on moving your tiny house more than once or twice, this foundation type may not be your best option.

What Are My Trailer Options?

Let's assume you've considered all the foundation options and have decided to build your tiny house on wheels. Next on your agenda is deciding what type of trailer you should build on.

Although there are many options for stock and used trailers, we highly recommend a custom-designed one specifically for your project. Everything you build on top of it will be influenced by your trailer's strength, stability, and overall quality.

Bumper-Pull Trailers

The most common type of trailer hitch setup is a bumper pull, which allows a trailer to be towed from a receiver hitch at bumper level. There are five classes of receiver hitches, and they all have different ratings for what they can pull:

- Class 1 and 2 hitches can only tow up to 3,500 pounds, so they're too small for towing a tiny house that can easily weigh 10,000 pounds and up.

- Class 3, 4, and 5 hitches can haul a lot more weight and are compatible with weight distribution systems. A weight distribution system is a receiver hitch attachment designed to distribute tongue weight across all axles including the tow vehicle and the trailer.

Tongue weight is the load placed at the point of connection between the vehicle and trailer, typically located at the hitch. Also referred to as hitch weight, this measurement is taken when the trailer is loaded to capacity and ready for towing.

At no time should the tongue weight exceed 15 percent of the gross trailer weight. It's better to keep things closer to the 10 percent range. If you overload the tongue, you might encounter trailer sway or worse—the hitch may rip off the tow vehicle.

A Class 3 hitch has a gross trailer weight rating (GTWR) of 8,000 pounds. However, if you're using a weight distribution system, that limit can often be bumped up to 12,000 pounds. The receiver tube for the hitch is typically 2 × 2 inches (larger than what's found on a smaller vehicle setup). Class 4 hitches also utilize 2 × 2-inch receiver tubes and can be used in tandem with weight distribution systems. This bumps up their towing capacity from 10,000 pounds to 14,000 pounds.

Class 5 hitches are a whole different beast. They're the biggest bumper-pull hitches available and have a towing capacity of up to 20,000 pounds GTWR. Because their towing capacity is very high, the use of weight distribution systems does little to increase that limit. We do still recommend these systems, though, because they help level the trailer and hauler, ensuring a safer and smoother ride. A Class 5 hitch uses either a 2 × 2-inch receiver tube or a 2½ × 2½-inch receiver tube. These hitches aren't commonly used for passenger vehicles, but if your truck can handle the tow capacity, you can certainly install one.

Ever hear of a pintle hitch? Pintle hitches are most commonly used in military applications and not as much in civilian day-to-day life. Pintle hitches extend from the bumper region of your vehicle but not from the bumper itself. They're secured to the tow vehicle's frame and are very easy to hook up to. If your tow vehicle can handle it, a pintle hitch can haul anywhere from 10,000 to 60,000 pounds.

A potential downside of using a pintle hitch is that there can be some movement in the coupling between the hitch and the trailer, causing some rattle and noise during towing. That said, if you need to haul a massive amount of weight, they can't be beat.

To be clear, Class 1 through 5 and pintle hitches aren't the same as bumper hitches. A bumper hitch attaches directly to your vehicle's bumper, limiting your vehicle's tow capacity to nothing much more than a bicycle rack. It's important to ensure your hitch matches the tow capacity of your vehicle.

To break down bumper trailers further, there are three main styles available:

Car haulers. A car hauler is probably what most people think of when they picture smaller trailers. The wheel wells are exposed above the deck height and the trailer deck is confined between the two wheel wells. The main advantage here is that the deck is relatively low to the ground, translating to more headroom in a tiny house. The main disadvantage of car-hauler trailers is that their decks are narrow, preventing one from taking advantage of maximum road-width limits. A narrow house can feel uncomfortable and make it more challenging to accommodate life's necessities since there's less square footage.

Deck overs. A deck over is a trailer where the deck is located over the top of the wheel wells, which provides room for a wider trailer than car-hauler styles. However, because the deck is so high off the ground, it limits the available interior height. Therefore, most deck-over trailers are used for single-story tiny homes.

Custom bumper-pull trailers. In our opinion, the best option for a movable tiny house is a custom trailer. With a custom setup, you can incorporate the best qualities of a car hauler and deck-over trailer. Your trailer manufacturer can build the deck as low as possible and extend the edges beyond the wheel wells, maximizing your head height as well as trailer width. The only downside of this setup is that the wheel wells will protrude into your tiny house structure. However, with creative design, you should be able to incorporate the wheel wells so they can't even be seen.

This illustration shows the difference between car haulers, deck overs, and custom tiny house trailers. The custom option maximizes the deck height and width.

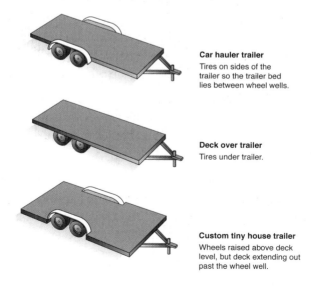

Car hauler trailer
Tires on sides of the trailer so the trailer bed lies between wheel wells.

Deck over trailer
Tires under trailer.

Custom tiny house trailer
Wheels raised above deck level, but deck extending out past the wheel well.

Goosenecks and Fifth-Wheel Trailers

Gooseneck and fifth-wheel trailers are very similar in design. Both connect via a hitch in the tow vehicle's bed, slightly in front of the tow vehicle's rear axle. These hitch systems are mounted to the tow vehicle's frame with an installation kit, enabling very high tow capacities. It's common for fifth-wheel trailer hitches to accommodate a GTWR of 25,000 pounds. A gooseneck hitch can typically handle a GTWR of 30,000 pounds.

The biggest differences between a gooseneck and fifth-wheel trailer are the hitch and ball configurations as well as how the connection is made. In a gooseneck, the ball is located on the tow vehicle and the hitch-receiving connector is on the trailer. In fifth-wheel trailers, the opposite is true. Because the point of attachment is located at the tow vehicle's rear axle, the tongue weight of gooseneck and fifth-wheel trailers is well distributed across the tow vehicle. This creates a smoother towing experience and provides a larger turn radius than a bumper-pull setup.

We recommend that any THOW above 28 feet be upgraded from a bumper-pull to a gooseneck or fifth-wheel trailer. The area located over a gooseneck assembly is often used as a bedroom or other habitable space. The head height in a room over the gooseneck is often quite generous and enough for an adult to stand in.

Permanent Foundations for Wheeled Structures

As of now, in order for a movable tiny house to be considered a permanent residence by the IRC, it must be permanently anchored to the ground. Exactly how you meet that requirement is up to you and your building department. Several permanent foundation options are available within the current IRC that a THOW or THOF could be built on top of, and it is likely that these options will be expanded with the adoption of the ITHP.

In some regions where the 2021 IRC's section R402.1 is acceptable, you can install a permanent wood foundation for your THOW. This system is relatively inexpensive and can be packed up and moved to a new location if need be. All that's required is plastic, gravel, pressure-treated lumber, and fasteners.

You can pour a concrete slab foundation with embedded anchors and attach your tiny house to it. This system would meet code requirements by resisting seismic and wind loads and is worth pursuing even though it's not specifically addressed in the IRC.

The intent of the IRC is to keep the public safe. Keeping this in mind when designing your project is important because if you can show your design follows the code, you'll have a better chance of winning COO approval. We highly recommend you hire a structural engineer to review your architectural plans. Their stamp of approval lends significant credibility within building official circles.

Ground-Bound Options

Perhaps you've decided not to build on a trailer but rather to build directly on a permanent foundation. There are various factors that help determine what foundation options are available such as soils, slope, site drainage, elevation above sea level, thermal mass potential, climate conditions, and budget.

Slab-on-Grade Foundations

Slab-on-grade foundations are the most common foundation systems in the United States. They're simple to build and deliver not only a foundation, but also a finished floor. When oriented to maximize solar gain, they also provide excellent thermal mass. They're easy to maintain and clean and have very long life expectancies.

On the downside, they're very hard and uncomfortable under foot. If you've ever looked at cashiers working on concrete floors, you might have noticed that they stand on thick rubber mats to minimize discomfort.

Pouring a concrete slab foundation is within the skill range of a well-researched DIYer. It's also quite easy to find a local concrete foundation contractor in nearly every community. The cost of a concrete slab foundation is also relatively low compared to other options.

Perimeter Stem Wall Foundations

Perimeter stem wall foundations, sometimes referred to as perimeter foundations, are quite common. They can be created with poured concrete or a combination of poured concrete and masonry block. Perimeter foundations require either a crawlspace beneath the floor or a basement. In areas in which deep excavation is required to get concrete footings below frost line, perimeter foundation walls make the most sense.

Although there are perks to building with stem walls, there are also downsides. They are typically more expensive and take longer to assemble, and they require more excavation and backfill as well as more material to assemble.

Pad-and-Pier Foundations

A pad-and-pier foundation is a simple system composed of two connected elements. The first is a concrete pad poured below frost line to support the loads placed upon it. The second is the pier, which is connected directly to the pad. In some cases, the piers consist of tall columns of concrete connected to the pad via rebar. In other cases, the piers are simply steel connectors embedded in the pads.

The adjustable length of the piers makes this system ideal for uneven ground. You're able to create level floor systems through the pier length adjustments with relative ease. Much is adjusted in the formwork, so you can check and double check your work before any concrete is brought onsite. Keep in mind that once cured, concrete is very difficult to adjust, so it's very important your forms are accurate.

Skids—the Secret Weapon

Skids take pad-and-pier foundations to the next level. A home built on skids can be placed on a pad-and-pier foundation for permanent attachment and then removed at a later date for relocation. This is possible because of the connection between the two. The assembly between the skids and the foundation is typically made with steel connectors, which are nailed or bolted onto the skid beams. Removing those connectors is all it takes to free the skids from the foundation, enabling you to load the home on a trailer.

Engineered Alternatives

There are other options available for foundations other than those we discussed in this chapter. These include foundations of permanent wood, poles, rubble trench, urbanite, stabilized earth, and more. Most of these foundations have been used for thousands of years, yet are not specifically called out in our codes.

If you want one of these systems, you'll need to hire an engineer to stamp your drawings. An engineer's stamp will greatly increase the potential of your project being approved. Sometimes building outside of code can be a great approach if the end result is safe and aligns with your overall priorities.

This construction sketch illustrates how a skid can be attached to a post-and-pier foundation system. The "T" strap can easily be disconnected from the framing post, freeing the skid itself if or when you want to move your THOS.

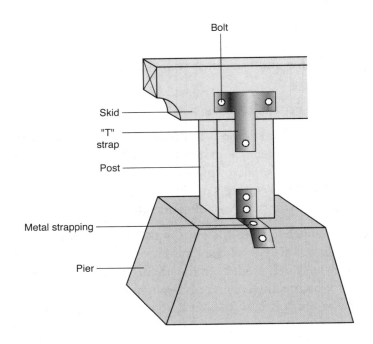

To Summarize

A wide variety of pros and cons are associated with the various tiny house foundation options, so it is important that you get clear on your priorities and constraints. Various foundation options exist for THOFs, too, ranging from concrete slabs to stem walls to pad and piers to skids. Several hitch classes exist for bumper-pull trailers, so ensure you get the right one for towing your tiny house. Goosenecks and fifth-wheel trailers are ideal for any THOWs more than 28 feet in length.

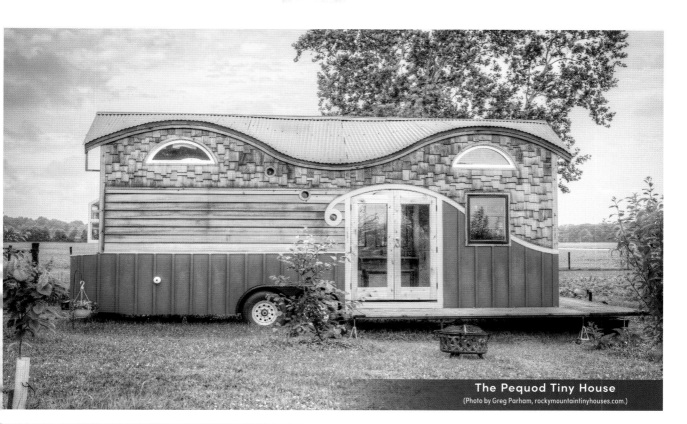

The Pequod Tiny House
(Photo by Greg Parham, rockymountaintinyhouses.com.)

METRO SIPs Tiny House
(Photo by Patrick Sughrue, artisantinyhouse.com.)

Nicole's Tiny House
(Photo by Christian Parsons of Tiny House Expedition.)

The Morrison Home Tiny House Kitchen
(Photo by tinyhousebuild.com.)

The Tangled Tiny
(Photo by Christian Parsons of Tiny House Expedition.)

The Matchbox Tiny House
(Photo by Christian Parsons of Tiny House Expedition.)

The Alpha Tiny House Exterior
(Photo credit of David Latimer, newfrontiertinyhomes.com; photography by Studio Buell.)

The Alpha Tiny House Interior
(Photo credit of David Latimer, newfrontiertinyhomes.com; photography by Studio Buell.)

The Klickitat Treehouse
(Photo by Christian Parsons of Tiny House Expedition.)

Stairs in the Morrison Home Tiny House
(Photo by tinyhousebuild.com.)

White Stairs
(Photo credit of minttinyhomes.com, copyright James Alfred Photography, jamesalfred.photography.)

Leaf Petal Stairs
(Photo credit of windrivertinyhomes.com; photography by Dillan 4C.)

Esk'et Spiraling Ladder
(Photo by esketbuilding.com.)

Ovida
(Photo credit of getaway.house; photography by Bearwalk.)

Clara by Getaway
(Photo credit of getaway.house; photography by Ball & Albanese.)

The Tiny Home at Dibble Creek
(Photo by Christian Parsons of Tiny House Expedition.)

The Polaris Tiny House
(Photo by Christian Parsons of Tiny House Expedition.)

The Morrison Home Tiny House
(Photo by tinyhousebuild.com.)

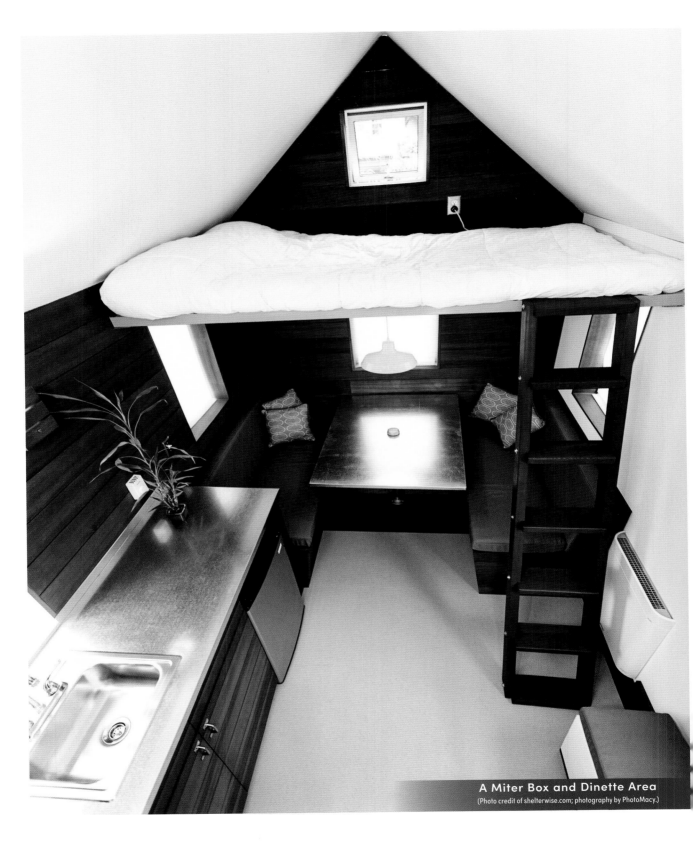

A Miter Box and Dinette Area

(Photo credit of shelterwise.com; photography by PhotoMacy.)

Tiny House Expedition
(Photo by Christian Parsons of Tiny House Expedition.)

Tiny House Expedition Interior
(Photo by Christian Parsons of Tiny House Expedition.)

Atlas Tiny House's Interior
(Atlas Tiny House by F9 Productions Inc., f9productions.com;
photography by McCall Burau Photography.)

Atlas Tiny House's Exterior
(Atlas Tiny House by F9 Productions Inc., f9productions.com;
photography by McCall Burau Photography.)

Tiny Bathroom with View into the Living Room
(Photo credit of Mint Tiny House Company, minttinyhomes.com; photography copyright James Alfred Photography, jamesalfred.photography.)

Tiny Bathroom
(Photo credit of New Frontier Tiny Homes, newfrontiertinyhomes.com; photography by Studio Buell Photography.)

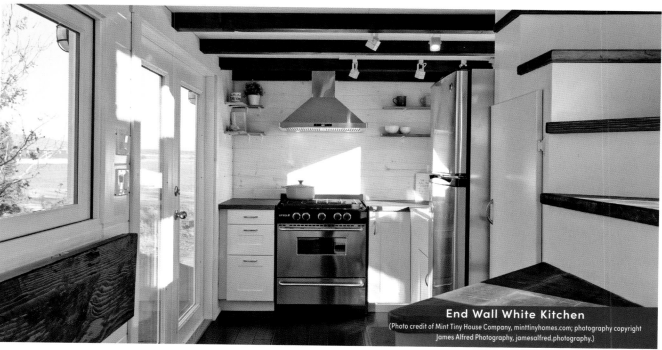

End Wall White Kitchen
(Photo credit of Mint Tiny House Company, minttinyhomes.com; photography copyright James Alfred Photography, jamesalfred.photography.)

Arched Loft
(Photo by Jan Sturman, albinocrow.com.)

Tiny Fellow's House
(Photo by Christian Parsons of Tiny House Expedition.)

Tiny House Shower with Wood Barrel Tub
(Photo by Christopher Tack, tackphoto.com.)

The Knot So Tiny House
(Photo by Christian Parsons of Tiny House Expedition.)

The Black Pearl
(Photo by Christian Parsons of Tiny House Expedition.)

CHAPTER 12

Designing Your Tiny House

Beautiful architecture has the power to inspire and invoke feelings of calm, contentment, inspiration, and joy. On the other hand, if a space isn't visually appealing and lacks practicality and functionality, it can make its occupants pretty miserable.

Many architects and designers have devoted their educational training and careers to this art form. Fortunately, by applying some of the tools of the trade, time, and energy, you can create your own beautiful set of tiny house plans, too. In this chapter, we show you how to choose a good set of existing tiny house plans, how to design your own tiny house, what software programs bring it all together, and how engineering is the best line of defense when it comes to safety. Let's get drawing!

Altering Existing Plans

Tiny houses are so personalized that it's unusual to find one that meets all your needs and wants. What's more common is to find one that's close, but requires some alteration to make it just right. An online search for tiny house construction plans should yield numerous options to get you started.

If you found a set that's close to what you want, you're off to a great start! Much of the preliminary design work has already been done for you. Although exciting, this can pose its own set of challenges, so be sure to choose wisely. Let's go over the factors you need to take into consideration when it comes to existing plans.

Choosing a Plan

High-quality and complete sets of tiny house plans do exist on the market, and more are being added regularly. If you're considering a set, be sure they contain all pertinent construction details, such as a clear floor plan, exterior elevations, construction sections, plumbing and electrical details, and engineering details.

Don't settle for an incomplete set, especially if you're a beginner builder. You'll likely end up wasting time and money if there are omissions. Look for ones that have been built by at least a couple happy customers and spare yourself the job of becoming the guinea pig.

Lastly, consider the level of customer service offered by the company selling the plans. It's always a good idea to send an introductory email with a few questions *before* you buy plans to see if the designer responds promptly. Because questions will certainly arise during the build, you'll appreciate the peace of mind knowing there's someone who can help you.

Every Change Counts

The biggest risk in altering existing plans is that a simple change can create an unforeseen and negative consequence. For instance, let's say you don't like the current placement of the kitchen in your purchased plans. You change it from a U-shaped configuration to a modified galley and place all the cabinetry and appliances on one wall. The other wall you leave relatively open and place only lightweight items along it.

What you don't realize is that the original kitchen layout was a key component in the weight distribution calculations made by the engineer. By moving the kitchen around, you've thrown the design out of balance. Before making any modifications to an existing set of plans, be sure you understand how those changes will affect your tiny house.

Changes in a tiny house layout can affect other aspects in a design as well. By moving a room, wall, sink, or other detail, you might start a chain reaction of challenges to overcome. Sometimes, if your changes are relatively significant, this effort can become so large that it might make more sense to just start from scratch.

There's nothing wrong with modifying an existing set of tiny house plans. That said, you must have a clear understanding of how a tiny house design comes together so you can predict the effects each change will have on the overall structure.

Knowing What's Important to You

A good tiny house design should be highly personalized to its residents. Knowing what to incorporate into yours depends largely on your day-to-day habits and needs. Do you work from home and cook often, or are you gone most of the time? Do you have a lot of sporting gear and extra stuff to be stored, or are you moving in with a light load? These are the types of questions you'll need to think about as you design your tiny house. Let's start the design process by dreaming big.

Start with Grand Ideas

Even though you're designing a tiny house, we encourage you to start out by dreaming big. Sit down with all members of your household (if there are others) and make a wish list of everyone's tiny house hopes and dreams. This is a fun opportunity to uncover what you value in a home.

The intention of this exercise is to get everything on the drawing board. No wish should be left behind. You don't want to regret omitting something later on because you didn't think it would fit. You might be surprised at just how much you can get in a tiny house when you use creative design.

Our hOMe wish list was gluttonous:

- Two bedrooms

- Home office for two

- Full-size kitchen

- Seating area

- Large bathroom

- Lots of storage

- TV lounge

- Comfortable stairs to the loft

To be honest, we worried we were being a bit excessive as we listed everything. After several redesigns, however, we managed to fit everything in our 28-foot tiny house.

Prioritize each item on your list from "very important" to "might be able to let this one go." If a downstairs bedroom is at the top of your wish list, put that in the number one spot. If there's more than one of you doing this exercise, create your lists either together or separately. If you do them separately, you can compile them into a single list later.

What You Really Need

After a week or two, review your wish list(s). Having some time off gives new perspective on what you included on your list. Are there items you can cross off the list right away or perhaps move their position on the priority list ranking? You might be surprised at how many wishes you're willing to part with without protest. Do this exercise several times, giving yourself a few days in between until you're left with a list that represents what you truly want.

As you learn to tell the difference between what you want and what you actually need, you'll start seeing opportunities to simplify your life, as well as the belongings you carry with you. You'll also get clarity on what needs to be on your dream list. Remember that going tiny is a process partly dependent on reprogramming old habits. This can take time, so be patient. The more time you can give to this process, the better your tiny house will turn out in the end.

Double Duty

Let's say you want a couch in your tiny house and everyone in your family agrees. The problem is that sofas are huge, and you shouldn't compromise your living space with something so large unless it serves at least two functions—maybe even three. Instead, look for a sleeper unit with embedded storage. Now your space-hogging sofa serves three purposes: seating area, guest bed, and storage unit. This combination of purposes might be enough to justify the loss of floor space.

The stairs in hOMe are a perfect example of multifunctionality; they provide not only comfortable access to our sleeping loft, but also 25 square feet of extra storage space. This is enough for our winter jackets, hats, gloves, shoes, keys, and more. We even plumbed it to fit a washer/dryer combination unit.

The hOMe stairs provide comfortable access to our sleeping loft as well as an extra 25 square feet of storage.

Introduction to Design

Designing a tiny house from scratch might seem intimidating, but if you know where to begin and what steps to take, it's fun and rewarding. Keep in mind that most tiny house dwellers designed their own home with no previous experience. If they can do it, so can you!

Sometimes the best approach to designing a tiny house is to start with a totally blank canvas rather than trying to fit bits and pieces of other designs into a floor plan. There's something to be said about approaching a challenge with a clear mind.

Visualizing the Layout

It's time to get creative, so grab your edited wish list! Don't bother drawing anything that looks like a house just yet. Instead, start by drawing simple circles and labeling each one to represent all the items on your wish list.

This process will transform your list into a picture of sorts called an *item-priority circle drawing*. Draw the size of each circle relative to the level of importance you've rated the item. For example, if you really want a full-size kitchen, use a large circle for that item. If, on the other hand, the bathtub is low on the list, draw a small one around it.

Bubble diagrams are an easy yet effective way of visualizing how a space flows together.

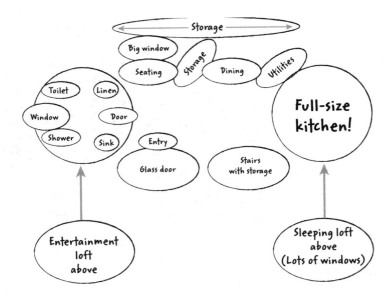

Next, turn your circles into a room-relationship bubble sketch, which is a series of simple hand-drawn circles that represent the rooms you want in your house. As before, the scale is important, and the size of each bubble should be relative to the size of the room it represents. The placement of the bubbles is also important. For example, don't draw the bathroom directly next to the kitchen unless that's where you want to place it. Bubble sketches are an easy way to assess the relationship between various spaces in your tiny house and to see how everything flows together.

With both the item-priority circle drawing and room-relationship bubble sketch complete, you should have a sense of which room goes where, what each one contains, and what the movement patterns between spaces look like. At this point, you can start laying out your plan in detail and working with graph paper or a computer program.

Designing Your Floor Plan by Hand

A floor plan is an architectural representation of a structure or room from a bird's-eye view. Even though it's just a two-dimensional depiction of a space, it gives detailed perspective and is a great starting place when embarking on the design process.

Floor plans should be drawn to scale, meaning that the proportions between all objects and lines should be true to form whether the house drawing is tiny or large. The most commonly used scale in American architecture is ¼ inch equals 1 foot. This means that a ¼-inch object or line represents 1 foot in actual space. If something is drawn to *full scale*, it's life-size and a bit difficult to carry around in your pocket.

The best way to ensure your drawing is accurate is by using an architectural/engineering scale. This triangular ruler is like a standard ruler. However, it contains several different scale options on it. You can draw with incredible precision by using an architectural/engineering scale. Always make a note on your sketch what scale you used for reference. A high-quality mechanical pencil as well as a nonsmudging eraser are the only other materials you'll need.

Here are the steps for creating a hand-drawn floor plan:

1. **Exterior walls.** Lightly draw the exterior walls of your tiny house. Use your architectural scale for precise lines. Be sure to incorporate the thickness of the exterior wall in your drawing. For the highest level of accuracy, the depiction of the exterior thickness also should include the framing material, siding, and interior finish wall materials. Although it's not common practice in residential architecture, it's important to include these items in a tiny house because of the extreme floor space and total width restrictions.

2. **Interior walls.** Again, be sure to draw interior partition walls using light lines. Account for wall thickness, too. It's easy to forget that information, but a miscalculation of even 2 inches can cause issues in a tiny house design. An improperly measured partition wall in one of our hOMe sketches nearly threw off our entire cabinetry layout.

3. **Doors.** Lay out your door(s). Erase any lines on the same plane your door openings will go. Draw a quarter circle to represent the direction the door opens. Refer to the floor plan image for instruction on how to draw a pocket door. A typical entry door is 36 inches wide.

This is a hand-drawn sketch of our 28-foot hOMe plans. Certain industry conventions are applied to floor plan sketches. When you learn what they all represent, you'll be able to understand any floor plan drawing.

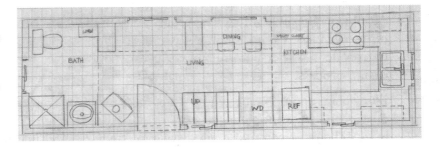

4. **Windows.** Windows can be depicted as boxes superimposed over the wall plane. For more information on window and door placement strategies, see "Windows and Doors," later in this chapter.

5. **Appliances, cabinets, and fixtures.** A typical lower kitchen cabinet depth and countertop is 2 feet. Uppers are generally 1 foot deep. Lower cabinets are depicted with a solid line while uppers are shown with a dashed line. Refrigerators and ranges/ovens are drawn just a tad deeper than cabinetry. Refer to the floor plan image for how to illustrate fixtures and appliances.

6. **Finishing up the first floor.** Clean up any smudges and label appliances and rooms if you desire. If you're pleased with this floor plan and feel fairly confident your exterior wall dimensions won't change, take a pen and go over the exterior lines. Make them pretty bold. We don't recommend you do this with your interior walls, cabinetry, and appliances, just in case you want to make modifications.

7. **Lofts.** If you plan on incorporating one or two lofts into your tiny house, take a separate piece of paper and place it atop the first floor elevation. With the exterior walls clearly marked in pen, you should be able to see them through the top piece. Copy the exterior wall outline (except for the windows) onto the second sheet, and draw out your lofts in pencil. Incorporate any second-story windows into that sketch.

8. **Mechanical and electrical systems.** Before you can really go into depth with this step, you'll need to research the following systems: water heaters, electrical panels, HVAC sources, water filtration systems (if needed), and mechanical ventilation systems. If any of them require a significant amount of space, be sure to account for where they'll be placed. Be sure to include a utility closet in your design for housing at least some of these items.

In terms of ceiling lights and switches, you might want to wait until you feel pretty set on your floor plan. Add those details once all the larger pieces have found homes. Don't race past this step, however. Lighting is incredibly important in any space, especially a tiny house. Be sure to give this adequate attention in the design phase.

As you go along, try to see your design through fresh eyes when possible. In one of our hOMe plan renditions, we realized we had forgotten to add a refrigerator! We were so focused on other details we completely skipped over it.

Windows and Doors

You've likely established your door placement, but perhaps you haven't determined where your windows will go. Windows are important not only for allowing light into your house, but also for augmenting your design.

There's an art to knowing how to make the most out of window placement. The *rule of thirds* is a great place to start. It's a composition concept used in photography, but the principle can be applied in architectural design as well. By dividing your tiny house design into thirds both horizontally and vertically, you create a grid of nine rectangles. Important elements (such as windows) should ideally align on any of the four corners of the grid lines. This adds visual interest to a design.

We incorporated the rule of thirds in our hOMe design by placing windows and the door toward the four corners as much as possible.

Another important consideration for your windows is line of sight. Optimize the placement of windows by anticipating your views from the inside out. If you plan on being parked in one location, be sure to incorporate views you want and minimize those you don't. If you intend on being mobile, design your sight lines for the best use of light and views in a general sense. You can always add multidirectional blinds later if your new view isn't as appealing as you had hoped.

Solar gain on south-facing windows can warm a space for free during cold winter months. It can also overheat that space in no time on a hot and sunny summer day if you don't plan for ways to protect the windows from that sun. A THOW has the unique advantage of being able to move with seasonal cycles, allowing you to take advantage of natural heating and cooling. Simply pull out into a clear open spot in the winter, orient your longest wall with the most windows toward the south, and in the summer, tuck it away under the shade of a tree.

Design Programs

A lot of design details are challenging to visualize without having a 3D perspective. Although some people are talented enough to build physical models or draw a house in 3D, the rest of us need other tools and solutions.

Luckily, we live in a world of computers, applications, and multimedia options made to simplify the design process. That said, some of them have steep learning curves even for those with a computer background.

There are several architectural design software programs available that can give you 3D functionality. There are new programs on the market all the time, so be sure to consider all your options before you get started. For example, we recently discovered an app that allows us to map out 3D spaces with our smartphone camera. By literally tracing our hOMe layout with the phone, this program translates that data into a floor plan. These technologies are getting more sophisticated every year.

Let's look at some of your options.

SketchUp

In designing hOMe, we used SketchUp (sketchup.com). We had never used the software before, so our learning process was slow. We invested a couple weeks working through free, online tutorials until we felt proficient enough to design our own tiny house. In the end, we were pleased with SketchUp's functionality and ability to create a working 3D representation of hOMe.

The biggest advantage of SketchUp is that the drawings are created in 3D from the beginning. Within this environment, you can move figures, furniture, and other details around easily. This makes checking the functionality of a space quite simple. SketchUp provides you with a human figure drawn to scale. As you move the figure through the house, you can double check that you've budgeted enough space for all components.

Pros:

- You can use the free version for most needs.
- Very powerful design options.
- 3D design for easy visualization of the space.
- Lots of online tutorials available.

Cons:

- Can be a steep learning curve.
- 3D only may make drawing the design difficult.
- Lines drawn in the wrong plane cause major problems with overall design.
- Pro version required for best results, which is fairly expensive.

You'll need to ensure that your lines are drawn in the correct plane or axis when working with SketchUp. Because you draw in three dimensions, a line placed even 1 degree out of plane can cause all kinds of headaches. Be sure your lines are precise and snapped to the correct axis to ensure the software works correctly.

You can do a lot with the free version of SketchUp. However, to create your tiny house design to its fullest, we recommend you upgrade to the pro version. There are a lot more add-ons and functions available with the pro version that make the overall job easier and faster.

AutoCAD

AutoCAD (autodesk.com) has been around for a very long time, and it packs a lot under the hood. It's most likely far more powerful than anything you'll need for a tiny house design, but it's a great resource should you decide to use it.

AutoCAD can be used to draw in both 2D and 3D. If you struggle with visualizing things in three dimensions, it might be easier for you to work in two dimensions instead. Because AutoCAD is such a well-known platform, many architectural programs allow you to import your 2D AutoCAD designs into its 3D simulator.

Pros:

- Very powerful design options.
- 2D and 3D design available.
- Interfaces with most other design software.

Cons:

- Perhaps overkill for your needs.
- Can be difficult to learn to use.
- You may need to create wall details from scratch, rather than importing existing details.

Home Designer Suite

Home Designer Suite (homedesignersoftware.com) is intended for conventionally sized houses, but you can use it on a tiny house design as well. It provides users with a questionnaire asking pertinent questions and generates a floor plan based on the answers.

With Home Designer Suite, you can view your 3D model from various angles as well as capture a video of the tour to share with others. One of the coolest features the program offers is the cost estimator. The program can create a spreadsheet with the cost of supplies you'll need to build your tiny house. Although not 100 percent accurate, it will give you a general idea of what to expect.

Pros:

- Offers cost estimating software.
- Relatively simple design features.

- 3D design for easy visualization of the space.
- Questionnaire may be useful in triggering thoughts you might not otherwise have about the design.

Cons:

- May be more than you need for a tiny house design.
- Doesn't interface well with other programs.
- Estimating software may not be as accurate as you would like.

SketchPlan

If you don't need something quite as robust as Home Designer Suite, check out SketchPlan.com. By simply uploading your floor plan with dimensions formatted to their needs, you receive a polished computer-generated substitute. You can even upgrade to a full 3D render of your floor plan, which allows you to take a virtual tour of your future home. The costs are very reasonable for this service, too.

Pros:

- Quickly generates 3D model for visualizing the space.
- Simple to use.
- Very reasonably priced.

Cons:

- You need to generate the 2D floor plan separately.
- Limited in its functionality and data representation.

Converting Your Designs into Architectural Plans

Having a floor plan—or a 3D version of your design—is a great starting place, but it's not the end. You'll need to create what are called working drawings from the current plans. Working drawings are what you actually build from. They contain all the necessary information to build the house, including dimensions, material choices, layout decisions, fixture locations, cross-sectional views, design details, and more.

For example, you'll need to decide whether you'll be framing your walls with 2×4 studs (16 inches o.c. or 24 inches o.c.), or perhaps using 2×6 studs. All that information needs to be laid out clearly in the working drawings.

It's all in the details, as they say, so the details need to be accurate. It's important to show things, such as how the window framing details and trim come together. It's also important to show construction details, such as the anchoring of the structure to the trailer. For better clarity, these details are typically done in a larger scale— ¾ inches equals 1 foot.

You'll want to create as many details and construction drawing pages as you deem necessary. Consider that taking time to draw the details is much faster than building them without fully understanding how everything comes together. It's cheaper to erase mistakes on paper than in reality.

The Importance of Engineering

Engineering is essential on a set of tiny house plans, especially if the home is going to be on wheels. Engineering documents ensure that if all construction details are followed correctly, the tiny house will perform as expected and won't pose a structural risk to you or anyone else. Because there are so many factors at play in THOWs, understanding how it all comes together can be difficult, even for a professional.

Licensed architects can provide their own engineering details on plans, but they often work with an architectural-specific engineer to ensure their numbers are correct. Designers, on the other hand, are required to subcontract out all engineering work to a licensed engineer.

Compared to conventionally built houses on fixed foundations, THOWs suffer a much larger range of loads and stresses as they're towed down the road. They must be able to endure earthquake-like movements, hurricane-force winds, and the stress of deceleration if the driver locks up on the brakes. It's essential that your tiny house plans be reviewed by an engineer to ensure your home can handle all those loads and forces.

Wind Loads

Any residential structure must be designed and engineered with potential seismic-, wind-, and snow-load burdens in mind. Various technologies offer solutions to each of these challenges, even in tiny houses. Knowing which ones to focus on will help ensure you end up with a safe design.

We've all watched news footage of the damage tornados can cause to structures. The biggest concentration of this destruction is often seen in mobile home parks. That's not because tornados have a personal vendetta against them, but because mobile homes are typically not designed to withstand high winds.

Mobile homes, now called *manufactured housing*, are more susceptible to wind damage because of their connection, or lack thereof, to the ground. Appendix AE of the 2021 IRC addresses this issue and specifies requirements for setting manufactured housing on foundations. Because of this effort and improved anchoring, manufactured houses are resisting high-wind forces much more effectively today than in years past. By following the details of IRC Appendix AE, or by using engineered alternatives, you can keep your tiny house safe in high-wind events.

Tiny houses on wheels must also deal with excessive wind loads when being towed. Imagine driving down the highway with your brand-new THOW at 45 mph. Wind is hitting your beloved tiny not only from the front but also from the left side at 50 mph as you near a storm front. Suddenly, an 18-wheel tractor-trailer passes you at 70 mph. Your poor tiny just got blasted with a hurricane-strength gust. You can practically hear it groaning. Knowing that your home has been engineered to handle these types of wind loads will help bring a sense of calm during a time of potential stress.

A THOW being towed down the road is subjected to significant wind forces from various angles at any given moment.

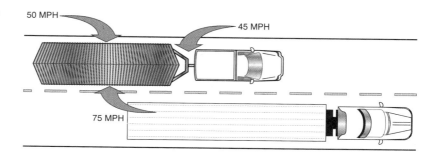

Seismic Loads

Seismic, or earthquake, forces exert a different type of pressure on a THOW. When an earthquake occurs, a sudden release of energy travels on the earth's surface as seismic waves. Those waves move both vertically and horizontally, causing violent shaking to a structure as well as a side-to-side motion that can easily overturn a house.

In the current residential housing codes, there's nothing that recognizes THOWs, so all building science that discusses the need for proper anchoring is aimed at foundation-bound structures. Within those findings, the evidence is clear that foundation-bound structures must be sufficiently anchored in order to better protect the inhabitants during a seismic event.

We expect the same data to pan out for THOWs as well. Therefore, be sure to pay adequate attention to your foundation options and how you plan on anchoring your trailer to the ground while parked. Even if you plan to move frequently, it's still a good idea to anchor the home while not in transit.

Snow Loads

Although the white stuff looks pretty and fluffy as it's coming down, it's actually very heavy as it accumulates. Tiny house roof spans are small, but they still must mitigate that weight in cold climates. In snow-prone areas, steeper sloped roofs are recommended over lower-sloped ones because they allow snow and ice to slide off more easily.

An important consideration when dealing with snow loads is rafter sizing. In a climate that's warm year-round, you might be able to get away with 4×4-inch rafters (assuming they structurally support the span) at 24-inch centers. In high-snow zones though, that rafter size is likely not appropriate. Increasing rafter sizes in a THOW is not simple because it translates to a decrease in loft ceiling height. Instead, you might be better off reducing the gaps between each rafter to strengthen your roof while not compromising your loft height. For example, move to a 12-inch spacing from the standard 24-inch o.c. layout.

Two feet of hard packed snow on a 28×8-foot tiny house weighs more than 6,000 pounds. If you framed your THOW in Florida with rafters sized for that climate but now find yourself living the dream as a ski instructor in the Colorado Rockies, there's a good chance you'll come home to a pile of splinters after the first major blizzard if you don't make some alterations to your roof design.

Building codes for roof framing vary from region to region depending on snowfall and other factors. Check the building codes in the snowiest area you think you'll visit with your THOW to ensure it can handle those loads.

It's essential you design your THOW to best match future plans. If those aren't clear, design the strongest and most versatile tiny house you can afford. This will give peace of mind not only to you, but also to any future homeowner that ends up moving the house to a different climate zone.

Additional Stress Loads

Imagine you're towing your THOW and are passed by a semi-truck traveling at 70 mph. As the truck passes you, you hit a pothole in the road. You just added an 8.0 seismic event for your THOW to manage.

But wait, it gets better. We have another force to throw into the mix—deceleration. This is the force exerted on the house when you hit the brakes. It could be slow and gradual or dramatic depending on how hard you hit the brakes. Are you getting the argument for engineering yet? We hope so.

On top of all these tiny house specific stresses, there are two standard load paths that all houses must deal with—dead and live loads. A load path is the path through which loads pass from the highest point in a structure through the wall systems, floor, foundation, and eventually to the ground. Dead loads consist of the weight of permanently attached aspects of the home. Examples of dead loads are framing members, fixtures, and any other load that doesn't change with time.

Live loads consist of any load that is not constant over time. Examples are movable furniture, people, snow loads, and the like. Each type of load affects a house differently, but they must all be considered in the design. Can you guess who can help you with that? Bingo! An engineer.

We imagine we've gotten you a bit rattled reading this section, so we want to reassure you by saying that these potential forces can be mitigated with proper design. Houses have been built to withstand hurricanes, earthquakes, and more for ages. RVs deal with these stresses on a day-to-day basis with pretty good success. Your THOW will do great as well, provided you plan accordingly. Be sure to include adequate bracing, anchors, connectors, and other construction details to your tiny house and it will stand tall and proud no matter what force comes its way.

Weight Distribution

Weight distribution in a THOW has a huge effect on towing performance. Properly balancing the loads over the axles and from side to side allows for a smooth towing experience. A poorly weighted tiny house, on the other hand, can instigate dangerous side-to-side sway.

When designing your house, pay attention to how the trailer is loaded. If you place a heavy kitchen on the right side and nothing on the left, your house will be unbalanced. Adding too much weight in front of the axles (on the tongue side) can also cause weight distribution problems. Conversely, adding too much weight behind the axles can create a safety hazard, too.

We highly recommend sway bars for trailers and tow vehicles for an extra safety measure. This after-market addition helps spread loads from the trailer to the tow vehicle's rear axle, offering stability and control above and beyond a well-balanced trailer design.

If you've balanced your home properly, your dead and live loads will all be accounted for. You'll be able to tow without any sway and will look and feel like a champ as you pull your tiny house down the freeway.

What Does This Thing Weigh Anyway?

As tiny housers, we sure have to deal with a lot of interesting challenges, one of which is knowing how much our house weighs *before* the trailer is even ordered. Because the strength of the trailer is completely dependent on how much the house on top of it weighs, you'd better have a pretty good sense of it all ahead of time.

If you aren't purchasing a set of tiny house plans with this information, an engineer can estimate the weight using weight tables and charts. You can also find similar charts by doing a web search for "common weights of construction materials." There are also books geared toward builders (not engineers) that outline material weights, too.

Large hardware stores offer the weights of all their construction materials as well as cabinets, finish materials, and the like, on their websites. Look under each product's information page for those specifications. In terms of the trailer, contact potential manufacturers and ask them for that information. Your trailer weight will need to be factored into your total load estimate as well.

For a general sense, you can calculate a rough lineal foot weight. The industry standard for most wood framed 8'6" wide × 13'6" tall THOWs says that you can expect a weight of 400 to 600 pounds per linear foot, including the weight of the trailer itself. That's a pretty wide range because there are lots of different finishes available.

We always recommend people err on the side of a larger-than-needed trailer than one not built strongly enough. Changing axles and increasing the strength of the frame is not easily done, and once the house is attached to the trailer, it's nearly impossible to remove that home in order to place it onto a new trailer.

To Summarize

It's best to start designing your tiny house by dreaming big and then whittling down to ensure you consider all your options. To maximize efficiency, each item you incorporate into your tiny house design should serve at least two purposes. Sometimes it's easier to purchase a complete set of quality plans and make modifications to it, rather than starting from scratch. Design programs have become highly sophisticated and can create beautiful 3D perspectives of your tiny house design. The best way to ensure your THOW will be safe while in transit and when set on-site is to hire a structural engineer to review your plans.

CHAPTER 13

Working with Design Professionals

If you have one too many peas on your plate and can't imagine adding "design my tiny house" to your multipage to-do list, fret not! There are some amazing and experienced tiny house design professionals out there who would love to help bring your tiny house dreams to life.

Finding the right design professional, whether it be a designer or architect, is an amazing feeling and something we hope to help you accomplish. In this chapter, we talk about when and how to hire a professional, the best ways to save money when hiring a pro, and how to make sure the contract protects you. We also introduce you to some engineering concepts you'll need to understand before the design process begins.

When to Hire a Pro?

Even if you're fairly certain you want to hire a designer or architect, we suggest you read Chapter 12 and follow the design exercises as far as you can. There are two reasons for this:

- You might find you actually *do* have what it takes to design your dream tiny house (in which case, you've just saved yourself loads of money!).

- The more you know about your needs and wants for your tiny house, the more effectively you'll be able to share that information with the design professional. This saves you hours of time, which translates to you saving money.

As soon as you make the decision to hire a design professional, you should start your search for the perfect match. Even though there are numerous tiny house–specific designers and architects out there, there's often more work available than professionals have time to complete.

You can also consider expanding your options by hiring a professional who hasn't designed a tiny house before. There are, indeed, some THOW-specific details that are helpful to know in advance of designing one; however, a quality design professional should be able to easily research and adopt them.

Finding the Right People

Great people make great company, and because you'll likely have many interactions with your designer/architect, it's best to choose one who understands your tiny house vision, hopes, and dreams. Be sure you will work well together and that they will be able to translate your wants into the design. As renowned architect Frank Lloyd Wright once said, "You can use an eraser on the drafting table or a sledgehammer on the construction site."

Ask for Referrals

The best way to find out about a designer's reputation is by asking for referrals. No matter how amazing someone seems on their website or how good their advertising may be, nothing says more about a professional than personal referrals. Because so many social media sites are dedicated to tiny houses, an obvious place to begin the hunt for recommendations is in those groups. If you can't find references within social media circles or via people you know, ask the design professional directly for some references. Be sure to call all the listed references and ask them the following five questions:

- Did you enjoy working with the design professional, and would you use them again on another project?

- Was their communication direct and clear?

- Were they easy to reach?

- Did they complete the job on schedule and on budget?

- Would you recommend them?

If a reference seems lackluster, be sure to ask follow-up questions. This is important for two main reasons. First, maybe the client and design professional were simply not a good fit. The reasons the client was unhappy may have been more to do with a personality clash than with an inherent flaw with the design professional. In that case, just be sure the same things that annoyed the client aren't huge triggers for you. Second, a longer conversation may surface details about the designer/architect that would be challenging for you as well. Perhaps they have an approach to working that you wouldn't appreciate either. It's always good to get the bigger story when possible.

Interview Multiple Design Professionals

If at all possible, you'll want to shop around a little bit and connect with at least three design professionals to see what options are available. You might find that you end up loving the first one you spoke with the most, but it's always good to make sure you've looked at multiple possibilities.

When interviewing design professionals, ask them the obvious questions, like "What's your experience?" and "What do you charge?" Don't be afraid to ask tough questions and expect good answers.

Here's a list of potential questions for you to ask the design professional during the interview:

- What do you find to be the biggest challenges when designing tiny houses as opposed to conventional houses?

- I want to know how difficult making changes will be along the way. Do you draft your designs by hand or on a computer?

- Do you have experience with off-grid living?

- Of your tiny house projects, how many were designed to be truly movable and how many were stationary?

- Do you have experience incorporating holding tanks for gray, black, and fresh water in a design?

- How many other projects do you have going right now?

- Are you available on weekends and holidays for conversations?

- Do you need to make a site visit or can you design from a distance?

- Do you work with an engineer that understands the unique challenges of a THOW?

- Can we set up a clear path of communication in case there are challenges that come up between us during the design process?

- What services are included in your price and what details would add cost to my project? How many revisions do I get with that cost?

- How long do you think it will take for my tiny house design to be completed?

The Importance of Communication

When you find a great design professional, you're ready for the next step: setting up the communication pathway. You'll talk quite a bit with your designer/architect, so having some contact parameters is a good idea. We suggest at least one weekly scheduled progress call. Try to schedule this appointment to fall on the same day and time every week so it becomes a part of your routine and consistency is kept.

Let's talk a little bit about how important honest communication is. It's easy to do when you love what your designer/architect is presenting and everyone is giving each other high fives. It's not nearly as much fun, though, when there's a challenge. The longer you wait to initiate a conversation in those situations, the sooner your molehill will turn into a mountain. If something isn't right, speak about it as soon as possible.

Here are some tried-and-true strategies that can be applied to challenging communications. We have personally used them ourselves in our years of working in the building industry.

- Don't speak from a place of anger or frustration. Speak by stating facts. Emotions won't likely help get your point across.

- Actually listen to the other person. Don't just wait for your turn to speak.

- When the person is done speaking, repeat to them what you heard, "I heard you say …."

- Let them agree or disagree with your statement of what you heard. If you were right, you're on the same page. If you misheard them, allow them the opportunity to explain their position again.

Your efforts will hopefully be rewarded by a simple and easy solution to the initial challenge, and if all goes well, you'll be back to high fives in no time.

What to Pay?

There are so many variables when it comes to design costs. These variables make it difficult to determine a fair price. That said, there are some basic parameters to keep in mind when looking for a design professional. We want to be clear that we're only discussing common price ranges here, so be sure to talk directly to your potential designers and architects to get a sense of what their current rates are.

You might have noticed that we've been talking mostly about *design professionals* and not designers or architects. That's because there are differences between the two, and how much they charge, which we will discuss here.

Designers

There are two primary differences between designers and architects:

- Designers typically don't spend time on the jobsite overseeing a build. Instead, they focus only on the design portion of a project.

- Designers typically charge less than architects. We have worked with a lot of designers and architects in our careers, and we have found outstanding ones with both titles.

Designers can charge less because they don't have the same overhead and start-up costs as architects. Designers aren't required to have the same amount of schooling, and they don't need to pay for the same licensing fees that architects must.

If you look online or read through design forums, you'll see that the average cost for work done by designers is between 50¢ and $2.50 per square foot. If you apply those averages to a house with very little square footage though, you'll see that a custom tiny house design could cost as little as $75. We can't imagine a professional designer creating a beautiful, custom set of plans for that little. The reality is that the smaller the house, the harder it is to design, so you should expect to pay more per square foot than you would with an average-size house. Any adjustment to one part of the plan heavily impacts the rest of the layout. It's not unusual for a design professional to have to start from scratch several times throughout the design process when working on a tiny home.

Designers charge, on average, anywhere from $45 to $80 or more per hour for their services. If you have a clear idea of what you want your plan to look like and just need someone to actually draw it up for you, hiring a designer by the hour may be the most cost effective solution. If you decide to work on a per-square-foot basis with a designer, you should expect to pay anywhere from $6 to $9 per square foot.

We recognize that these prices end up being close to those on conventionally sized house, but the reality is that designing a tiny house can easily take as much time, if not more. Tiny houses present special challenges, which take a lot of creativity and time to resolve.

Architects

As previously mentioned, architects are more expensive than designers, and for good reason. They've paid for years of schooling, must maintain specific licensing within their state, and are certified to perform both design and engineering services for your home.

We don't recommend architects over designers or vice versa. Instead, we recommend you find the best person to work with within your budget. Hire the person that sees your vision most clearly and that has the best ability to translate your wants and needs into a full set of architectural plans.

Similar to designers, architects typically charge for their projects in one of three or four ways. For a tiny house project, they might charge per square foot ($8 to $12 per square foot), by a percentage of the total construction cost (5 to 20 percent), or per hour ($125 to $200 per hour for a principle architect or $50 to $65 per hour for an architect intern).

In some cases, it makes sense to combine all these options in a contract. You can include aspects that will be billed per hour, others that are charged per square foot, and others that will be charged based on a percentage of construction costs. These types of contracts are created to protect both the architect and client on projects that have some areas of stability but also some areas that contain unknowns.

Here are the payment options for design professionals:

- **Cost per square foot:** $6 to $9 (designer), $8 to $12 (architect), depending on their experience.

- **Cost per hour:** $45 to $80 or more (designer), $65 to $175 or more (architect), depending on their experience.

- **Percentage of construction costs:** 8 to 15 percent (more common for architects than for designers).

- **Combination:** Some designers and architects combine cost per square foot, cost per hour, and percentage of construction costs to create either a more fluid contract or a project-based, fixed-price contract.

Reading the Fine Print

How many times have you signed a contract without reading the fine print? Let's be honest, many—if not most of us, are guilty as charged. The trouble is that in a contract, and in a court of law, every single word counts—including the itty-bitty, tiny ones.

As overwhelming as long contracts can be, they can create clarity for all parties involved. Nobody wants confusion during the job, so having everything laid out ahead of time is ideal. Including details such as deadlines, payment, and other important terms can prevent a lot of frustration down the line.

Confirm whether or not site visits are included in the arrangement. For foundation-based, conventional homes, it's common for architects to make weekly site visits to check on progress. Perhaps they are willing to do so for a THOW as well. These visits can be very useful, but they come at a price. Having an extra set of professional eyes on your tiny house build, especially if you'll be the general contractor, may very well be worth the extra money.

To Summarize

More and more design professionals are specializing in tiny houses, and more nonspecialized design professionals are looking to get involved in tiny houses, so you should have a wide range of professionals able to assist you. By talking with referrals and asking the right questions, you'll have the best chance of finding a perfect fit for your build. What you'll pay for your design professional's services depends on their title—architects tend to be more expensive than design professionals. You can save a lot of money by presenting them with a clear idea of what you want in your tiny house design. Scheduling weekly progress-check meetings is a great way to be sure that your vision is being materialized. The best way to ensure that your contract with a design professional has your best interests in mind is to read it carefully until you fully understand all the ins and outs.

CHAPTER 14

Reading Construction Drawings

Architectural plans provide the vital information you need to build a house, but until you learn how to read them, they can appear as perplexing as a 1,000-piece puzzle. Fortunately, with time and guidance, you'll start to see the method behind the madness and understand how it all comes together.

In this chapter, we cover details on how to read a set of architectural plans. We talk about each set of components and how to make sense of it all. We also illustrate three examples of tiny houses:

- A 28-foot THOW with a loft
- A 24-foot THOW
- A 20×18-foot tiny house on a fixed, permanent foundation

What's Included?

A quality set of working drawings should include the following:

- Title page
- Foundation plan
- Floor plan
- Electrical plan
- Plumbing plan
- Elevations
- Framing plan
- Sections
- Details

Let's explore each component and learn what information each contains.

Title Page

Title pages contain important pieces of information about a construction project. Although a lot of the text is in small print, it's very important that you read and understand it all. It might contain important disclaimers from the designer or notes on how to proceed with local building departments. Title pages should also contain a table of contents as well as a symbol legend defining the notations used throughout the plans.

Study the symbol legend on the title page closely so that you understand exactly what each one's telling you. Let's follow along with the symbol legend in the following figure, which was taken from a set of tiny house plans. When looking at the building section flag, note that the bottom number calls out the page on which the section detail is found. In this case, the building section flag is referring to page A3.1. The top figure indicates that the actual building section number is (1), and that it is on page A3.1.

There's an arrow, of sorts, on the building section flag as well. This arrow shows the orientation of the building section. Finally, the long line that extends down from the flag shows the precise location in which the building section is cut on the floor plan.

The detail flag identifies areas that are illustrated in more precise detail on a different page. The top number identifies the detail number, and the bottom number identifies the page on which the detail drawing is located.

The final symbol on the legend is an exterior elevation flag. Like the building section flag, this symbol has an arrow, which depicts the direction of view. This symbol also shows the same breakdown of page and elevation numbers as shown previously.

Each of these symbols contain important reference information. Learn how to read them before starting your construction process to optimize your build.

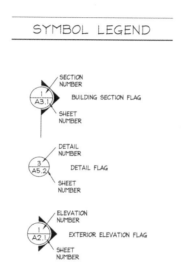

By studying the plans and following the detail paths, you can learn a lot about the house—from general notes to the finest details. Be sure to familiarize yourself with the plans before you start construction or order any materials.

In some cases, you might find discrepancies between the general plans and the construction details. In those instances, it's customary to heed the more detailed instructions rather than the general instructions. However, to be safe, read the title page fully and make sure the architect/designer didn't specifically address how they want you to handle those situations.

For homes built on permanent foundations, a title page includes plat information on a plot plan and details exactly where the house should be built on the lot as well as all setback details from property lines, wells, septic systems, waterways, and the like. Homes built on wheels likely won't include a plot plan because they're mobile in nature.

Title pages might include other notes, such as a glossary of terms and abbreviations, design load criteria, building data (for example, square footages), and safety notes. Be sure to read all this information!

Foundation Plan

Because the home will be built on a trailer, many tiny house plans don't include a foundation plan per se. Instead, they'll typically include trailer construction plans from which a reputable fabricator can create the trailer. Engineered tiny house trailer plans are essential for a safe THOW build. Most off-the-shelf, non–tiny house–specific trailers aren't engineered to support the weight of a tiny house.

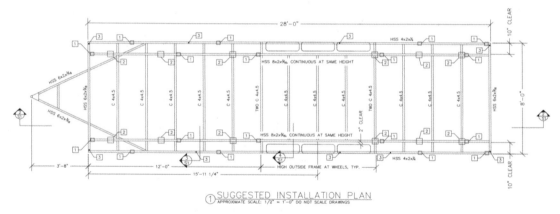

In a complete set of THOW plans, you should find trailer plans, which can be taken to any reputable trailer manufacturer.

Trailer plans should include framing member dimensions as well as callouts on the type and grade of metal required. They should also include details on axles and their placement on a trailer. Hold-down locations should be marked, including anchor points for the house to the trailer, as well as anchor points for the trailer to the ground anchoring system.

For homes on permanent foundations, plans should include details on concrete footer locations, as well as specific construction details. If you're building a concrete foundation, you should see notes for the inclusion of rebar, as well as the overall size of the foundation walls. Finally, you should see details about proper drainage away from the home along with information on any in-ground drainage lines necessary to keep the foundation dry.

Floor Plan

Floor plans outline a structure's layout and should include information on things such as heating appliances, utilities, flooring types, specialty cabinet locations, room layouts, window and door locations, and more. You can see examples of floor plans later in this chapter.

It's common for window and door schedules to appear on the same page as the floor plans. These schedules describe window and door details, including rough openings, finished sizes, glazing requirements (for example, tempered glass), number of each unit in each size, and header heights. You should be able to place your window and door order directly from these schedules and know exactly what size openings your framing should use.

You might find some general notes on a floor plan as well. It's not uncommon for architects and designers to call out specific safeguards such as "general contractor to verify all dimensions," or "home to be constructed in accordance with all local laws and codes." As much as these notes offer protection to the architect, they also raise important points that should be followed.

As mentioned earlier, the symbols used on a floor plan direct you to other views, such as elevations, building sections, and construction details. Always follow the information in the symbols to the most detailed drawing in the plans before starting any aspect of the build. In other words, start on the floor plan, zoom in to a building section, and zoom in again to specific construction details.

Let's look at an example set of plans to explain this concept. Find the flag in the left image that says *1/A3.1*, which is located on the top of the image toward the middle. This flag is telling you to look at Detail 1, which can be found on page A3.1.

Now look at the right image. It shows you building section 1 on page A3.1. You can see several other detail flags and a building section flag on Detail 1. If you had the full set of plans in front of you, you would follow each of these detail paths until you reached the last one.

The good news is that this system is used in nearly all residential construction drawings, so once you learn how to read plans, you'll be able to decode pretty much any of them.

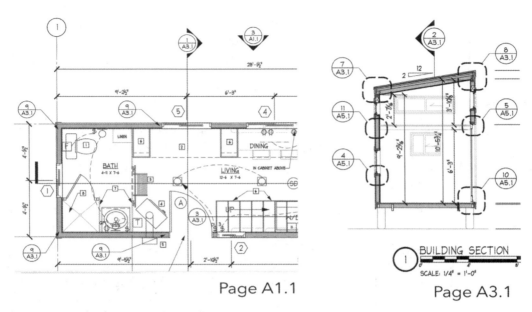

Page A1.1   Page A3.1

In this figure, two images illustrate how to read building section flags and details.

Electrical Plan

In smaller homes, electrical layouts are often included on the floor plan itself. You can study this detail in figures later in this chapter. Sometimes, however, they're placed on a separate drawing. An electrical plan doesn't show where to place your wires. Instead, it depicts the locations of switches, plugs, lighting, and safety detectors. An electrical plan also marks the location of the main electrical panel and anything else specifically related to the electrical system.

Exactly how you run your wiring is up to you. Also, you won't find specific information on how many circuits should be used or which parts of the home should be connected to the same circuits. That's up to you, too. Be sure to plan out your circuits ahead of time.

Other details not typically included on most electrical plans are the recommended wire type and gauge. The most common wire type used in residential construction is nonmetallic sheathed cable or NM-B (Romex). The most common sizes are 14g and 12g. There are specific requirements for some circuits within a home, which is dictated by the National Electrical Code (NEC) and something you'll have to investigate per local requirements.

Plumbing Plan

Most architectural plans don't include an actual plumbing plan; usually those details are left for a professional plumber. Designing a plumbing system is challenging in a THOW with height restrictions when it comes to vent stack designs. You might want to discuss your proposed plumbing layout with a plumber before you start framing to make sure it will work as intended.

On plans with plumbing details, you'll typically be shown the layout in 3D perspective, enabling you to see how the vent, waste lines, and water lines all interact. Plumbing plans also include gas lines, if applicable, in their layout.

Elevations

An elevation drawing enables you to see a proposed structure in a 2D view as though you were looking at it from street level. You can view examples of elevations on figures found later in this chapter. Sometimes an interior view might be represented in elevation form as well, such as a kitchen or bathroom cabinet layout.

It's common for elevation drawings to contain information on siding type, trim details, finish floor materials, overall building heights (marked from grade), and window identification badges that relate to both the floor plan and the window schedule. A window or door identification badge is simply a number or letter assigned to the window or door that's labeled in the window or door schedule. This enables you to see which windows and doors go where clearly.

Framing Plan

Framing details provide information on framing member sizing, spacing (such as 2×4 studs, 16 inches o.c.), as well as any sheathing that should be included in the wall assembly. Also, you'll find any specific notes regarding nailing patterns if they vary from industry standards and codes. Specialty hardware, anchors, strapping, or other fasteners will be included in these framing plans, too.

In some cases, a general note about framing details will be placed alongside a long arrow to describe a specific area. That note might read something like "4×4 ceiling joists, 24 inch o.c. placed over the loft frame."

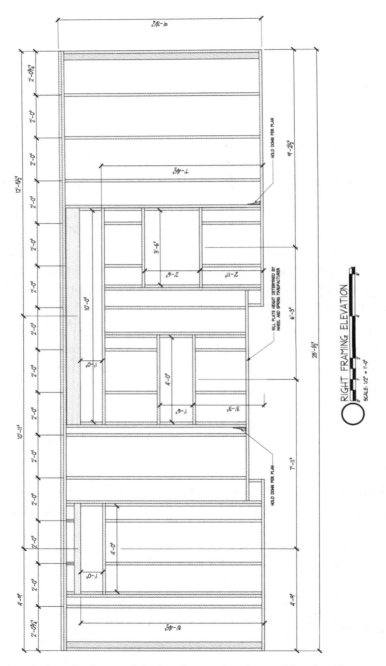

Framing plans outline how wall, floor, ceiling, and roof assemblies should come together.

Sections

In order to understand sectional views, imagine cutting a house with a knife along a specific line (section line), and then laying that view flat. By dissecting the house this way, you can see the inner workings of the walls, roof, floor, and anything else the section line intersects. As mentioned previously, this plan is where you'll most likely see wall assembly details.

You'll most likely find two sections in a tiny house, one cutting each direction across the house. In more complex homes, you may see more than two sections. It's customary to see detail circles on each section. These circles indicate that there are even more comprehensive views available to describe a detail. As mentioned earlier, be sure to follow those detail paths all the way to the highest level on the plans.

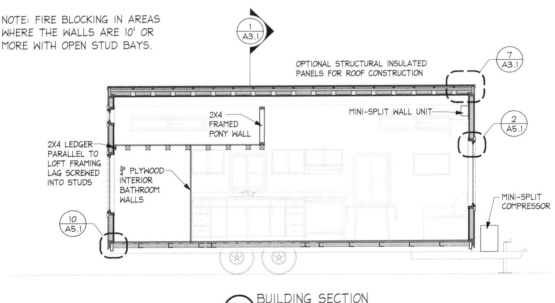

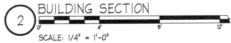

Building sections illustrate what a house looks like if you slice it along the section line. They provide a glimpse into framing and finish material systems.

Details

As the name implies, details provide the closest, most accurate view of any aspect on a set of plans. They're often used to show how roof intersections should be built, how the house to foundation or trailer connection should be made, and/or how the trim details should come together.

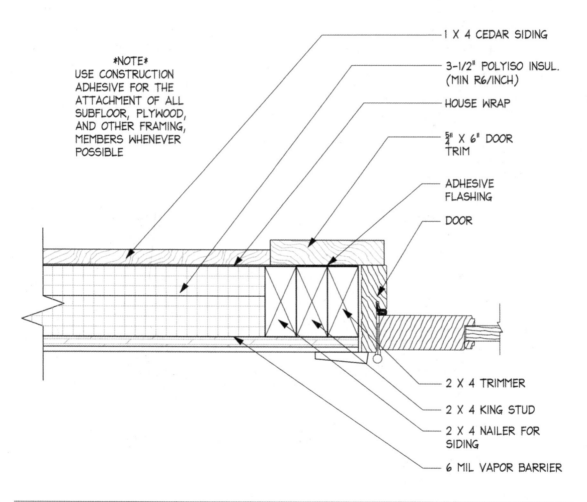

NOTE
USE CONSTRUCTION
ADHESIVE FOR THE
ATTACHMENT OF ALL
SUBFLOOR, PLYWOOD,
AND OTHER FRAMING,
MEMBERS WHENEVER
POSSIBLE

1 X 4 CEDAR SIDING

3-1/2" POLYISO INSUL. (MIN R6/INCH)

HOUSE WRAP

$\frac{5}{4}$" X 6" DOOR TRIM

ADHESIVE FLASHING

DOOR

2 X 4 TRIMMER

2 X 4 KING STUD

2 X 4 NAILER FOR SIDING

6 MIL VAPOR BARRIER

DOOR JAMB, PLAN VIEW

6

0'   3"   6'   1'

SCALE: 3" = 1'-0"

Construction details illustrate how various assemblies come together. A good set of construction drawings could have a dozen or more details.

The more details a set of plans contains, the easier it will be to construct the house. After all, you'll have a greater understanding of how everything comes together when you can see it in detail and from several angles.

Three Sample Tiny House Plans

In this section, we share three floor plans and elevations showcasing some tiny house examples. They might be a great point of inspiration as you begin to design your own dream tiny house. Two of these tiny houses are on wheels while one is on a fixed foundation.

24-Foot THOW

This 24-foot version of the hOMe tiny house is great for those wanting something a bit easier to tow but with enough space for day-to-day living for one to two people. One of the great features of this tiny house is that it offers a downstairs sleeping area. The original design calls for a sofa sold by IKEA, which converts easily into a queen-size bed while also providing storage for the bedding during daytime.

You can easily build a loft over the kitchen and bathroom area and have enough space for a set of stairs (as shown in the drawing). If you don't want the loft, the space where the stairs are could be incorporated into the kitchen, thus creating more counter space.

If you prefer not to sleep on a sofa, you can certainly place a mattress and frame where the sofa currently sits and incorporate back cushions so that the bed becomes a comfortable seating area during the day. If you opt for the loft option, you can fit a queen-size mattress up there as well as clothes storage furniture.

This 24-foot tiny house boasts a comfortably sized galley kitchen large enough for regular appliances. There's space for a washer and dryer combo and a comfortably sized bathroom with its own full-size sink. It incorporates a dining/work table large enough to comfortably seat three people. The table can be folded down during the day when more open floor space is desired.

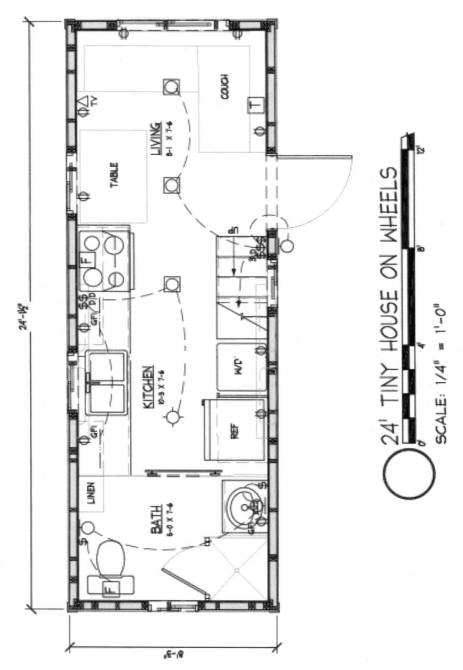

This 24-foot version of hOMe can be built with or without a sleeping loft. It boasts a nice size kitchen, bathroom, and comfortable seating area, which can convert into a bed at night.

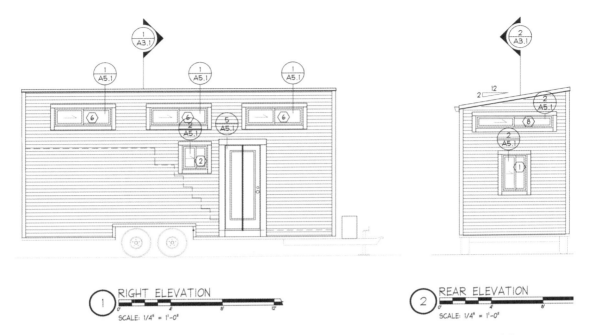

RIGHT ELEVATION
SCALE: 1/4" = 1'-0"

REAR ELEVATION
SCALE: 1/4" = 1'-0"

This elevation shows the 24-foot hOMe on wheels, which can be built with or without a loft.

THOW with Two Lofts

This 28-foot design is what we've been calling home since 2013. It's large enough for us to live and work in full-time. It's also spacious enough that it served as a home base for both of our children who lived full-time with us on that land. Although they did have their own sleeping cabins just a few feet from hOMe, the tiny house is where we all spent the bulk of our days.

The 28-foot hOMe design incorporates a comfortable set of stairs, a full-size kitchen with full-size appliances, tons of storage, a home office for two, a comfortably sized bathroom, and two lofts. It's also large enough for our two dogs and one cat.

This 28-foot layout can also be configured to incorporate a downstairs sleeping area. The U-shaped kitchen can be reconfigured into a galley setup in the middle of the tiny house; then, the end space can be used as a separate bedroom, creating the potential of three separate sleeping areas (two lofts and one downstairs bedroom).

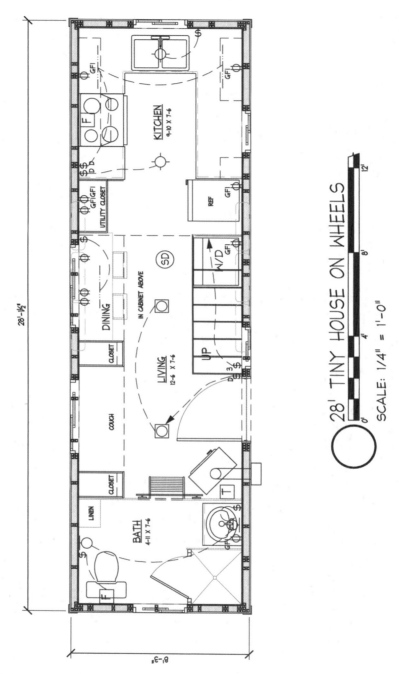

This 28-foot version of the hOMe tiny house contains two lofts, a set of stairs to the main loft, a full-size kitchen, and a comfortable bathroom.

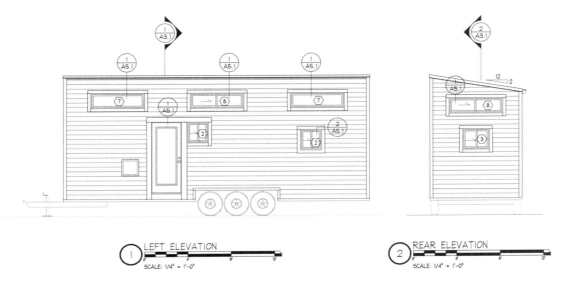

This elevation shows our 28-foot hOMe.

One of the lofts could be eliminated and then the kitchen could be moved to the center of the home. A raised floor could be added in the living area on the opposite end of the bathroom. A sliding bed frame can be hidden under a raised floor during the day and pulled out at night. Because beds are typically only used during sleeping hours, it's very efficient to create a bedroom scenario that doesn't take up any space during waking hours.

THOF

This tiny house designed by Chris Keefe of Organic Forms Design, LLC, is only 377 square feet, but it packs a surprising number of features. A full-size bathroom is large enough for a standard bathtub as well as a stacked washer and dryer unit. The sink vanity is quite spacious as well.

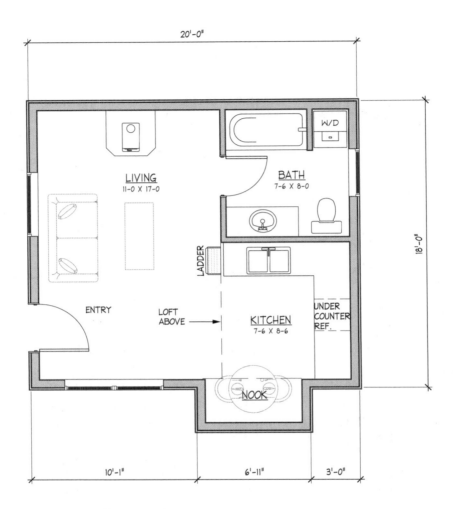

FIRST FLOOR PLAN   377 sq. ft.

SCALE: 1/4" = 1'-0"

This 377-square-foot THOF is large enough for a full-size bathroom, functional kitchen, eating nook, standard furniture, free-standing wood burning stove, and a sleeping loft above the kitchen. Also, the loft can be extended on top of the bathroom.

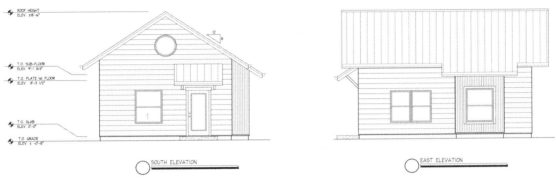

This elevation shows the 377-square-foot tiny house on a fixed foundation.

If desired, the kitchen is large enough for standard appliances as well as full-size upper and lower cabinets. The eating nook comfortably seats three or four people.

The bedroom is in the loft, but you could certainly incorporate it into a studio setup with either a Murphy bed in the living room or a sleeper couch serving as the bed. The living room can be configured in various ways with either a sectional couch or smaller seating units, allowing more open floor space for movement.

You can install a wood-burning stove or open up that floor space by installing a mini-split or wall-mounted heater. As you can see, there are various options for how to set up the living room, and plenty of space exists for adding storage cabinetry.

The space behind the front door is perfectly suited for a coat rack and shoe storage area. The large window between the front door and eating nook could be swapped out with a patio door leading to a deck.

The overall height of this 377-square-foot tiny house is 18'6". Because it's not on wheels, the owner is free to make it as tall as desired. Adding this height translates to a sleeping loft that's much more comfortable for moving around.

Though this cabin is still technically a tiny house, you can see just how much space is available. This space is certainly large enough for two adults to live in full-time and could even work for a family of four. By extending the loft to pass over the bathroom as well as the kitchen, two bedrooms can easily fit upstairs.

To Summarize

Numerous details and components go into a set of architectural plans, so learning how to read them is a huge—if not necessary—asset. A good set of architectural plans should include a title page, foundation plan, floor plan, electrical plan, plumbing plan, elevations, framing plan, sections, and details. When you learn how to read one set of plans, you'll have the skills to interpret a wide range of them.

Building Your Tiny House

All this talk about tiny house lifestyle and design has likely gotten you excited to start your actual build. Constructing shelter with your own hands is part of your DNA, so don't be surprised if you begin to experience a deeper sense of satisfaction as you get farther along in the process.

There's a lot to cover in Part 4, from working with contractors and subcontractors, to knowing what the best tools for a tiny house job are. We also discuss the meat and potatoes of the project such as raising the walls, installing utilities, building envelope considerations, and all the fun finishing touches. We cover options for off-grid power generation in a tiny house and how to supply water to your home if you're not connected to city services.

So grab your tool belt, and let's get to work. There truly is nothing like standing back at the end of a house build and seeing the results of your craftsmanship standing there in front of you.

CHAPTER 15

Identifying Your Team

Building a tiny house can be a fun and exciting project, but it's not for everyone. Perhaps you want to hire a builder to do the whole thing for you, or you want to do some aspects of it yourself while leaving others to subcontractors? If you want to hire someone for any part of your build, you'll need to know how to assemble the best team possible.

In this chapter, we cover the various aspects of working with builders and subcontractors from the hiring process and understanding quality contracts, all the way to scheduling and managing your subcontractors. We also cover strategies for staying sane, happy, and productive on your jobsite, no matter how busy your life may feel during your build.

Working with Contractors

Your builder will be in charge of the day-to-day construction and management of your tiny house, but you'll still play an important role in the dream home's creation. Be sure to choose a builder who appreciates the significance of what this tiny house means to you and who's enthusiastic about your project.

We know of a few cases where tiny house clients were left with unfinished homes, an absent builder, and a lawsuit to deal with. To minimize risk, it's important to have an overall understanding of the big picture so that you can ensure tasks are completed in a timely, legitimate, and cost-effective manner. Let's go over ways for you to get the best builder at a fair cost.

Ask for Referrals

Referrals are your best resource when it comes to finding the right builder for your tiny house project. Ask for a list of clients for whom they have completed projects and call each of them. Keep in mind that the builder specifically wants you to talk with the people they've had positive experiences with, so don't be shy to ask them for a couple other names that weren't on the original list. Call those clients as well and ask for an assessment.

To be fair, bad clients are as frequent, if not more so, than bad builders, so take any referral with a grain of salt. Rather, look at the overall trends in the feedback. If three out of four clients have positive reviews, you're probably looking at a good builder. If it's a 50-50 split though, you might want to either find out more about the builder or move on to another contractor.

Ideally, the builder will have a current job you can swing by to check on the quality of work being done. Look for site cleanliness and organization. If the jobsite is chaotic and disorganized, there's a good chance that the builder doesn't pay a lot of attention to details or organization. See if you can speak with the current client and ask how things are going. If the builder has a crew, ask to meet them as well.

Get Multiple Bids

If possible, obtain at least three bids on your project—although this can be challenging considering there aren't nearly as many tiny house–specific builders as conventional ones. This will give you a sense of what you can expect to pay for your tiny house and also give you the opportunity to weed out over- and underpriced bids.

Typically, you want to choose bids that fall in the middle of the two extremes. Bids that seem too good to be true usually are. In those cases, you often risk ending up in one of two scenarios:

- The builder uses the low bid as a tactic to secure the job. When it gets started, they hit you with multiple change orders—an amendment to a contract to add, remove, or alter the scope of work—to significantly increase their original bid.

- The builder is subpar and doesn't understand the full scope of the project. In the end, they can't complete the build on budget, on time, or to the quality you were expecting.

In either case, you'll find yourself in a tight spot because you'll have signed a contract that obligates you to meet the specifications of the agreement. If the builder doesn't blatantly break their end of the deal, you may find yourself trapped in an unpleasant situation.

Solid Contracts Are a Must

A quality contract is vital to the success of any business partnership. The more detailed and clearly it's written, the better things will turn out for all involved. A contract is most successful when it protects everyone, not just one side of the equation. Nobody wants to feel like they're at risk.

There are several different contracts commonly used in the construction industry. Builders typically create them, so you may not be afforded a lot of input on the details. Regardless, it's vital not only that you understand what you're signing, but also that you're comfortable with all the details. Construction contracts are upheld in a court of law, so take this part of your research seriously.

There are five common types of contracts a contractor may present:

- Lump sum contract
- Time and materials contract
- Incentive contract
- Cost-plus contract
- Guaranteed maximum price contract

Let's take a look at each.

In a lump sum contract, also known as a fixed-price contract, the client and builder agree to a fixed price for the work to be completed. An accurate set of construction plans is required for these contracts. Without them, a builder can't accurately estimate the job.

In a time and materials (T&M) contract, the contract enables the builder to charge an hourly rate for their labor plus the cost of materials. Any subcontractor charges billed through the general contractor are forwarded on to you as well. Builders typically increase material and subcontractor costs by 15 percent to cover their own overhead and profit margins.

T&M contracts are typically used when the job's scope isn't clear enough for an accurate lump-sum estimate. Such contracts can be risky for clients because they're open-ended and the builder doesn't have an incentive to work quickly.

In an incentive contract, built-in provisions in the contract reward the builder with bonuses when they hit certain targets (quality, deadlines, and the like). This contract is a great option on builds with tight deadlines or other specific needs.

In a cost-plus contract, the client pays the builder for all construction costs plus an additional fee to cover the builder's profit and overhead. If costs get out of control, there's no cap to push up against, making it a high-risk contract for clients, especially if all the details aren't clear from the onset.

In a guaranteed maximum price (GMP) contract, contract caps are set in place to protects clients. It's a good contract for builders as well if they add enough cost to protect themselves from overruns. GMP contracts can be used as stand-alone contracts describing the scope of the work as well as a not-to-be-exceeded price. They can also be an added feature to other contracts. For example, a T&M contract can have a GMP clause added to protect the client.

The following eight elements of a quality construction contract are required and are essential to the success of your project. It doesn't matter which contract your builder ends up using. With any of these elements missing, your contract will have gaps that leave one party unprotected. Other elements may be added to the contract as long as they don't detract from the power of these eight:

• Full name, address, and contact information of both parties to the contract plus their respective signatures

• Financial terms, including cost and payment schedule

- Detailed scope of work to be performed
- Schedule of the work and the project's completion date
- Builder's license, insurance, warranty, and bond information
- A clear description of the change order process
- The tradesmen's right to lien details
- Details about the subcontractor payments and responsibilities

Beyond just the builder's basic contact information, you'll want to secure multiple phone numbers, email addresses, website contacts, social media pages, and more. This information not only helps in overall communication but also provides potential safeguards should the builder disappear mid-job.

The contract's financial terms are crucial and must be clearly laid out. You'll want to specify the type of contract used, the overall contract cost, and the payment schedule. It's vital to know when payments are due. For example, if these terms aren't in writing and your builder requests a 50 percent down payment before getting started, you'll have to come up with the funds even if you haven't made accommodations to access that much money so far in advance. A moderate down payment of 10 to 20 percent is customary, but the majority of payments are actually paid as distributions once the work is completed, not as large lump sums ahead of time.

Listing out what are called line-item costs is a great way to define a payment schedule. In this scenario, when the builder completes a task such as framing, rough plumbing, and so on, they get paid the amount specified on that line of the contract. If your builder doesn't offer this approach initially, encourage them to do so.

Be sure to include a provision to hold back 10 percent of the contract price until the final walk through and delivery. This protects you from the builder walking away from your house when it's nearly done. A punch list, which is a checklist of items to be finalized before the contract can be considered complete, is a helpful tool to ensure that all the work has been finished. After the walk through is concluded and all punch-list items have been completed, you can release the final 10 percent payment to the builder.

We've already mentioned the importance of detailed construction drawings. A detailed description of the specific scope of the work is equally important in a contract. By clearly defining all tasks to be completed, there can be no gray area and thus a lot less potential for unexpected change orders from the builder.

To be clear, there are almost always details that will be missed in contracts, so all you can do is your best to anticipate what may come up. Having the vast majority of the details covered in your contract will make any moments of potential negotiation less painful.

Be sure to include a schedule of work and a completion date in your contract. Some clients choose to include incentives, such as bonuses for projects completed ahead of schedule. In other cases, the incentive is actually more of a punishment in disguise; the most common being a cost-per-day fee charged to the builder for each day they are late in completion and delivery of your home. This penalty helps to offset any unexpected costs for you associated with the incomplete project such as hotels and food expenses. For the builder, the incentive is avoiding these costs entirely.

Be sure your builder is licensed, bonded, and insured. Without those safeguards, you could be left out in the cold if something goes wrong. Check the builder's license and standing with the state board of contractors *before* you sign any agreement. Include the contractor's license number in the contract to show you've done your due diligence.

Changes happen. Even the most well-planned construction project can see unexpected events. Sometimes the client creates the alterations, other times the builder does, and sometimes it's external forces such as weather. As such, it's important to understand what will happen when changes occur.

Change orders are the industry standard for tracking alterations in a construction project. They typically include a new scope of work description, the cost for said work, and the impact on the schedule. Both parties are required to sign any change orders before work can resume.

If you've prepared your build plan well and have a quality builder, you won't need too many change orders. That said, if you continually suggest alterations during construction, change orders are going to come at a fast and furious pace. Stay the course with your plan the best you can to maintain your budget and time line.

The last two elements are somewhat intertwined. It's vital you understand the role of subcontractors on your tiny house build. Because the general contractor or builder hires the subcontractors for the job, he or she is responsible for paying them. The subcontractors have an option that protects them from not being paid, which is the right to place a lien against your property. A lien is the right to keep possession of a property owned by another until any debt owed is paid off. It may seem unfair that a subcontractor can encumber your house and land if the builder doesn't pay them, but that's how things work. You can see the importance of ensuring that the builder does indeed pay all of their subs.

The Importance of Communication

No matter the size of your house, there's a lot on the line during the construction process. The success of your build is dictated in large part by how well you and your builder communicate through any changes and unexpected events. Small things can blow out of proportion in short order if your communication isn't good. Before you sign any contracts with your builder, check in with your intuition. If you have a hunch that you shouldn't trust them, or that you won't be able to let them know when something needs to be dealt with, listen to that inner voice and don't sign any documents to work with them.

If you want to be present on the jobsite daily, schedule your visits for the end of each day while the builder is gathering up their tools. It gives you a chance to review the day's work and have a conversation with the builder while not interrupting them. You want them focused on your house, not on answering your questions throughout the day.

Mind If I Help?

If you want to work alongside the builder on the construction of your tiny house, you'll need to establish a clear outline of what that looks like in advance. Believe it or not, you might end up raising the cost of the build if you don't have a lot of experience. If you're a skilled builder and want to help out, though, you may be able to save some money on the contract if your builder is willing to work alongside you.

Working with Subcontractors

If you plan on being the general contractor (GC) on your build and only intend on hiring subcontractors for specific tasks, you'll need to understand the role of a GC. General contractors are in charge of scheduling, payments, management, and much more. In short, they're responsible for the success (or failure) of a build.

General Contractors vs. Subcontractors

A major difference distinguishes general contractors from subcontractors: responsibility. GCs are in charge of all aspects of a build from start to finish. If something goes wrong, the buck stops with them. Subs, on the other hand, specialize in one job aspect and are only responsible for their portion of the work. For example, a plumber is not responsible for the electrical work completed by an electrician. A GC, on the other hand, is responsible for not only their own work, but also that of the electrician and plumber and all other subcontractors used on the job.

It's important to recognize that as the GC, you're the responsible party. You may save financially by doing it yourself, but if you don't run a tight ship, you may end up actually losing money and sleep throughout the process. Being a GC works well only when the future homeowner is organized, pays attention to detail, and is able to schedule and manage others.

Knowing Which Subcontractors to Hire and When

The first challenge in hiring a subcontractor is knowing when to bring them onto the jobsite. Ensuring you have the right amount of overlap from one subcontractor to the next is important to the overall job flow. Let's consider who you might want to hire and how scheduling that subcontractor should play out.

Many tiny house DIY builders hire out the plumbing, HVAC, and electrical, so we'll assume you'll do the same. Who should you schedule first? The answer is typically the HVAC company. As a rule of thumb, the trades installing the largest and hardest-to-adjust components get first crack at a house. Generally, the plumber is brought in next, followed by the electrician.

This can all change completely, though, if for example the HVAC team wants power wired to the house before they get there to ensure their installations are working properly. In that case, you'll need to adjust the order of operations. You must be clear on your subcontractors' needs and expectations well before you have them come onsite. We suggest a half-day overlap between subcontractors if possible so they can communicate any pertinent details from one tradesperson to the next.

Managing Your Subcontractors

Your biggest job as a GC pertaining to your subcontractors is ensuring they're on task, on time, and on budget. You'll also have other jobs on your project, but this must be your main focus.

Be sure to have a solid contract with each of your subcontractors, just as you would if you hired a GC. You need to confirm that they're licensed, insured, bonded, and carry workers' compensation insurance for any employees. You don't want to be left responsible should something go wrong. Remember that as the GC, ultimate responsibility falls back on you. If you have builders' insurance, your insurance carrier may require your subcontractors to list you as an additional insured person on their policy.

Additional insured is a person (you in this case) that benefits from being insured under an insurance policy underwritten for someone else (the subcontractor). An additional insured policy typically applies to liability coverage and is often applied by means of an endorsement added to an original policy. When you are an additional insured, you'll either be identified in the policy by your name or by a general description under a blanket additional insured endorsement.

The best way to keep your subcontractors happy is by paying them on time. As soon as you receive a bill for work completed send their payment. That is assuming, of course, that you've reviewed the work and accept it as complete.

Scheduling and Managing a Build's Time Line

With signed contracts in place, you can start scheduling your jobs. In order to limit the risk of missed appointments with subcontractors, stay in close contact with them. Put in a reminder call at the beginning of the week and follow up with a reminder the day before they're scheduled to show up.

It's not uncommon for subcontractors to miss a scheduled appointment. After all, they juggle lots of jobs, and if a problem shows up on another project, it may impact their ability to make it to yours on time. A subcontractor missing a scheduled day of work on your project can throw off your entire critical path. They'll be more likely to make it up to you as soon as they can if they are reminded that you're on a time line. Placing those phone calls is one way you can communicate the importance of time lines to your build.

Time Management

As a general contractor, you're responsible for all aspects of the job including subcontractors, suppliers, and insurance. This responsibility includes creating and maintaining the schedule, too. All this while still maintaining healthy relationships with your family and friends. This might be new for you, so know that things might be hectic for a while until you get used to your new role.

You might sometimes feel like you're herding cats as you try to keep everything flowing smoothly. The good news is that there are some useful strategies that can help you stay sane.

SMART Goals

There are regular goals and then there are SMART goals. Regular goals are frequently unrealistic or unbounded. As such, it can be very hard to achieve them. A SMART goal, on the other hand, is a clear and measurable goal that has the best chance of leading you to success. It is described as follows:

- **S:** simple and specific
- **M:** measurable
- **A:** attainable
- **R:** relevant
- **T:** time-bound

Set your goals smartly by clearly and specifically stating your goal, what your end result should be, how you can attain it, and the time in which you want to achieve it.

Don't Multitask

For years, we've been told that multitasking is the best way to get a lot done. However, research repeatedly shows that multitasking only leads to stress and subpar results. We encourage you to focus on one task at a time, especially once you've started building your house.

As a general contractor, you'll wear many hats. You'll be the builder, the site foreman, the superintendent, the bookkeeper, the office manager, the office assistant, the supply manager, and so on. If you try juggling all those roles at once, you're certain to drop something. If you focus on each task individually, your chances for success increase exponentially.

It's all about managing your time effectively. If you know you have to do several different things, you need to break up your day into bite-size chunks. Create a schedule to bring order to a chaotic day. Focus on one job at a time while being methodical and deliberate with each task and you'll minimize financial and time-consuming mistakes and have time along the way for fun and a little relaxation.

To Summarize

Working with a contractor can either be a pleasant or terrible experience, so it's important to know how to find the right fit for you and your project. You can feel secure that you're paying the right price for your contractor by getting multiple bids and contacting the contractor's previous clients for recommendations. Contracts don't have to be scary when you know what to look for. Being a general contractor can be a great experience when you know how to perform the job well and in a timely manner, but it is not a suitable option for inexperienced builders.

CHAPTER 16

Tools, Glorious Tools

Tiny houses are small, but they require many of the same tools found on conventional jobsites, which can add significant cost to a tight budget. If you need to build your tool arsenal, knowing which ones are necessary and which ones you can live without will save you a lot of money on your tiny house build.

In this chapter, we cover important strategies for staying safe on the jobsite, what tools you'll need to have on hand to get the job done, and the most cost-effective ways of obtaining them. With creativity, you can gather up nearly every tool you'll need for a very low financial investment.

Safety on the Tiny House Jobsite

Staying safe on the jobsite is of paramount priority. After all, nothing slows down a construction site more than a visit to the emergency room, especially when you're the only builder! If you don't have experience with the tools you'll be using on your construction site, take time *before* you start building to learn how to use them properly.

There can be a false sense of security when working on a tiny house, so it's important to keep the risks in mind and to be careful when building. Just because the scale of the structure is small doesn't mean your risks are. It's still a construction site, and you can still get hurt (or worse) if you're not prioritizing caution throughout the build.

The Occupational Safety and Health Administration (OSHA) reports that falls are the most common cause of death and injury on a jobsite, and 27 percent of those incidents occur on ladders just 10 feet tall or shorter. Because a THOW is typically 13'6" in height, you'll be spending quite a bit of time on ladders, so please be careful.

The tools you'll be using can be dangerous as well. We highly recommend you learn how to use them properly before you start your build. A great way to do this is by hiring a professional builder for a few hours on a weekend and asking them to give you a safety course. Another option is to contact a local trade school to see if you can hire one of the construction-tech teachers. They are typically pros at imparting safety guidelines to beginner builders.

Be sure to wear safety glasses, hearing protection, gloves, appropriate clothing, a respirator or dust mask (depending on the task), and any other pertinent protective gear. Protecting yourself is the first step in staying safe.

What Tools Do I Need?

A tiny house build is unique in that the owner typically doesn't have enough space in their new house for storing tools after the build is done, so knowing which ones to purchase versus renting or borrowing is particularly important. Let's go over each option so you'll know how best to invest your money.

Basic Hand Tools Required

Let's start with the most important one of all: your tool belt. Get one that's comfortable with an abundance of pockets to fit hand tools, nails, and other construction must-haves. We recommend suspenders for comfort and less wear and tear on your hips—these things can get heavy fast.

Levels and measuring devices ensure a square, level, and plumb build. A high-quality measuring tape is as necessary as a set of levels. We recommend a torpedo level in addition to a 2-foot and a 6-foot level.

Another jobsite requirement is a speed square. Nothing is handier during roof framing layout. It serves several other functions as well, is inexpensive, and fits snugly in a tool belt.

If you intend on doing most of your build alone, a plethora of clamps is a necessity. They serve as an extra set of hands on tasks that require at least two people. We recommend at least two 8-inch C-clamps, a few spring clamps, and a set of trigger clamps.

Even the best builders make mistakes on the jobsite and need to remove nails from time to time. A cat's paw nail puller is a simple but mighty tool for this task, so we recommend you keep one in your tool belt.

If you plan on installing your own electrical system, add a high-quality set of wire strippers to your list. Realistically this is the only electrical tool you'll need because there aren't many plugs and switches in a tiny house. If you'll be plumbing your tiny house, you'll need to decide which system you'll use (PEX, copper, and so on) before buying or renting any tools. Each plumbing solution requires very different installation tools.

The following hand tools are considered to be minimum requirements on a tiny house construction site:

- Safety glasses
- Gloves
- Hearing protection
- Dust mask
- Tool belt
- Levels

- Speed square
- Measuring tape
- Clamps
- Hammer
- Utility knife
- Wrench set

- Caulk gun
- Linesman pliers
- Hammer tacker
- Electrical wire strippers

- Needle nose pliers
- Screwdrivers
- Cat's paw

There are other basic hand tools you might decide to pick up as well. For some, less is more, while others prefer having the appropriate tool for each task. Consider your budget as well as your storage capacity for all these tools after your job is done. If you're limited in both of those aspects, you might want to opt for the fewest number of tools possible and get creative if you don't have the exact tool needed for a task.

Recommended Power Tools

There's no doubt that the most versatile power tool on the jobsite is the circular saw. It can be used for almost everything from cutting lumber and sheathing, to metal roofing and pipe, simply by switching out the blades. It can even be used for finish work once you master its use.

Our preference for circular saws are *worm-drive* models. They have inline motors, which make them more powerful than standard box saws. The blade is set conveniently on the left side of the saw, which means that a right-handed cutter can keep their eye on the blade itself during the cut. Left-handed carpenters might find it easier to use standard circular saws so they can follow the blade directly.

A reciprocating saw makes fast and easy work of cutting through nails, wood, metal, and just about any material out there. This tool is invaluable on a jobsite when a mistake, such as framing a window incorrectly, must be fixed. You might think this is a demolition tool and, as such, not needed on a new construction jobsite. However, mistakes happen, and having the ability to easily deconstruct things is valuable even on new projects.

Jigsaws and routers are typically not necessities on the tiny house jobsite, but they do save a lot of time and effort in certain situations. For example, a plunge router with a specialty bit makes cutting window openings through sheathing as easy as can be. However, because you won't use it often, you might be better off renting a plunge router if necessary. We also recommend a Dremel tool on the jobsite.

Let's get to the big stuff now: table saws, miter saws, and nail guns. These puppies are essential to a high-quality project. They not only speed up the process, but also make it more accurate. They aren't cheap, but they're worth the investment on any tiny house jobsite.

Table saws enable you to accurately perform rip cuts—cuts parallel to the long direction—on materials such as sheathing, lumber, siding, and finish trim. A standard tabletop can accommodate materials of various sizes, from very small to 4-feet-wide, heavy-duty plywood. Miter saws, on the other hand, are the best option for precise cross cuts—cuts perpendicular to the long direction—in lumber, trim, and other materials. In terms of capacity, a 12-inch sliding compound miter saw can cut dimensional lumber up to a 2×16-inch piece at 90 degrees.

There are various types of nail guns out there, so select one that can be used for at least a couple different purposes on your tiny house build. A good option is a framing nailer with nail size adjustments. These enable you to easily change nail size as you switch tasks—something that you will do often during the build.

Lastly, you'll want to invest in a quality power drill and driver set. Drills are designed for creating holes, but drivers are made specifically for inserting screws and bolts into construction material. Some drills are hammer actuated and have much more power than drills. We recommend a standard drill bit set to go along with your drill with everything from $\frac{1}{16}$- to $\frac{1}{2}$-inch bits, a spade bit set, and larger hole saws for creating openings for vent lines and so on. In addition, we recommend a driver set that contains drill bits of various shapes and sizes as well as common-size ratchet drivers.

Lowering Your Tool Costs

There's nothing that sobers a giddy builder browsing through the tool aisles more than price tags. Tools are expensive, and if you're not careful, you can blow a significant part of your budget before you even start building. Some tools are worth buying, but others are not.

Now that you know what tools are essential on your jobsite, you'll need to decide which ones to buy new, which ones to rent or borrow, and which ones to buy used. If you plan on keeping your tools long after your tiny house is complete, buy the best quality you can afford whether new or used. You truly do get what you pay for. For tools that will only be used once or twice (e.g., a plunge router), look into renting. Just be sure you consider how many days you'll need it. Some rental yards are so expensive that after just four days of rental, you might as well have bought the tool new.

Trade schools, community colleges, and high schools sometimes have tool rental options for community members. It's worth mentioning here that many schools around the nation are now using tiny houses to teach their students hands-on construction techniques. Consider approaching your local educators and seeing if they're interested in building yours or working together on the build.

Another great option is a tool-sharing co-op. These tend to exist only in larger communities, so if you don't have one near you, consider starting one yourself. In reality, not every single household needs all these tools, so it makes so much more sense for a community to own them collectively. Because the costs are shared among all members and the tools are available for use to all members as well, the co-ops have been quite successful where adopted.

Borrowing or bartering tools are potential options as well. These situations always end best when there is a win for both parties involved. Consider exchanging either a tangible good or your time for the use of a tool. Perhaps your neighbors who happen to have a well-stocked tool shop/garage could use some help with yard cleanup or would appreciate you taking care of their plants when they go out of town. Come up with an agreement ahead of time that addresses how to proceed if one of the tools breaks or you need to use it longer than anticipated. With good, clear communication, these are great options that can save you hundreds of dollars.

Depending on how you approach the acquisition of tools, you could spend thousands of dollars or just a few hundred. If you plan on purchasing everything and combining some new tools with lightly used ones, your price tag will likely land somewhere in the $1,500 to $2,000 range.

To Summarize

The best way to stay safe on your jobsite is by learning proper tool etiquette from an expert and being exceptionally careful on ladders. Not a lot of hand tools are required for a tiny house build, but knowing which ones you need (and which ones you don't) will save you a lot of money. Tiny housers need to consider what they'll do with their tools after the build is complete. Most tiny houses won't have adequate storage to keep all the tools long term. By being resourceful and reaching out to your community, you can access all the tools you need for your tiny house build at a very low cost.

CHAPTER 17

Raising the Walls

If you've never built anything significant before, don't fret. After personally teaching more than 4,500 participants at our construction workshops since 2006, one thing has become crystal clear. You *can* build your own house. We've seen it done time and time again by novice builders, so we have complete faith that you can be successful with your build, too.

Most people living in their self-built tiny houses have no previous construction experience either. What they did have was determination, passion, and a desire to learn a new skill. We can tell this describes you, too, because, after all, you're investing your time and effort right now by reading this book and learning as much as you can.

In this chapter, we cover tiny house floor frame systems and important framing terms, compare wood framing to other options, and learn how to fasten our tiny house to the ground, to the trailer, and to the roof.

Flooring Systems

You have two options when it comes to floors in a THOW:

- Use a trailer frame as the base for your floor sheathing.
- Add a secondary floor system over the trailer frame.

There are advantages and disadvantages to each approach.

By adding your sheathing directly to the trailer frame, you'll maintain maximum ceiling height in your structure because you won't have additional floor framing competing for interior space. The downside is that you'll increase the potential for thermal bridging through the trailer frame into your conditioned interior. Thermal bridging refers to the process in which heat moves to areas that are colder. This is also known as heat loss. When materials such as metal are used in construction, they provide a path for that heat loss. When directly connected to the interior of a structure, these materials create a bridge for that heat loss.

You can minimize thermal bridging by adding a framed floor system on top of your trailer frame. By creating space for additional insulation, your trailer will be much more isolated from your interior space. Your interior head height will decrease, but you'll enjoy the benefits of warmer toes in the winter and be able to install utilities within the subfloor rather than through the ceiling.

You'll want to create this floor frame with smaller lumber, such as 2×4s, to minimize the loss of ceiling height. Be sure to install the framing material either directly above the trailer frame members or perpendicular to them.

If you want to eliminate thermal bridging completely, consider using structurally insulated panels (SIPs) as your floor frame. SIPs, which are custom factory-built structural systems with embedded high-insulation foam, are very strong and provide a complete thermal break. They come in different options, and the thicker you go, the better your insulation potential. SIPs can be built to fit nearly any design, typically cost the same as wood-framed construction when labor is factored in, and allow for smaller heating and cooling systems in a structure. (More on SIPs later in this chapter.)

Wall Systems

Various wall system options exist when it comes to tiny houses, ranging from conventional wood framing, steel, SIPs, and more. Some of them cost less but take longer to yield results. Others cost more but reduce framing time by 90 percent. Factors such as your budget and time availability will greatly affect which option you choose.

Framing Defined

It's important to familiarize yourself with framing terms. Not only will they help you understand the material we're about to cover, but they'll make it easier for you to discuss specific needs at the lumberyard or with building professionals. Bear in mind that terms may vary slightly by geographic location. Let's go over each one and define it.

Wall Framing Terms

Let's review some basic wall framing terms:

Wall stud is a vertical framing member—typically a 2×4 or a 2×6—and a key element in construction.

Cripple stud is a vertical framing member installed above and/or below doors, windows, and headers. Cripple studs never touch both the bottom plate and top plate at the same time.

King stud is a vertical framing member placed on either side of a door or window, running from bottom plate to top plate.

Trimmer stud is a vertical framing member placed on the inside (toward a window or door opening) of a king stud, running from the bottom plate to the top of the window or door header.

Header is a horizontal framing member placed above a door, window, or other opening.

Corner stud assembly is a vertical framing member placed at corner locations, typically built of three studs.

Rough sill is a horizontal framing member placed below a rough window opening. It attaches to the cripple studs below as well as the trimmer and king studs on the side.

Top (upper wall) plate is a horizontal framing member fastened to the top of the wall studs. A secondary (double top plate) is always connected to the top plate, overlapping at the corners, to increase the overall strength of the wall assembly.

Bottom (sole, lower wall, base) plate is a horizontal framing member placed atop the floor sheathing and to which studs are connected.

Rough opening (R.O.) is the space left open in a framed wall assembly to accommodate the future placement of a door or window. Check with manufacturer specifications for door and window R.O. callouts before framing the wall.

Learning these wall framing terms will make your construction process a lot smoother.

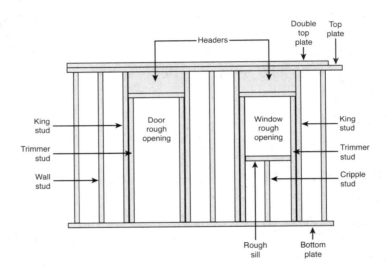

Roof Framing Terms

Following are some basic roof framing terms:

Loft joist is a horizontal framing member installed to support the loads above it.

Ceiling joist is a horizontal framing member connected to the double top plate or to a ledger that creates a ceiling overhead. If the construction also results in a floor above, these joists may be referred to as floor joists rather than ceiling joists.

Rafter is a framing membrane that supports the roof sheathing. Rafters attach to the ridge (when present) and to the double top plate.

Ridge beam is a horizontal framing member—typically a 4× beam or greater—that supports the end of rafters at the ridge. The beam is supported by posts, which transfer the roof loads to the foundation. Note that a shed roof (roof without a gable peak) doesn't have a ridge beam.

Ridge board is a horizontal framing member—typically a 2× board—that's supported by the end of rafters at the ridge. The beam isn't supported by posts, but rather the rafters themselves. Because it's supported by the rafters, collar ties are necessary. Note that a shed roof (roof without a gable peak) doesn't have a ridge board.

Collar tie is a horizontal framing member connecting two rafters on a gable roof. Collar ties are vital for roof safety and prevent rafters from collapsing when stressed by excessive loads such as snow or road rattle.

Learning these roof framing terms will give you a leg up when ordering materials and talking about construction with professionals.

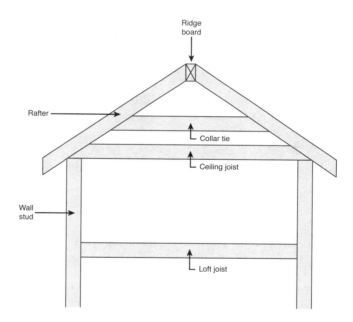

Wood Framing

Wood is the most commonly used material in residential construction. It's forgiving, easy to work with, and any mistakes can be fixed with relative ease. Although power tools make the job easier, they're not required because you can accomplish a lot with just a saw, a hammer, and some nails.

Another advantage to wood framing is that the materials (framing, sheathing, and fasteners) are readily available in pretty much every location across the country. Whether you shop at a local lumberyard or a big box store, you'll likely find everything you need with ease.

The most common layouts for wall stud spacing are 16 inches o.c. and 24 inches o.c. This means that when measured from the center of one stud to the center of the other, the space is either 16 or 24 inches wide. Tighter spacing makes for stronger walls. However, wider spacing is acceptable and provides for better insulation values and less weight.

Residential construction in the United States calls for 2×6 walls to meet insulation code in most cases. For tiny houses, the most common framing size is 2×4 walls because of the space savings. You'll have to decide if you want extra insulation value or extra floor space when considering which framing members to use.

Be sure to lay out your walls correctly so that your sheathing lands on the centerline of your framing members. A 16- or 24-inch o.c. frame requires you to adjust your first stud location back by ¾ inch (half the framing member's thickness) for the rest to be on-center. Measure your first framing member location to 15¼ or 23¼ inches and then strike a new measurement from that point every 16 or 24 inches.

Screws vs. Nails

Although many people believe that screws are the better fastener for a THOW, construction physics prove otherwise. The fact is that screws don't have any shear strength, which is vitally important in a mobile tiny house. Let's say you placed a nail in the wrong spot while attaching two pieces of wood. To remove the nail, you'll have to pry it back and forth and work it out with some effort. This ability for nails to bend and flex is an integral part of their shear strength.

On the other hand, if you strip a screw while driving it into a wall, you simply need to give the head a whack with your hammer for it to easily snap off the body. This is an illustration of the lack of shear strength in screws. Whereas a nail can flex significantly, a screw simply can't tolerate that same force.

All that said, there are two situations when it's appropriate to use screws for framing and sheathing:

- When you are using structural screws. These are specialized screws rated for structural use. They are *not* deck, drywall, or any other standard screw. You'll know you're getting the right ones when you just about keel over as you look at the price.

- When you can use screws in tandem with nails. Sometimes it's handy to use a few screws to hold up sheathing before you come around and nail it all off.

It's important to use wood glue wherever you can join two surfaces to create the strongest connection possible between framing and sheathing. Wood glue is considered cheap insurance and something you should add anytime you make a wood-to-wood connection. By using the right fasteners, your THOW will be able to withstand all the stresses it will endure while being towed mile after mile.

There are various types of nails on the market, and they vary in material, size, head shapes, and tip shapes, as well as shank texture (smooth or ringed). There's some method behind choosing the right-size nail for the task at hand, but the best approach is to check your local building codes to see which nails are used where. This is important because using a 16d nail to toe-nail (or angle nail) a stud to a plate can actually blow out the stud and make the connection fail. (That location requires an 8d nail.)

A very basic approach is to use 8d nails when toe nailing and attaching sheathing to the frame, 16d nails for all framing connections other than toe nailing, and teco nails for all hangers and straps. You can use 10d nails for some specific applications, such as hangers and straps. However, it's best to know exactly what nails are required where, especially when working with structural metal hangers and straps.

Nail sizes are typically called out by units of *d*. This harkens back to many moons ago in England when nails were named for how much it cost for 100 of each size. That means if 100 nails cost six pence, they were referred to as *6-penny nails*. Today, the letter *d* refers to "penny." Why? Because the *d* stands for the Latin name *denarius*, which was the Roman equivalent of a penny. Pretty neat, huh?

The most common framing nail sizes are as follows:

- **8d:** 2½ inches

- **10d:** 3 inches

- **16d:** 3½ inches

- **Teco:** 10d × 1½ inches (for hangers and straps)

Steel Framing

Although steel framing isn't as common as wood in residential construction, it's a good option for a THOW. Let's go over the advantages of this material. Light-gauge steel framing is considerably lighter than wood. Some claim that 60 percent of the total frame weight can be saved on a tiny house by substituting steel for wood.

Steel studs are structurally very strong. In fact, they're often considered to be stronger than wood. This means you can use less material to create the same strength rating. Steel studs aren't solid like wood. Rather, they're shaped like the letter C (thus the name C-channel) in a cross-section. This specific shape creates excellent strength while minimizing materials and weight. The hollow core provides an additional benefit by allowing insulation to be placed *inside* the studs, limiting thermal bridging.

One thing to be aware of is that steel studs are at risk for condensation issues. To mitigate this, it's customary to wrap the exterior with rigid insulation. Unfortunately, this will reduce some of your interior square footage. If you use 2-inch rigid foam, your overall room width will be reduced by 4 inches.

Steel studs connect with structural screws, not nails. This process intimidates some novice builders. It's not as forgiving as wood framing either. Cutting the studs leaves the edges of the material sharp and is either loud and full of sparks (if you use a saw) or slow and uncomfortable (if you use straight aviation cutters). You'll have to decide whether the added strength and reduced weight of the material are worth the effort.

In fact, most people who choose to build with steel frames don't do the work themselves but rather hire it out to professionals. It's much easier to work with a custom steel frame through a shop or construction company that specializes in that type of work than it is to do it yourself.

Structural Insulated Panels (SIPs)

Many tiny housers are turning to SIPs for their wall and roofing systems. As mentioned previously, SIPs are a sandwich system in which a foam insulation core is laminated between two skins of oriented strand board (OSB). SIPs are structural so they require no other wall or roof framing systems to support them. Because they include a foam core, they provide the insulation envelope for your walls at the same time.

Although they might appear like a complex building option, SIPs are actually quite easy to work with. SIPs manufacturers can take any set of construction plans, create a custom SIPs package, and deliver it directly to your jobsite. They factory-cut all your window and door openings and provide channels for utility conduits as well.

SIPs show up on the jobsite as large panels. This greatly reduces the time it takes to frame and roof a tiny house. With several helpers onsite, you can realistically erect an entire tiny house frame (including the roof) in a day or two. Remember that this includes your insulation envelope as well, reducing your construction time even more. Insulating a tiny house can actually take a significant amount of time to do well.

Making last-minute onsite changes to a SIPs house isn't easy, but it's not impossible either. That said, it's best to invest adequate time getting the design just right and working closely with the factory to eliminate the need for changes in the field.

Some of the foams used in the SIPs industry are considered unhealthy by some. One side argues that the foam is inert; others suggest that it emits unhealthy fumes. We highly recommend you research the foam your SIPs factory uses and ensure that it meets your needs and addresses your concerns. Two options becoming increasingly popular are polyurethane foam and graphite-based foams. Both claim to be inert and not to emit any toxic fumes. Ask your SIPs manufacturer if they offer either as an option.

There are currently a couple companies specializing in SIPs for tiny houses, but any reputable SIPs manufacturer can handle the job. They typically need a little lead time to have an order delivered to the jobsite. Sometimes you can have your design delivered within the month. However, it could take longer depending on how busy the factory is, so plan accordingly.

Although SIPs might appear to cost more than wood framing at first glance, it's important to remember that the insulation is also factored into the cost. Therefore, the price difference is not huge. In terms of weight, they weigh about the same as a stud-framed wall.

Tiny House Shells

Several tiny house companies are now offering dried-in shells for THOWs. The term *dried-in* refers to the stage in construction when the structure is protected from the elements and the following are completed: rough framing, exterior wall sheathing, windows set, and roof waterproofing material installed. This is a particularly attractive option for people intimidated by framing and also for those with a tight deadline. Prices are actually pretty reasonable for the most part, especially when considering you'll be spared weeks and potentially months of framing, siding, and roofing.

Typically, shells come with windows set, siding adhered, and the roofing material installed. The tiny house owner is left with tasks such as plumbing and wiring, insulating the interior, installing finish materials and cabinets, as well as fixtures and appliances.

One thing to keep in mind when considering a tiny house shell is that if you aren't 100 percent certain where you want your door and window openings to go, you can simply ask the builder to not install them. Instead, you can cut them out when your shell is onsite, when you have a better sense of where you want them placed.

When the shell is completed, you can either pick it up yourself or have it delivered. Because transit costs can be high, you might want to look for a shell builder that either builds locally or has distributors relatively close to you. Quality matters here, so choose a builder only after you've had a chance to inspect their work.

Anchoring Systems

No matter what framing system you choose, you'll need to ensure you have adequate anchoring to connect the house to the trailer. Without it, a tiny house could literally disconnect from the trailer frame, and that would be a terrible start to a road trip. Next, we'll discuss the three major points of connection to consider.

Ground-to-Trailer Connections

The first type of connection to consider, even if you're building a THOW, is attachment to the ground. By residential building codes, all forms of housing, except for recreational vehicles, are required to anchor to the ground in some capacity. The intent of this provision is to minimize damage and injury caused by high winds, earthquakes, or other natural disasters.

There are several options for connecting a THOW to the ground and which one you choose will be affected by site soil conditions, topography, regional natural disaster potentials, as well as climactic influences. Your local building department can help you identify the best option for you. You can also speak to local contractors and engineers.

The most secure way of attaching a tiny house to the ground is by connecting it to a perimeter concrete foundation. This requires the removal of the wheels and potentially the axles as well. Though tedious, removal of the tiny house from the foundation is possible if relocation is necessary. However, this isn't the best option if you plan on moving your house with any regularity. In fact, if you plan on moving it more than once or twice, this may be a burden not worth implementing.

Another option is to pour a concrete slab with engineered anchors embedded into the foundation and to then attach the tiny house to those tie-down locations. It's important to also use strategically placed jack supports under the trailer frame that can take the weight off of the wheels while parked. This is a relatively simple solution compared to other options because the axles and wheels can remain on the THOW.

It's important to provide support for your loads (dead and live), as well as resistance against uplift and tip over. This is why both anchors and jacks must be employed together. In terms of what foundation system to use, several options are available other than those listed here.

If you plan to move your house often, a permanent foundation system is not a great option for you. Instead, consider using something that can quickly and easily be put into place and removed. A common approach is to place the trailer on jack stands while parked. You can also ask your trailer manufacturer to weld hooks onto your trailer that can be anchored to ground anchors in your location. There are screw-in ground anchors available on the market that can be perfect for temporary anchoring.

Trailer-to-Wall Frame Connections

The next level of support is the connection of the house to the trailer. When done correctly, the house can't disconnect from the trailer, no matter how many potholes the driver manages to drag it through. There are several ways to accomplish this task.

A common anchoring system in the park model industry is the use of metal strapping. Each piece is installed behind the siding and in front of the framing and house wrap. The straps run from one side of the trailer frame, up and over the roof, and all the way down to the other side of the trailer frame. Each strap is then welded to the frame and further attached to the stud framing with nails. These straps are typically only installed in two to four locations across the entire house.

If using metal straps is too cumbersome or expensive, you can choose anchor bolts. Where to place them and which ones to use varies with the tiny house, so please consult with an engineer or purchase plans that specify this information.

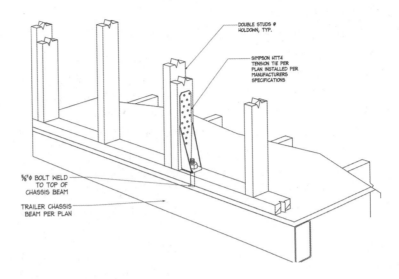

The most common anchoring system for THOWs is anchor bolts. Depending on your trailer manufacturer, they will come installed upon delivery or you can install them onsite.

Most commonly, anchor bolts are welded to the frame in predetermined locations designated by the architectural plans. These bolts extend up from the trailer frame and through the bottom wall plates. They are secured in place with heavy-duty metal brackets (Simpson HTT4). The HTT4s are then tightened down with a locking nut and nailed to the studs in line with the manufacturer's specifications.

This connection attaches the wall frame to the trailer with incredible strength. The HTT4s are used in high-seismic-risk areas around the country and are thus resilient enough for a THOW application.

Some tiny house trailers can be custom built with frames that allow for the installation of anchor bolts *after* the walls are erected. If your trailer doesn't have that feature, you'll need to lift your framed walls up and over the bolts, which are welded in place on the frame.

One important point to mention with any of the anchoring systems is that once your walls are enclosed in finish material, you'll no longer have access to the nuts and bolts. For that reason, you'll need to be 100 percent certain that everything is fully tightened before you close up your walls. Be sure to use locking nuts, thread locking fluids, or any other time-tested fastening system.

Wall Frame-to-Roof Connections

Now that your walls are connected to the trailer, you'll need to ensure your roof doesn't fly off while in transit. The best way to do this is by using hurricane clips. The most common clip we see in residential construction is the Simpson H2.5. It's easy to install (nailed on to framing members with manufacturer's recommended nails), very strong, and relatively simple to hide behind most wall finish materials.

To Summarize

You can minimize thermal bridging in your tiny house by installing a raised floor system atop your metal trailer. Although wood framing is the most common for tiny house construction, other options such as steel and SIPs are being used with increasing frequency. When building a tiny house, you need to securely anchor your wall framing to the trailer and to the roof to ensure it doesn't all come apart while driving down the road. Several anchoring system options are available, ranging from metal straps to hurricane clips to HTT4 anchors. Be sure to select the options that make the most sense for your specific build and lifestyle.

CHAPTER 18

Utilities and Envelope Considerations

Discovering the right HVAC system for your tiny home can be daunting. In this chapter, we will guide you through the tangled web of these systems, as well as others, including plumbing, electrical, sewer lines, venting, roofing, insulation options, siding, and finally, window and door installations. Additionally, we will review the options available to connect your THOW to the internet.

Choosing and Sizing Your HVAC Systems

It's important to properly size your HVAC systems for your tiny house. One that's too small will find you wearing nine layers on a cold winter night, while one that's too large will leave you wanting to wear nothing more than a bathing suit.

To determine the right fit, fill out a web form on an online British thermal units (BTU) calculator. You'll need to collect the following data about your tiny house first:

- Square footage

- Height

- Number of exterior walls

- Number of doors and windows

- Number of occupants

- Insulation R-values

If the form doesn't ask for this level of detail, find another one because detail is the key to your success.

Calculating BTU will show you how much energy it takes to raise the temperature of 1 pound of water by 1 degree Fahrenheit, which is the standard unit of measurement when comparing heating and cooling appliances. When you know how many BTUs are required to condition your space, find the unit that can deliver that amount at the best cost.

The form will tell you how many BTUs are needed to heat and cool your space. Look for units that meet those requirements. If your BTU value falls between two potential models, choose the larger of the two. Assuming your unit can be thermostatically controlled, it can always be set to turn off when the temperature falls out of programmed range.

Grid-Tied Electric HVAC Options

Not all climates require air conditioning to keep inhabitants comfortable. (We don't have air conditioning in hOMe.) Some places, on the other hand, never use heaters, but they would become dangerously hot without air conditioning. If you plan on moving your THOW through various climates, look for a unit that combines both cooling and heating functions. Our recommendation for that scenario is a mini-split system.

Mini-splits are simple, compact, energy-efficient, affordable, and ductless, and provide both heating and cooling and mount seamlessly to a wall. They work in conjunction with a small compressor, which installs to the exterior of a house (usually on the trailer tongue on a THOW).

Mini-splits are reasonably priced and quite energy efficient (compared to other electric units). They look pretty sleek and can be mounted high up on a wall, taking up no floor space. They come with a thermostat and operate reliably, even in extreme climates.

There are also other electric heat sources that work well in a tiny house. One such option is radiant floor mats. They're typically used in bathrooms in conventionally size houses; although because tiny houses are so much smaller, they can work as the primary source of heat here, too. The mats install under the finish flooring, giving off lovely heat to warm the toes while taking up no additional space. Be sure to choose a model that produces enough BTUs to comfortably condition your space. Some are quite small and insufficient for cold winter applications, even in a tiny home.

Some tiny housers choose to simply use portable oil-filled radiant heaters, electric fireplaces, wall panels, plug-in baseboards, and the like. These options install easily and are inexpensive. Similarly, a lot of options exist for electric air conditioning units as well. There are certainly enough grid-tied options to ensure that you will be able to find a system that is the perfect fit for your THOW and the climate it's kept in.

Off-Grid HVAC Options

Those of us living off-grid don't have the option of electric heating systems. Even the most efficient ones draw too much power and require an enormous and expensive solar system. Instead, we look to wood and propane heaters to warm our spaces.

There are now several small wood-burning stoves appropriately sized for a tiny house. It's especially important to choose one that's not too large because you won't have the option of controlling your temperature with a thermostat.

With a wood-burning stove, you'll need to budget space for storing kindling and logs. You'll also need to factor where you'll place your vent stack if you plan on being mobile. Remember that measurements for road restrictions are taken at the widest and tallest parts on a trailer. You might want to install a vent that can be removed with relative ease as needed.

Wood-burning stoves typically produce a significant amount of heat and are very hot to the touch. Therefore, they require quite a lot of clearance and space around them. Search for a unit with minimal clearance requirements and low weight.

In terms of propane heaters, we only recommend direct-vent units in which fumes and vapor are carried outside. Though some claim that nonvented heaters are safe for indoor use, we can tell you from personal experience that they smell bad and create a significant amount of indoor condensation, even when windows are left partially open. They're tempting because the costs are so much lower and the installation is so easy, but we can tell you that after three days of trying a couple different models, we ran to the store to invest in a direct-vent unit. Important options to look for are thermostat control, nonelectric ignition (in case of power failure your unit will still work), and proper BTU sizing.

Many units are quite large and put out way more heat than needed. Fortunately, there are a couple wall-mounted and freestanding models being used successfully in tiny houses today.

We chose the Hampton H27 for hOMe. It mimics the appearance of a wood-burning fireplace and produces enough heat to keep us toasty warm even when it goes down to –10 degrees Fahrenheit (–23°C). It does take up quite a lot of space and wasn't inexpensive, but we like that it comes with a remote thermostat and requires very little safety clearance. We have no complaints about it at all.

Ventilation

It's essential to provide adequate ventilation in your home because moisture and stale air accumulate very quickly in a small space. The most obvious locations for vents are in the kitchen and bathroom. We're often asked if it's important to install them in both, and our answer is always yes.

If you only install a kitchen vent, all the moisture (and odor!) produced in the bathroom will be pulled through the house to the kitchen vent. On the other hand, if you only install a bathroom fan, all the steam, grease, and exhaust produced in the kitchen will be dragged through the house before exiting. Thus, it's best to add both.

Kitchen fans not only mitigate food odors and grease but also exhaust dangerous carbon monoxide if using gas appliances. Tiny houses are more susceptible to the buildup of noxious gases than conventionally sized homes because of the minimal square footage. If you use a gas oven, cooktop, or range, you absolutely must install a vented range hood.

We highly recommend you install a moisture sensor switch connected to your bathroom fan. This simple and inexpensive device automatically turns on and off as moisture levels in your home rise and fall. You decide what ambient internal humidity level you want it set to (varies with the season and external temperature), and the switch does the rest. It can work in conjunction with any fan on the market and simply replace the wall switch that activates the unit.

It is important to note that regular bathroom fans often fail to fully remove moisture because homeowners don't leave them on long enough. Over time, this moisture can penetrate walls and cause mold issues. The use of a moisture sensor switch completely mitigates this issue and can save you thousands of dollars on repairs.

Let's assume you've built a tight home with very few air gaps and leaks. When your kitchen and bathroom fans are on and pulling air from the interior, where will the replacement air come from? Without adding what's called make-up air (the outside air used to replace exhausted air in a structure), your tiny house will be forced to pull air through gaps in the insulation envelope. That's a terrible idea because you're literally forcing moisture laden air into the cracks of your home, and that's exactly what you want to avoid for the long-term health of your home.

Instead, we recommend you install a passive make-up air vent to provide replacement air. Bringing air in through a controlled pathway eliminates the risk of moisture getting trapped inside the wall cavity. Perhaps more importantly, controlled make-up air eliminates the risk of pulling air back through the exhaust vents from places such as your greasy stove vent, the stinky composting toilet vent, or sooty wood-burning stove vent.

You might also want to consider adding an energy recovery ventilator (ERV) or a heat recovery ventilator (HRV) to your tiny house. These provide conditioned, fresh air to your home by means of exchange. Stale interior air is dumped to the outside, while fresh air is brought in through an exchanger. These systems only have a 10 percent temperature loss between the intake and outtake air, saving you energy and money. HRVs and ERVs also help eliminate interior moisture buildup by condensing excess water and draining it to the exterior.

Having a source of fresh air is important, especially if you live in a tightly sealed home. Nobody wants to breathe stale air all day long. Provide yourself with a healthy, fresh alternative by using the techniques we've laid out.

Plumbing and Gas

Although not particularly glamorous, rough utility lines are a vital component of any house because they enable water and gas to travel to the right locations. The effort you put in here will keep you safe, warm, and clean once the house is done. Let's go over various considerations.

Gas Lines

Two types of gases are used most commonly in residential construction: natural and propane. Unless you intend on hooking your tiny to a municipal system, your best option is propane. Plan for the location of each gas appliance in the design process, and install the lines after framing is complete.

There are three main material options when it comes to gas lines:

- Copper
- Black pipe
- Flex line

Let's review each option.

Copper comes in long rolls and can be relatively easy to install. The biggest challenge is the flare fittings at each connecting point. Copper is soft, so be sure it can't rub onto hard surfaces such as your trailer as this may cause it to break over time. Bed the lines in flexible and soft material (or use minimal expansion foam) wherever they penetrate the house.

Black pipe is perhaps the easiest material for a first timer to work with. It's strong and durable and offers fittings of nearly every shape, length, and size you could possibly need. Secure the joints with the appropriate pipe thread tape. There are lots of potential options, so make sure you choose the ones specifically rated for propane. Use two pipe wrenches to tighten the fittings and connections, ensuring there are no leaks.

It's a good idea to protect black pipe from rubbing at the house penetrations in the same way we outlined for copper lines. In fact, we suggest you take this precaution with *any* material you choose. Wherever gas lines terminate at an appliance, install a shut-off valve so you can easily disconnect the appliance for service if needed.

When calculating the lengths of runs in black pipe, you have two main options available: purchase standard-length pieces off the shelf and use couplers to create the length you need, or have custom lengths cut and then rethreaded at the store.

Flex line requires a special permit to purchase and install. You *can* get a permit with some simple training, so you need to decide if it's worth the effort. Flex line is great because it installs easily, is flexible (important when you're towing your THOW), and comes in long lengths. The fewer connections you have in any system, the fewer potential locations for leaks, so the long uninterrupted runs of flex line are very advantageous.

After your pipe is installed, perform a leak test. Close all shut-off valves by each appliance and install a pressure gauge with an air cock on it at the initial tank or point of system-entry location. Fill the system with more air pressure than you intend on having for the gas. In other words, if you plan on running your gas at 40 pounds per square inch (psi), test your system at 50 psi. The best way to discover the pressure of your system is to contact your propane supplier and ask them what their tanks are charged to. It's important to also know the manufacturer specifications for all your appliances to be sure they don't require higher or lower pressures than what your tank supplies.

Leave the system charged for 24 hours. When you return to the gauge, the pressure should be exactly the same. If it's less by even a tiny amount, fill a spray bottle with soapy water and check every joint by spraying it. Start at the pressure gauge and work your way back through the entire run, looking for bubbles. Take your time, and get it right. After you connect the gas source to your lines, be sure to check that the connections to the main line (from the tank to the house) are leak free as well.

There is no room for error here, so pay attention. If you're not completely comfortable working with gas lines, there's nothing wrong with hiring a pro to tackle this important job.

Sewer Lines

Providing sewer/waste lines is the first step of the plumbing process. You want to install them *before* you install the supply lines because they're harder to adjust around existing utilities. Water supply lines, on the other hand, can always be shifted around waste lines if necessary.

There are two main options for waste line materials: *ABS* and *PVC*. ABS, short for "acrylonitrile butadiene styrene," is resistant to abrasion, durable, nontoxic, and slightly easier to install than PVC. It's more durable and has a higher impact strength, but it's more likely to deform when exposed to UV rays. It does not contain BPA (bisphenol A). PVC, short for "polyvinyl chloride," is resistant to abrasion but less durable and has a lower impact strength than ABS. It's nontoxic and slightly harder to install. It does contain BPA.

Whichever material you choose, stick with it throughout the build and don't mix and match. In addition, use the proper adhesive for that material. Each waste-line type has its own specific glue, and in the case of PVC, a special primer is also required.

There are some important details regarding sewer-line installations such as the angle of the fittings as they meet the main lines, what fittings are appropriate when, and more. Therefore, we highly recommend you find a reliable resource, specific to plumbing installations, that can outline this process for you in more detail than we can provide here. A poorly draining sewer line can cause more issues than just an odor buildup.

It's crucial to install in-line vents with your waste lines. Without these vents, water in your P-traps will completely drain after each use. This water is necessary to provide the seal from sewer gases entering your living space. These gases and odors will present an issue if you don't provide vented P-traps whether you're on a municipal, septic, or black water tank system.

If you're wondering what P-traps are, take a look under your kitchen sink. That curved section of pipe below the sink drain is a P-trap. Water remains trapped in that curve, creating the seal needed against sewer gas.

In many locations, air admittance valves (AAVs) are a code-approved, under-cabinet vent solution. These are great for THOWs because they don't require a penetration through the exterior house walls. Instead, they work by providing a break in the suction that would otherwise drain your traps, the same way an in-line waste vent would but without penetrating the roof.

AAVs must remain accessible, so they can't be hidden inside walls unless there's an access panel. In time, AAVs need to be replaced because they'll stop working when the seal eventually gets too brittle to fully work. This could be every 5 to 10 years, depending on usage.

If you prefer not to use AAVs, you can install standard roof stack venting. The issue for a THOW is that the venting needs to extend above the roofline. If you plan on being mobile, you'll need to either factor that consideration into your design and lower your roof height or remove the stack each time you relocate. Check your local code requirements, however, as you may be required to provide one roof-penetrating vent line in the home.

Waste lines can be drained into a municipal system, a septic tank, a black water tank, or to the ground if you're using a gray water system and a separate black water system. Whatever option you choose, be sure to provide a safe and approved shutoff at the end of your main lines where they exit your tiny house. This way you can close off the systems when traveling. The people driving behind you will appreciate the gesture.

If you plan on installing a gray water tank, an RV black water tank, or a fresh water tank under the trailer, remember to include the weight of the full tank(s) into your weight-distribution calculations. Also, place them in a location that will minimize the risk of damage during transport. An installation toward the rear of a THOWs may be riskier as you change road grade and potentially scrape the bottom of your tiny house.

Air admittance valves (AAVs) are good options for THOWs because they can be installed inside a cabinet, eliminating the need for a conventional vent line through the ceiling and beyond the roof line in most cases.

Water Lines

The next step is installing the water supply lines. We recommend you plumb your entire house with PEX (or cross-linked polyethylene). This flexible material is easy to install, reliable, resistant to breakage during freezing events, and color coded (red for hot, blue for cold).

Drill holes in your framing members to create channels for the water lines. Make the holes just large enough to fit the PEX spacers or anchors but not so wide that the wall's structural integrity becomes compromised.

Keep the holes as close to the center of each framing member as possible. This minimizes the risks of puncturing lines with nails while attaching wall finish materials. It also leaves room for insulation around both sides of the water line. If you end up placing the hole too close to the edge of the framing member, nail a steel plate over the hole location to protect the water line. These steel plates can be found at any plumbing or electrical supply store and are specific for this purpose.

Use spacers/anchors to protect your water lines from rubbing when the house is in motion. If you can't find spacers, use spray foam to protect the lines as they pass through the framing.

As far as couplers and fittings go, we recommend a system made by Shark Bite. Although individual fittings are expensive, they're incredibly simple to use and very reliable. They also don't require any special or expensive tools during installation. We used them in hOMe and were very pleased with the product.

There are other systems, but some require special training and expensive tools, while others lack durability and quality. Look for something that's within your budget and skill level.

Install individual shutoffs at each point of use and charge the system to pressures above the usage level. Let it sit for 24 hours as you did for your gas system and check for leaks. Although the risk of explosion is nonexistent, a leak can still cause major damage to your house over time.

The Shark Bite system is incredibly simple to use and nearly impossible to mess up during installation.

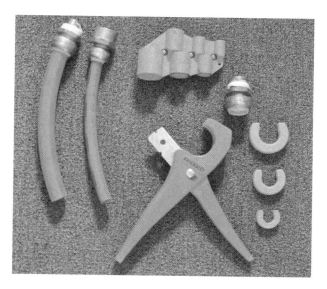

Electrical

As was the case with gas line installation, electrical work can literally kill you if you make a significant enough mistake. We don't mean to incite panic, but we also don't want you to take this job lightly. Do your research before you even think about starting this process. Be sure you're being extremely mindful while working. Even the pros sometimes suffer injuries and death when they lose focus for a few seconds.

Never ever attempt to work on powered-up electrical lines. In the early stages of setting up your system, this is easy since there won't be any electricity in your structure anyway. This caveat applies to the time after everything's hooked up. Always turn off the power at the breaker before you make any modifications to your electrical system.

With that said, wiring your own tiny house is definitely possible. Many tiny housers with no previous building experience brought light to their home safely and successfully.

When installing the actual electrical lines, be sure to place them in the middle of the framing members in the same way you did with plumbing lines. You don't want to risk puncturing a line with a nail in the construction process. If you do drill a hole for the line too close to the edge of the framing member, install a steel plate on the stud right over the electrical line location.

When electrical lines are running perpendicular to the framing members, they don't need to attach to the framing and instead, can simply suspend in place. However, when they run parallel, they must be attached to the frame every four feet with fasteners specifically rated for the job. Those fasteners should also be placed within 6 inches of a turn and within 6 inches of electrical boxes.

The type of fastener you use depends on whether you're working with wood or steel framing and whether all your electrical is running in conduit (such as when you're working with SIPs). You can choose to surface mount your electrical wiring in conduit. If so, be sure to use proper anchors to hold the lines in place. That said, the most common application is the use of insulated electrical staples on wood framing.

There are several different options when it comes to electrical boxes. The most common are plastic, fiberglass, and metal. Metal boxes need to be grounded because they can conduct electricity. To ground metal boxes, simply attach a pigtail off the ground wire from the line that enters the box to the ground screw provided. A pigtail is a small length of wire attached to the main wires inside an electrical box that can be used to make connections to the fixture or to the box itself when grounding metal boxes. Plastic and fiberglass boxes, unlike metal, don't require grounding.

The most commonly used boxes are the blue plastic ones which come with self-mounted nails for wood stud construction, which make installation easier. They even provide small tabs allowing you to space the box's face edge exactly ½ inch (standard drywall thickness) beyond the framing member. This feature allows for a flush installation of the electrical box face with your finish wall material.

The most common wire installed in residential construction is known as *Romex*, a nonmetallic sheathed wire. The two gauges most commonly used are 14g and 12g. Which one to use depends on your specific project, so be sure to research your options ahead of time.

There are requirements about which gauge of wire is used where so be sure to investigate what you need. For example, you must use 12g wire on two separate 20-amp circuits for your kitchen plugs. Another example is in bathrooms where a 20-amp circuit, wired with 12g wire, is required.

There are also requirements about what type of plugs to use and where, as well as the number of circuits in rooms such as kitchens and bathrooms. For example, you must install a ground fault circuit interrupter (GFCI) in each bathroom at the exterior of every entry door and in any other potentially wet location. Furthermore, arc fault circuit interrupters (AFCIs) are required in all bedrooms and might, in fact, be required for all outlet circuits not protected with GFCI technology. Check with your local electrical inspector to confirm what you need and where.

There's a lot to know about electrical wiring and how to install it correctly. Whatever resource you choose, be sure they can be trusted and that you understand each step.

If wiring a house doesn't seem the least bit appealing, any reputable electrician can help. If you do opt to install your own, please hire an electrician to come for a site inspection before you close up your walls or power it on. An electrical report is actually required for some tiny house insurance policies, so if nothing else, get one for this reason.

Remember to always install smoke and carbon monoxide detectors. Many municipalities require them to be hard-wired (not battery operated) into the main panel. You may as well buy the extra peace of mind by installing yours this way, too.

Internet and TV

In today's modern world, internet access is nearly as much of a necessity as electricity or plumbing. The good news is that connecting to it is becoming easier, even for those of us living in THOWs.

The simplest way to tap into the web when living tiny is by connecting to a personal hotspot. A hotspot is a Wi-Fi network created by a smart device such as an iPhone. It pulls data from a cellular phone plan, which is then shared with a computer via a protected Wi-Fi signal. A cellphone signal is required for this system to work.

Of course, using free Wi-Fi at a business, library, or other location is an option. It won't allow you to have internet within your tiny house (unless you park in range of a signal), but perhaps it will help create a new routine in which you don't have web access in your home 24/7.

Satellite is another option for tiny houses. If you plan on being mobile, look at the RV industry for mobile solutions. It's very slow and quite expensive when compared to other options, but if you live remotely, it may be your only hope.

No matter what system you use (unless you're completely remote), we recommend you add a virtual private network (VPN) to your devices. A VPN protects your devices from hackers in public Wi-Fi areas by encrypting your personal information and data. After enduring a couple cyberattacks on our computers, we never use our devices (smartphones and computers) without connecting to our VPN first. VPN services can be purchased in subscription services at reasonable costs.

Insulation Options

There are many options when it comes to insulation for a tiny house, whether mobile or fixed. To find the right one for you, consider your budget, what R-value you're aiming for (more on R-values in a second), whether you want to use natural materials or not, how thick your walls will be, and how easy you want the installation to be.

Roughly put, an R-value refers to the insulation potential for a material and how well it resists the tendency of heat loss. The higher the R-value, the better the insulation. Although not a perfect measure, it's the most standardized option out there and a good starting place when comparing various insulation materials.

Natural Choices

The market for natural insulation has grown in recent years and there are now many materials available. You can choose from sheep's wool, denim, hemp, cork, cellulose, rock wool, and more. Their major advantage is that they don't emit chemical fumes.

Natural materials are generally more expensive than other options. Some, such as denim and wool insulation batts, tend to slip down the walls when forced to endure motion while in transit. To minimize this risk, use an insulation adhesive on the sheathing and studs to help secure the insulation in the stud bay.

Standard Choices

The most commonly used insulation in construction is fiberglass batting. It's available practically anywhere and is one of the less expensive options out there. It also has one of the lowest R-values per inch, and the paper facing is prone to mold issues if there is any water penetration. If you choose fiberglass insulation, look for formaldehyde-free options to reduce the health risks of the material.

Rigid foam is a high efficiency material that can be a great option in a tiny house. It's a bit tricky to install properly because of its lack of flexibility. Rigid foam comes in three common types: expanded polystyrene (EPS), extruded polystyrene (XPS), and polyiso (ISO). They come in varying thickness and can be found in either 4×8-foot sheets or 2×8-foot sheets. Costs are moderate when compared to other options.

Electrical wiring, plumbing, and other obstructions make it challenging to neatly place in each stud-bay. This foam can cause a significant decrease in a wall's potential R-value if gaps in the insulation envelope are left unaddressed. Use low expansion spray foam in conjunction with the rigid foam to fill any potential gaps. Take your time here as a fully sealed insulation envelope is very important for not only the energy efficiency of your home but also its long-term durability.

SIPs panels are another option. The insulation value within them varies with thickness and the foam material used for the core. In a standard assembly comprised of white EPS foam sandwiched by two exterior layers of OSB (oriented strand board sheathing material), you can expect an R-value of 16 on a 4-inch panel. In a graphite gray EPS/OSB combo, you can expect an R-value of 20 for the same thickness. Keep in mind that the higher the R-value, the better the insulation potential of a material.

Spray Foams

There are two types of spray foams out there: closed cell and open cell. In both cases, a two-part mixture made of Isocyanate (Side A) and resin (Side B) combines at the tip of a spray gun and forms an expanding foam. There is conflicting evidence on the safety record of spray foams, so be sure to do your own research and assess the risks before opting for this choice.

Closed-cell spray foam insulation is denser than open-cell foams and offers excellent air- and moisture-barrier properties. Unlike open-cell spray foam, it's rated for use in external walls. It won't sag over time and is the best insulation on the market when it comes to minimizing air leakage. Although it can be installed by the DIY builder, it can be difficult to locate the necessary equipment, so you may end up contracting it out in the end.

In open-cell foam, gas pockets intertwine with each other, like a bath sponge. Although nonozone depleting, water-based varieties can be eco-friendlier than closed-cell foams, they're not recommended for exterior wall applications. Even though several people have used open-cell foam in exterior wall locations, we still recommend that you consult a local installer to ensure it's a proper use for your project.

The Importance of Roof Venting

Roof venting is sometimes overlooked by novice builders, so we want to stress how essential it is. Roof venting allows for vital air flow in the gap between the ceiling/roof insulation and the underside of the roof sheathing. Without it, your sheathing, rafters, and insulation will succumb to moisture damage in as little as one to two years. The fix for the damage? Tearing off the roofing material and sheathing and replacing any rotten insulation, rafters, and the like. It's no small task.

It's imperative you leave an unobstructed ventilation gap directly below the roof sheathing and provide screened vents at the bottom and top of the roofline. There are several materials available on the market that make this process very simple. Called insulation baffles, they simply install directly below the roof sheathing. The insulation can then be pressed up against the baffles.

By design, the baffles provide an air gap above the insulation and below the roof sheathing. This gap allows air to move up and across the sheathing's surface, removing any condensation that might otherwise form as warm, moisture-laden air from the house meets the cold surface of the roof sheathing.

To provide access for air, you'll need to install screened vents at the bottom of the rafters, where they meet the double top plate and at the ridgeline in a gable roof or the top of the rafters in a shed roof. These vents are installed in between the rafters in the blocking that supports each rafter.

The need for air vents and gaps below roofing sheathing can be eliminated if you use closed-cell foam insulation. It's the only insulation currently on the market that provides a complete air seal and doesn't require any venting at all.

Installation Tricks and Know-How

The most insidious risk to any home is water or moisture intrusion. If any of the wet stuff becomes trapped in your walls or roof assembly, your house will develop issues. Depending on how conducive your environment is to mold spore growth, you could be facing a significant issue in as little as one year.

For years, there was a concentrated push to create airtight homes. Unfortunately, some of the adopted practices created more problems than they fixed. For example, the use of plastic vapor barriers—sheet plastic installed on the interior of homes—in walls and ceilings ended up actually trapping moisture, rather than eliminating it.

What the construction industry learned from this is that the biggest focus needs to be on stopping the free movement of air. Air is laden with moisture, so a gap in an air seal can allow moisture to build and become trapped in the walls when it hits the plastic barrier.

Steps you *should* take in a tiny house include sealing all window and door gaps with low-expansion spray foam insulation, installing a moisture barrier (*not* a vapor barrier) to seal air from entering the home, taping all housewrap joints with the manufacturer-specified vapor tape, and using foam gaskets on all switches and outlets under the finish plates. A moisture barrier, which is typically referred to as housewrap, is placed on the exterior face of wall assemblies and is designed to eliminate the movement of water and air in the house. Unlike vapor barriers, moisture barriers allow water vapor to escape the home. These simple techniques will do far more to protect your home than wrapping a plastic barrier around it.

Envelope Options

Keep your interior walls dry by installing a good hat (roof) on your tiny house and wrapping it with a waterproof jacket (siding). As previously mentioned, keeping your place dry is the best insurance policy you can invest in.

Roofing Considerations

Your roofing material choice is important. Get it wrong and all those months (and possibly years) of construction could be ruined in just a couple heavy rainfalls. Choose something that's been tried and approved not only by the building industry, but also by tiny housers.

Factor aesthetics into your decision, and choose something that brings out the best in your tiny house. As always, consider weight and how it will perform in sustained high winds. There are many roofing options, and most should work well in a THOW application.

Metal roofs are an excellent choice. They can be installed on low-sloped roofs when others can't. They do an outstanding job of shedding moisture and perform well in high-wind conditions. Metal roofs are relatively easy to install on a shed or gable and are highly durable with a 50-year expectancy.

We recommend you hire a local company to custom make your roofing package. They'll provide you with all the hardware, installation tools, and flashing required.

Flashing is a thin piece of material in construction that stops the penetration of water into a structure in places such as window seams, roof penetrations, wall joints between the roof and vertical wall, etc. Look for companies that offer standing seam metal roofs. These are the best option, in our opinion, because they are designed in such a way that the fasteners on the roof panels are completely hidden and no longer exposed once the installation is complete. The only exposed fasteners are on the flashing details, and those come with a rubber gasket.

Composition roofs have improved dramatically both in aesthetics and performance in recent years. You can find some with a whopping 50-year warranty. Composition shingles can tear off a roof at high rates of speed, so look for options rated for high-wind events.

There are other choices ranging from rubber shingles to wood shakes and beyond. Consider your needs, budget, and aesthetics, and choose the option that best matches your wishes and wants.

No matter which choice you make, use high-quality roofing felt beneath. Better yet, use an adhesive membrane such as Grace Ice and Water Shield, which seals around fastener penetrations and creates the most waterproof and durable shield for your tiny house's roof. This material fully seals to the roof deck and eliminates the risk of water damage from ice dams, wind-driven rain, and more.

Gutters and Catchment Systems

In most residential construction, gutters and downspouts are ubiquitous. Their purpose is to direct water away from the structure, providing an extra layer of protection from moisture intrusion. Why do we rarely see them on THOWs then? Because a tiny house is measured from the two widest points, and because gutters are included in that dimension. Most people don't want to lose 5 inches (on a shed roof) to 10 inches (on a gable roof with gutters on both sides) from their tiny house interior to accommodate them.

If you get pulled over by a police officer when towing your THOW and your gutter(s) extend past the 8'6" highway limit, they may issue you a ticket. If you want to install gutters, either have a wide-load permit while towing, or take down the gutters before transit and reinstall them when you reach your next parking spot.

If you do want gutters and don't plan on moving often, you can remove them during relocation and re-install them after you're parked. You'll need to decide if having gutters is worth the hassle. Keep in mind the potential damage that water can do to your home and what a hassle fixing that damage would be.

Siding Choices

Nobody has ever walked up to a house and said, "Wow! The rough plumbing and electrical work looks great!" Instead, they see the finishes. If your siding looks amazing, people will be impressed. If it looks like you dragged some wood out of the forest and nailed it to your house, most people won't have very nice things to say about it.

Consider weight when making decisions for a THOW. For this reason, an option such as fiber-cement board isn't ideal. Instead, look for materials such as wood planking, shakes or shingles, lightweight metal siding, or anything else that can weather the storms but not weigh you down.

Different siding materials require different fasteners, so be sure to research which ones are right for your project. Nongalvanized nails may leave rust streaks on your pine siding after a couple rainfalls. Therefore, galvanized nails are the best option for most siding materials. However, cedar siding doesn't work well with galvanized nails and may actually eat through the nails over time. That's why stainless steel is required when working with cedar.

In terms of attaching siding, you can choose to blind nail (hiding nails from view) or face nail (keeping nails visible). Both approaches are acceptable. Face nailing provides better resistance against wind but makes the siding more prone to expansion and contraction as the fastener swells and shrinks with external temperatures. This can cause holes in the siding, leaving the wall behind it susceptible to water intrusion. Blind nailing doesn't provide the same resistance against wind, but it conceals the fasteners and eliminates the issue of leaks developing at fastener locations over time.

Prime both the back of the siding and all the ends with stain or paint to provide protection for the material and significantly increase longevity. Caulk any butt-joints to seal your building envelope.

Rainscreens allow for trapped moisture behind siding to escape. An easier alternative is a housewrap with built-in crinkles and waves that serve the same function and allow moisture to drain out from behind siding.

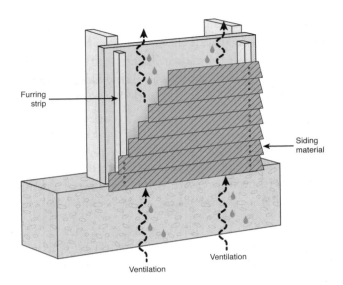

Furring strip

Siding material

Ventilation

Ventilation

Ventilation

Install a rainscreen to add protection to your tiny house. Rainscreens allow moisture to escape rather than become trapped behind siding. A ventilation gap between the sheathing or housewrap and the back of the siding prevents condensation and moisture buildup, adding years of longevity.

Instead of a rainscreen, there are housewraps that provide the same protection through the use of ridges and dimples in the material itself. These ridges provide a drainage channel for any moisture buildup. It's a lot easier to install than a full-blown rainscreen.

Windows and Doors

There are several window and door material choices to pick from. You really do get what you pay for, so you should invest in the highest quality possible. The more energy efficient your windows and doors are, the more power and money you'll save over the life of your home.

Many manufacturers use their own specific rough-in measurements. We'll use vinyl windows as an example. When ordering one that's listed at 3 feet wide × 2 feet tall, you need to frame your rough opening to 3 feet wide × 2 feet tall. The window will arrive ½ inch smaller in each direction to allow for shim space, so you can plumb and level the unit within the rough opening.

A custom wood window, on the other hand, might be a totally different situation. You may need to frame the rough opening at 2 feet, 11¾ inches wide × 2 feet, ½ inch tall so the window will actually fit. Always choose which window manufacturer and what material you're going to install *before* you frame out the rough opening (R.O.).

To be clear, a rough opening call-out is very different from the actual window size. It is simply the opening into which a window (or door) is installed.

Be sure to flash your window and door openings correctly. These areas are major sources of water penetration in any house. It's best to start with a counter-flash pan of some sort. This can be a rigid material but is more commonly created with self-adhesive flashing materials around windows and three lines of caulk below door thresholds.

After the pan is installed, install your window or door into the rough opening. Once set, be sure to use self-adhesive flashing around the unit. As is the case with any waterproofing material installed on a home, you always install from the bottom up so that water is directed *away* from the structure, not back into it. This is called shingling your flashing.

You might choose to install a metal flashing over the top of the window, door, or trim above them as a final safeguard. Check the manufacturer's recommendation because many units now come with a similar flashing already installed on the unit and another one may not be necessary.

To Summarize

Several electrical heaters and air conditioning options exist for tiny houses, but far fewer options are available when only considering propane. If possible, integrate systems that have the option of switching between electric and propane to maximize efficiency. Plumbing ventilation is more challenging in a THOW because vents need to expand beyond the roof line. Air admittance valves (AAVs) are a viable venting alternative to traditional venting methods. Most insulation options available to conventional houses are appropriate in tiny house applications; however, some are better than others in this context. When installing your insulation, be sure to create a moisture barrier and not a vapor barrier to prevent mold issues. Venting your roof assembly is vital. Without it, moisture-laden air will become trapped under the roof sheathing, causing significant mold damage over time. There are so many factors to consider when approaching utilities and envelope considerations; it is essential that you spend adequate time parsing through your options. A lot of literature is available on the various insulation installation methods, so research ahead of your build which option will be the right fit for your home.

CHAPTER 19

Finishing Touches

It might seem like ages ago that you were learning about downsizing and saving for your tiny house build, and here you are reading about adding finishing touches to your house. How far you've come!

In this chapter, we discuss options for bringing the beauty of your tiny house to life. We also cover appropriate choices for tiny house trim, cabinets, and loft access. Lastly, we discuss steps in getting your mechanical systems totally trimmed out. Let's get started!

Interior Wall Finishes

For a long time, the most common wall finish in a tiny house was simply exposed wood (most typically pine). Today, numerous options are available, and nearly every design aesthetic can be satisfied. The key factors to consider when looking at interior wall finishes for THOWs are weight, environmental impact, ease of installation, long-term maintenance needs, and cost.

An often underestimated factor is maintenance and upkeep. Many finishes look beautiful upon installation but show signs of aging much sooner than they should. For example, if you install tongue and groove planking in your interior, eventually all those cracks and gaps will begin to collect dust. Furthermore, if you opt for a material with a less-than-smooth surface, wiping the walls down will be just shy of impossible. These considerations are especially important if you plan on traveling a lot or placing the home on rural property along a dirt road.

Most conventional houses on permanent foundations are finished with drywall. This wall finish is an option for tiny houses on wheels as well, but it poses two significant challenges:

- The first is weight. Unless you purchase special lightweight drywall, it's quite heavy, requiring the trailer plans to reflect the added load.

- The second concern is that taped drywall joints tend to crack. With enough movement, it's likely that joints will crack. That said, there are some current tiny housers out there who are very happy with their drywall choice.

If you decide to go with wall paneling as your finish material, you need to choose this well in advance of the actual installation. Because typical paneling is thin, it tends to bow and bend in between studs if the framing members are spaced 24 inches o.c., which is often the case in THOW wall systems.

You have two options in the previous scenario:

- The first is to install the wall's plywood sheathing to the interior side of the studs (rather than the exterior which is customary) and use it as a paneling backer.

- The second is to frame the THOW with a 16- or 12-inch o.c. stud layout. This option adds materials, cost, and of course weight, so be sure to budget for those factors in your design.

In looking for wall material options for hOMe, we came across some high-end panelized systems that yielded a clean, modern look, but we practically fell off our chairs when we saw the prices. We set out on a mission to re-create this panelized look but at a more budget-friendly cost.

We chose a super inexpensive and lightweight vinyl subfloor plywood product called IronPly and hung the sheets on our walls. We created thin gaps between each 4×8-foot piece by temporarily installing nails at each corner. Because we had installed our sheathing on our inside walls, we already had a backer material in place, which created a solid surface to which we could adhere the thin IronPly. After a couple coats of paint, our budget-friendly interior wall finish looked like its more expensive cousins.

A great way of adding aesthetic details to a house is by using accent walls. An accent wall is an area within a larger wall finished differently with the intention of creating a visual point of interest. You can add materials such as faux tile or lightweight metal siding, or you can simply paint a specific location a different color.

Several options are available on the market today. The hard part might not be finding something that works. Instead, the hard part might be paring down your options. You could choose from metal, dozens of patterns of paneling, and even materials not typically used on walls, such as IronPly. Get creative and have fun!

You will need to decide what type of wall finish material you plan on installing before completing the design process. Because different materials are affected by factors such as stud spacing and location of wall sheathing, you'll need to know which option you're going with to ensure that your framing can properly support the system.

Flooring Options

There are so many flooring options on the market today, and as a tiny houser, you can actually choose from nearly all of them. You can use hardwood, floating laminate, nail-down laminate, glue-down laminate, glue-down wood tiles, cork tile floors, cork strip flooring, bamboo floors, carpet, linoleum, vinyl, and more. If you plan on being quite mobile, ceramic tile might not be the best option because it's heavy and grout lines are susceptible to cracking when subjected to movement.

No matter what flooring you choose, be sure to make your selection early on. There are different installation details associated with different finishes, so you'll want to know how each option will affect your overall interior height. Your ceiling heights are measured from the finished floor up. That means if you budget your design for a ¼-inch-thick finish floor but end up adding ¾-inch-thick wood, you'll lose ½ inch from your ceiling heights. This might not seem like a big deal, but it could trigger a failure in a code inspection if you're going the legal route.

The two most common finish floor options used in tiny houses are wood (laminate and true wood) and sheet materials, such as linoleum and vinyl. Preparing for sheet flooring is quite simple, but there are some important details to keep track of.

The subflooring needs to be perfectly smooth. If it's not, any imperfections will show through the material and potentially cause premature failure of the flooring. The best way to create a perfectly smooth base is by adding a new layer of material to the rough-floor sheathing. It's best to use a lightweight and thin plywood option, such as IronPly, rather than heavier particleboard. Whatever material you choose, keep it as smooth as possible and butt the joints as tightly as possible to eliminate any gaps.

If your tiny house walls aren't completely square to each other, choose finish flooring materials that won't highlight that fact. Choose a pattern that will softly hide any imperfections, and stay away from sheeting flooring with a lot of squares or straight lines on them.

When it comes to the installation of the wood flooring itself, there are some basic steps to take for a quality end-result. Wood expands and contracts as ambient temperatures and humidity levels change. If the wood flooring you purchased was previously stored in a climate-controlled facility and you then installed it in your tiny house before it was properly conditioned to the new location, the flooring would suffer the effects.

If the new climate is more humid than the previous one, your wood flooring will be subject to buckling as it swells in its new location. Conversely, if your house is extremely dry compared to the previous space, you'll likely see cracks and gaps in the flooring after installation. The only way to avoid these issues is by acclimating your wood flooring for at least three days in its new location.

Ideally, your climate control systems will already be in place in your tiny house before installing the flooring so that you can regulate the acclimation process. If part of your plan is to leave your tiny house unconditioned for extended periods of time, a more synthetic flooring material might be a better option.

Always leave an expansion gap around the flooring edges where they meet the walls. This is true for both laminate flooring—whether nailed down, glued in place, or floating—as well as true wood floors. Typically, a ¼-inch gap is suggested, which is enough to provide adequate expansion for most wood materials. Neglecting to provide these gaps will cause floors to buckle at the joints. Baseboard trim hides these gaps between the flooring and the walls.

Getting Up and Down

If you plan on including a loft or two in your design, you'll need a means of accessing the space. There are four common approaches to loft access, and each has its advantages and disadvantages. We'll begin with our favorite—stairs.

Stairways

One thing we were clear on before even starting our tiny house design process was that we didn't want to lumber up and down a ladder every time we had to access our bedroom. Because we work from home and spend most of our time here, we're constantly going up and down. For us, the only option was stairs.

There are several advantages to stairs, the most obvious being ease of use. It's also our belief that they're safer and stronger than ladders. Their downside is that they take up quite a bit of floor space, which can pose a significant issue if you have very little square footage to begin with. Stairs in tiny houses that are much shorter than 24 inches might prove quite challenging.

We built our stairs out of custom-made plywood boxes stacked on top of each other. The construction process was very simple and resulted in a strong staircase that could easily support two people walking on it at the same time. An important feature of the stair design is the additional 25 square feet of storage space provided below the steps, which is enough to house shoes, jackets, hats, gloves, and much more.

One thing that's not currently possible for most tiny houses is a stairway that meets International Residential Code (IRC) standards. This is because the required rise and run of an IRC-compliant stairway is too large for a tiny house. This could change as tiny house-specific codes are implemented, but for now, you might have to build outside of code if you want stairs in your THOW.

This set of stairs can easily be built by assembling custom-made plywood boxes strategically stacked on top of each other.

Ladders

As mentioned earlier, ladders are perhaps the most common loft access devices in the tiny house world. We've already mentioned some of their downfalls, but on the upside, they take up very little space and can be hung out of the way when not in use. This is a major advantage when compared to stairs. If your tiny house is so small that stairs are simply not an option, a ladder could be the perfect solution.

Always ensure the ladder has full and connected contact where it meets the loft. In other words, install the ladder in such a way that it can't slip during use. You might even consider extending the length of one of the side rails beyond the loft floor to make the approach to the ladder safer for the user.

You can purchase premade ladders or custom make them yourself to match the look and feel of your tiny house. You can also purchase an inexpensive attic-access drop down ladder assembly and extract the ladder from the frame. This will give you a lightweight yet strong means of access to your loft.

To attach the ladder to the loft framing, you can look online for library ladder assemblies or create something less expensive. Even just black pipe from the plumbing department held to the wall with basic C brackets can act as anchoring points for the ladder hooks. The point is that with creativity, you can create a comfortable loft ladder for $100 or less.

Ships Ladders

Ships ladders are a hybrid of stairs and ladders. They're most commonly built at angles between 65 and 75 degrees, which means they're easier to walk up and down on than standard ladders. In addition, their treads (the part that you step on) are larger than those found on standard ladders. If you've never seen them before, picture a sturdier version of a simple loft ladder.

Unlike standard ladders, a ships ladder isn't something that can easily be put away and it certainly can't be hung on a wall. That might be a disadvantage, but their footprint is significantly smaller than a full stairway, making them a great choice for many tiny houses. As always, a handrail is recommended for safe access while getting up into and down from the loft.

An IRC provision for the use of ships ladders states that they're allowed as a means of egress from a loft space. However, they can't be used as the *primary* means of egress, meaning that some other form of access must be included as well. There isn't enough room in a tiny house for two modes of stair and ladder egress from one loft. Therefore, until we see changes in the code that allow ships ladders as a primary means of egress, they won't be IRC compliant.

Alternating Tread Devices

Alternating tread devices (ATDs) are a great way to access a loft space. They take some getting used to, but ATDs provide safe loft access with a minimized footprint. Because the stair treads alternate left to right as they ascend, the space needed to ascend the same distance is greatly reduced over that of a traditional or ships ladder. (See Chapter 6 for an example of an ATD.)

Alternating tread devices are included in the IRC. However, similar to ships ladders, they cannot function as a primary form of egress. That said, they're used in all kinds of commercial applications, such as warehouses, restaurants, and even in some of NASA's buildings.

Cabinetry and Counters

When most people think about cabinetry, they typically think about kitchens. That makes sense, but cabinets can also make great additions in other parts of a tiny house. Because standard furniture can be hard to fit in a tiny home, using modular cabinetry as both storage and furniture can be a great way to go. For instance, upper cabinets placed on the floor can serve as ideal frames on which to place cushions and create sofas with built-in storage.

No matter where you install cabinets in a tiny house, you'll need to consider factors such as weight, style, budget, and ease of installation. Be sure to optimize every inch of your cabinet layout. In the old days, people used filler blocks for thin areas between cabinets to hide dead space. However, today, you can use that space for slide-out drawers creating a perfect slot for baking sheets, dishtowels, and other thin items. You can also install under-cabinet drawers in the toe-kick area for further storage capacity.

The weight of off-the-rack particleboard cabinetry is significant in a THOW. If you plan on driving around a lot and want the lightest house possible, look for custom-made units or lighter-weight options from the RV industry. Furthermore, be sure to anticipate the weight distribution of those cabinets on your overall trailer design so you don't end up with an improperly balanced tiny house.

No matter what style cabinet you use and from which source you purchase it, you'll need to understand some basics about cabinet installation:

1. Be sure to measure where your cabinets are going to be installed before you order them. In other words, don't trust the plans on this one. Even if you built to plan, there's a chance that a small hiccup here or there could have changed your layout.

2. Check your space to ensure it's square. If you only measure along one wall and don't check that the intersecting wall falls square to your reference wall, you may find your cabinets don't fit during installation. If things are indeed not square, come up with an action plan for correcting the issue ahead of time. The most common repair option is shimming the cabinets so that they appear tight to the wall, even if they're not.

3. Be sure your trailer is level before taking any further action. If the trailer isn't level when the cabinets are installed, the cabinets will remain unlevel later. If your floor is truly not level, start by setting cabinet bases at the high end of your layout and shim everything up to meet the level line.

Our personal preference is to install upper cabinets in a kitchen before the base units. It enables us to stand comfortably while hanging heavy upper cabinets. It's common practice to mount uppers so that the distance between the countertop and the bottom of the uppers is 18 inches. Because a countertop is typically 1½ inches thick, you can mark a line on the wall 19½ inches above the top of the base cabinet's height.

To find and mark the base cabinet's height before it's actually installed, you'll need to identify the high side of the floor, mark a level line, and then measure up from that line a distance equal to the height of the base cabinet: typically, 34½ inches. It's from this line that you'll measure the distance to the upper cabinets.

Avoid unexpected issues with your electrical plug and switch layouts by deciding where to place your cabinets during the design stages and prior to setting up your rough electrical wiring. Be sure to plan ahead for under-cabinet lighting and other details that rely on proper placement within your cabinets.

There are many choices for countertops, which can make it difficult to make a selection. Again, refer back to factors such as weight, cost, and practicality when making your selection. No matter what material you go with, you'll have some installation guidelines to follow.

The first step is to ensure the space is square. One thing you'll notice about countertops is that they often come with a backsplash, which provides a convenient way of hiding any wall planes that are out of square. By scribing the exact contour of your wall onto the backsplash with a compass and pencil, you can use a belt sander to remove excess material until it's a perfect reflection of the wall contour.

The best way to ensure your counters fit snugly is by starting with a dry-fit assembly. Place each counter piece against the wall as if you were going to install it. Mark the wall undulations on the backsplash and make any scribe cuts as necessary. Continue this practice until all joints are tight and the transitions from counter to wall look good.

Once you're happy with how things look, start making other cuts for items such as sink openings, faucets, and any other penetrations. Finally, create the permanent installation by gluing the miter joints together and locking them to each other with under-counter clamps provided by the manufacturer. Attach counters to the lower cabinets with L brackets or wood blocks. Be sure to use screws that don't penetrate through the countertop surface.

Trim Work

Trim plays an important role in home construction. It hides gaps and adds beauty to any project. Trim layout style and material choice impact the overall look of your house, so be sure to select something that compliments the house's design aesthetic.

The most common trim materials are real wood, engineered wood, plastic, vinyl, and medium-density fiberboard (MDF).

Real wood yields the highest quality finish but is more expensive. MDF is inexpensive but swells with the slightest contact with moisture. No matter what material you choose, there are many different profiles or cross-sectional designs to choose from. You can use one style for the entire house, mix and match, or even build up several styles in one location for a more sophisticated look.

The most common joints used in trim work are miter joints (45-degree cuts that come together to make a 90-degree angle) and simpler butt joints (square cuts where two pieces of trim butt into each other). You can create more elaborate joints if you prefer, but the skill required jumps up exponentially. We recommend using glue on all joints to help keep things tight as the house travels down the road.

Use a small-gauge nail gun to install trim. Gauges between 22g and 16g are considered adequate for trim installation and will minimize the amount of patching needed to hide nail holes. These nails are so small, especially in the 22g realm, that you can often just leave them open without any patch work at all.

If you do find that a nail needs to be driven deeper into the material to hide the head, be sure to use a nail set—a small metal tool designed to allow a nail head to be pushed below a material's surface. These allow a person to hit only the nail head, sparing the wood around it and making for a much cleaner installation job.

Paint and Stain

Paint adds a protective layer over the substrate and provides years of longevity to a material. Stain, on the other hand, actually penetrates the material and changes the color of that substrate on a much deeper level. Staining must be sealed to protect it, making it a multistep application process.

Both materials can be applied by roller, brush, or sprayer. If you choose to spray your material, be sure to protect surrounding areas from overspray. It's easy to lose track of this and completely ruin surrounding objects such as your neighbor's cat without even realizing what's happening.

When applying paint or stain with a sprayer, you'll still need to take the additional step of rolling or brushing it into the material for full adhesion or penetration. Be sure to paint all surfaces on all sides of the material in question to ensure the best quality results possible. This includes the end-cut surfaces.

Finishing Mechanical Systems

We've been talking about cabinets, trim, paint, stain, and countertops. However, now we are moving to the final stages of construction as we cover electrical, plumbing, and HVAC installations.

Electrical

As we mentioned in the section on cabinet heights, some details surrounding electrical systems potentially come into play much earlier than during the finishing process. Consider electrical plugs in a kitchen, for example. If the boxes are set in the wrong locations, you might have to cut the countertop backsplash to accommodate their position, which never looks good.

Ground fault circuit interrupter (GFCI) plugs are required in all wet locations and areas at risk of moisture, including bathrooms, kitchens, and outdoor plugs. Conversely, arc fault circuit interrupters (AFCIs) are typically required in bedrooms. However, be sure to check local code requirements because some jurisdictions now require AFCIs in all locations in which GFCIs aren't used. Take the time to learn the requirements to keep your installation safe and successful.

Choose lighting options that highlight your favorite features in your tiny house. Mood lighting can be created with dimmer switches and warm-toned lightbulbs. Incorporate brighter lights over any work areas, and set them up to operate on separate switches from the regular lights.

You can choose between recessed-can lights for a clean modern look or hanging pendant lights for a more whimsical feel. Track systems are very sleek, and wall sconces provide a nice traditional look. In terms of bulbs, LED technology has come a long way not only in efficiency but also in cost and aesthetics. Where they used to emit a stark light, they can now emit much softer and warmer tones.

Plumbing

Rough plumbing is typically not considered a glamorous component of a residence, but finish plumbing certainly has a wow factor. Various options exist and almost anything available in conventionally sized homes works in tiny house applications as well.

Because each manufacturer has its own installation requirements, it's best to follow the instructions that come with each fixture you purchase. You may need specialty tools to complete the installation, so check the packaging for guidance while still at the store.

Be sure to use caulking anywhere water might find its way through the holes made for the fixtures. Water damage can appear quickly or over long time periods, depending on the severity of the leak. Neither is something you want to deal with, so put in the extra effort to seal all points of water entry to minimize issues down the road.

One secret that we learned some time ago is that it's much easier to install faucets in a countertop *before* the countertop is in place. If you wait until the countertop is installed, then you'll have to work on your back to fit the fixture tightly into position. Instead, install the fixture while the countertop can be flipped over.

HVAC

HVAC system installation is one of the final steps in house construction, so when you reach this point, you know you're nearly done! HVAC systems include bathroom fans, kitchen fans, and heating and cooling components. By this point, you've likely already installed your climate control components, so this is the time to trim and finish them out completely.

Be sure to install your fan covers and any filters in the HVAC systems in such a way that you can easily access and remove them later. It's important to keep your ventilation pathways as clean as possible and free from dust, cobwebs, and grime. This will extend the life of the unit and make it more effective in day-to-day use.

One specific location in a tiny house may pose a challenge when it comes to ventilation—the range hood above the oven/stovetop. There are requirements about how close a vent hood may be from a range top. This is rarely, if ever, a concern in a conventionally sized home. However, in a tiny house with lowered ceilings under a loft, meeting these requirements can be an issue.

Make sure your hood vent gets placed far enough from the stove. On gas units without electric burners, the hood should be at least 26 inches above the surface of the cooktop. For electric stoves, the hood can be dropped to within 24 inches of the top.

Be sure whatever unit you use meets the requirements for exhaust (how many cubic feet of air it moves per minute). Also, install a vent hood that's 6 inches wider than the unit for which it's proving ventilation. For example, if you have a 30-inch-wide oven range, install a 36-inch-wide hood vent. This will collect steam and smoke that might otherwise escape the vent draw.

By this point, there's not much left to do except sit back, admire your work, pat yourself on the back, and sleep for a few weeks straight. Congratulations! Your house is now move-in ready!

To Summarize

Choose finish materials that are lightweight, cost-effective, and as eco-friendly as possible. Most finish options available for conventionally sized houses are available for tiny houses as well. Effort put into the proper installation of finish materials pays off greatly in the overall look and feel of a completed tiny house, so take your time in this process.

CHAPTER 20

Off-Grid Living

One of the aspects we've enjoyed the most in our experience of living tiny and minimally all this time has been being off-grid. Our ritual of manually tracking the sun by turning our panels several times per day has gifted us with an intimate understanding of the seasons and climate. It feels good knowing where our power comes from and that we're sourcing it as locally as possible.

Each property offers unique natural resources, and discovering the gifts yours has to offer is a fun and rewarding process. In this chapter, we cover how to calculate your power needs, how to create solar electricity, and what to use as a backup power source. We also discuss options for bringing water to your tiny house if your land is undeveloped. Let's get you onto the path to power independence.

What Is Off-Grid Living?

Depending on who you ask, you'll find a couple definitions of what off-grid living is. Most are willing to grace the term *off-gridder* to anyone disconnected from the main electrical network. Others are adamant that any outside reliance on energy (for example, propane or gasoline for a generator) or water (delivered via truck) to sustain a house disqualifies them from truly being off-grid.

In an ideal world, everyone would be responsible for creating 100 percent of their energy and would have a reliable onsite water source. A lot of emerging technologies are getting us close to that point, but we're not completely there yet. Hopefully in the next 10 to 20 years, we'll see existing solutions become even more compact, available, and cost effective, so that we can reach the goal of total energy independence.

The Joys and Challenges of Making Your Own Power

Making your own electricity is fun! Even being off-grid as long as we have been, we still marvel that the sun can generate our power. Another advantage of sourcing electricity from an onsite system is that the amount of energy dissipated during transit from power plant to point of use is decreased significantly, thus reducing the burden on the power grid and minimizing our reliance on foreign power sources.

Off-grid living fosters a lifestyle of mindfulness and connection with nature's cycles. It can also be an opportunity for a bit of time travel and whimsy. Old technologies used by our own ancestors can suddenly be helpful again: hand coffee grinders, metal flat irons, oil lamps, and so on.

There's even a sense of romance in living off the grid. It's so much nicer to sit around candles while drinking wine or tea with friends than underneath bright electric lights. Of course, although you can keep using your modern gadgets, you might enjoy a new lifestyle in which the earth seems to spin just a little bit slower and you live in a day-to-day connection with the rhythms of the sun and weather.

If you've never lived off the grid before, you might experience a steep learning curve. There's a lot to understand, and some lifestyle adjustments to be made. It's all manageable, but it's not as easy as just turning on a light switch or opening a faucet without any consideration at all. A lot of issues come down to planning and anticipating the day's energy needs. One thing is for certain if you choose to pursue an off-grid lifestyle: you will develop a much better understanding of your consumption and environmental footprint.

Basic Solar Terms

There's a lot of jargon in the world of alternative power. We'll introduce you to several terms throughout this chapter, but for now, let's start with very basic definitions:

Watt (W). When it comes to sizing an alternative energy (AE) system, as well as assessing how much power an appliance uses, you'll be evaluating the data in units of watts. When a product's specification sheet states that an appliance uses 100W, they're referring to watts per *hour*, not per *day*.

Kilowatt-hour (kWh). 1 kWh = 1,000W sustained over an hour. This is the unit most often used by utility companies when talking about how much energy is being consumed.

Voltage (V). If you imagine that electricity flows like water through a hose, voltage is the equivalent of water pressure. Your options for a solar system are 12V, 24V, and very rarely, 48V.

Ampere (amp). The measure of the amount of electricity in a circuit.

AC power. *AC* stands for alternating current in electricity. Conventionally built houses run off of AC power as do nearly all appliances.

DC power. *DC* stands for direct current and is typically only seen in off-grid applications. Electricity is delivered from batteries as DC power. DC systems are more efficient because there's no need for an inverter in a DC system (which loses a lot of power during conversion). However, DC systems require separate wiring and specialty appliances.

Amp hour (Ah). This is the amount of energy charge in a battery. This is the standard unit used to compare batteries.

How Much Power Do I Need?

Put your best foot forward when starting down the road to energy independence by choosing systems that are as efficient as possible. The efforts you make in selecting energy-efficient insulation, appliances, and lighting will pay off in spades when it's time to size up your AE system.

Knowing how big your system needs to be is challenging. You can calculate this information yourself or ask a solar installer for assistance. We highly recommend the good folks at Backwoods Solar (backwoodssolar.com). Their focus is on DIY builders, and their telephone support is outstanding. We've spent many hours talking with them over the years and have always been very impressed with their service.

To estimate your AE system size, you'll first need to take stock of *all* the appliances you plan on installing in your tiny house. A lot of online sizing calculators tell you to refer to current utility bills to obtain your usage numbers. This will be of no use unless you happen to live in a grid-tied tiny house already. Instead, you'll need to research the energy loads of each appliance. Fortunately, this information can be easily found online.

In terms of calculating the power burden of your small appliances, the handiest gadget you can get is a Kill-a-Watt Meter. Simply plug this small device into any electrical outlet and install your appliance into the device's power port. The Kill-a-Watt Meter will display various pieces of data about your appliance, including how many watts it draws.

Remember that watts are represented in terms of how much power is drawn *per hour*, not per day. So if you have a laptop that draws 60W per hour and you typically leave it plugged in for three hours per day, your daily electricity need to power it is 180W (60W × 3 hours = 180W).

In hOMe, we used a 1.6 kWh system. This is enough to power the following appliances daily for nine months of the year without any need for generator backup:

- 2 laptops, 6 to 8 hours per day

- 2 laptops (kids'), 2 hours per day

- 18-cubic-foot electric refrigerator

- 15 LED lights spread out among cabins

- LED TV screen, 2 hours per day

- DVD player, 2 hours per day

- Food processor, 10 minutes per day

- Clothes washer, 1 hour per day

- Propane clothes dryer, 1 hour per day

- Charging small electronics, such as smartphones, 3 hours each day

- Printer and scanner, 10 minutes per day

- Hair dryer, 10 minutes per day

- Propane water heater, 1 hour per day

- Composting toilet fan, 24 hours per day

- House bathroom and kitchen fans, continuous

- Generator, 2 hours per day during sunless winter to fully charge our batteries (A 5-gallon gasoline tank lasts 1 week.)

We highly recommend the off-grid system size calculator on at unboundsolar.com /solar-information/offgrid-calculator. It's comprehensive, free, and considers all the factors that play a role in an AE system. Once you have your watt estimate, you can take this information and apply it to *any* off-grid system you're considering, whether it's solar, wind, or hydro. Commit this figure to memory because you'll refer to it dozens of times while researching systems.

The following list gives an idea of how much power is drawn by basic tiny house appliances:

- Washing machine: 500 to 1,000 watts

- 18-cubic-foot electric refrigerator: 500 to 750 watts

- Blender: 300 to 1,000 watts

- Desktop computer: 200 to 400 watts

- 32-inch LED TV: 50 watts

- Laptop: 20 to 75 watts

- Small printer: 15 to 75 watts

- DVD player: 15 watts

- Cell phone: 5 to 10 watts

- LED lights: 5 to 10 watts

- Composting toilet fan: 4 to 15+ watts

- Propane hot water heater: 2 to 10 watts

Keep in mind that some appliances run continuously when powered on (for example, composting toilet fans, computers, TVs, and DVD players). However, some appliances run only intermittently on any given hour (refrigerator, water heater, printer, and the like). As you calculate how much power you need, make adjustments to reflect this because you likely won't be printing for an hour straight or blending your food for more than 3 to 5 minutes at the most.

Solar Systems

By far, the most commonly utilized source of alternative power in a tiny house is solar. Compared to other solutions, solar is moderately priced, can be mobile, and is fairly compact. There are two other options: wind and hydro, but they're so rarely used in tiny house applications, we're going to stick to solar in this book.

Solar 101

Solar solutions used to be incredibly expensive, but they've become more affordable with each passing year. When you pair today's prices with government rebates and incentives, you end up paying a mere fraction of what you would have just three years ago. You can find up-to-date rebate offerings by zip code in the United States on dsireusa.org.

Sometimes, building a solar system is much more cost effective than connecting to the grid. Bringing electricity just 400 feet from the road to our home site would have cost between $25,000 and $30,000. Instead, we paid about $12,000 for our 1.6 kWh system and cashed in on 40 percent worth of rebates and tax incentives, lowering our total investment to $7,200.

Our system was quite expensive by tiny house standards because we power not only hOMe where we work full-time on our computers, but also both of our kids' cabins and a pretty large electric refrigerator. There are complete solar packages on the market that can be bought in the $2,000 range. As we mentioned previously, the key is minimizing power needs in the design process. If you plan on installing the solar system yourself, we recommend you hire an electrician for a final inspection to ensure that you haven't created an electrical hazard.

Numerous components go into the process of converting sunlight to electricity. Although it seems like magic, there's a lot of science behind it. Let's go over how it works.

System Voltage

For starters, you'll need to decide on the system voltage (12V, 24V, or 48V) that's best for your battery bank. A 48V system is really intended for much larger homes, so we can safely eliminate that option. A 24V system is appropriate for installations in the 1 kWh to 5 kWh range, whereas a 12V system is perfect for smaller solar systems. Most likely, you'll be looking at 12V systems for your tiny house.

Charge Controllers

These wall-mounted devices protect the batteries from overcharging when too much electricity travels from the panels. Without a charge controller, batteries can become permanently damaged.

To calculate the size of your charge controller, you must first determine how many amps are required. Divide your solar system size by battery voltage. For example, if you have a 700W system and a 12V battery bank, (700W/12V), you'll have a 58-amp load, which can be met by a 60-amp charge controller.

Inverter

If you want to run standard (AC) appliances in your tiny house (not specialty DC units), you'll need an inverter to convert the DC power emitted by the battery bank into AC current. Because inverters are one of the most expensive components of a solar system, we recommend you purchase a unit larger than you think you'll need just in case you end up expanding at any point in the future.

You can roughly calculate the inverter's size by establishing your tiny house's peak load. To do this, add up the wattage of all electric appliances that might run simultaneously in a peak hour of usage. This sum will tell you the minimum inverter size you need. Choose a Pure Sine Wave inverter for a steady current, which will protect appliances from any surges.

Batteries

Deep-cycle batteries are ideal in solar applications. Preferably, you'll invest in solar specific models to get the most out of your system. Flooded deep-cycle batteries are used most commonly in off-grid applications. They're affordable, easy to maintain, long lasting, and reliable.

The formula for calculating how many batteries are needed is somewhat complex:

1. Multiply your daily estimated power need (for example, 800W) by 1.5 to create a buffer for those times when there's heavier usage (800W × 1.5 = 1.2 kWh).

2. Decide how many days you want to have power stored before needing to recharge batteries (for example, 2 days). Bear in mind that the more days you add, the more expensive your system will be.

3. Multiply the buffered daily wattage estimate by how many days you want power autonomy (1.2 kWh × 2 = 2,400).

4. Next, multiply this number by 2 (2,400 × 2 = 4,800).

5. Divide this number by 12V or 24V, depending on which system voltage you chose. For this example, 4,800 ÷ 24V = 200Ah. That means your minimum Ah capacity is 200Ah.

6. Divide this number by your battery's rating, and you have the number of batteries needed.

Batteries are extremely heavy and can weigh more than 100 pounds each. Finding a place to install them in a THOW is challenging not only because of this weight, but also because of the required venting to the exterior. Many tiny house folks end up installing batteries on the tongue side of their trailers in small, custom-made utility closets. Remember to factor this weight into your load distribution calculations to ensure a safe and pleasant towing experience.

Solar Panels

There are various options on the market and they differ in material, size, power capacity, and cost. Solar panels can be installed on THOW roofs, but remember that overall height is measured to the tallest point of a trailer. Be sure you stay under the legal height limit.

Consider installing some type of removable protective panel that can cover your panels while you're in transit so as not to damage them. Park your THOW so that the solar panels face south. To maximize solar gain, mount the brackets on the roof so they install at approximately a 30-degree angle.

This photo of Andrew shows the size of a 1.6 kWh solar array mounted on a pole. The pole is 8 feet deep and supported by tons of poured concrete to prevent any uplift in case of high winds.

You can find tiny house–appropriate solar solutions and options in the RV industry. Look for roof-mount options as well as portable solar kits. For example, depending on your power needs, you could potentially get away with the totally portable Goal Zero Yeti 1250 Solar Generator, which weighs just 103 pounds. The Goal Zero solar panels can be roof-, wall-, or ground-mounted.

Use these steps to calculate how many panels are required:

1. First, you'll need to know your daily power needs (for example, 800W).

2. Add a 25 percent cushion to that value (800W × .25 = 200W; 800W + 200W = 1 kWh).

3. Calculate how many hours of sunlight you can expect in your area (found on the internet on a solar map).

4. Divide your daily kWh needs by the number of daily peak sunlight hours, which is 5 hours in our area. That means 1,000 ÷ 5 = 200.

In this example, a 200W solar panel sitting in 4 hours of sunshine should produce enough electricity to get you through the day.

Backup Power

When the sun isn't shining and the 10-day forecast looks bleak, you'll need a way of charging your deep-cycle batteries. The most common backup source is a gas-powered generator. There are numerous models and sizes out there, so choose the one that can recharge your battery bank's capacity.

Spare any neighbors (and yourself) tons of noise pollution by choosing a unit with whisper-quiet technology. Seek out models with an eco-throttle option and save on gas, too. If you don't plan on running large power tools from your generator, a smaller one should do the trick. If you plan on being mobile, you'll likely place the generator in the living area during transit and then move it outdoors once you're parked.

Sourcing Water

If you plan on parking or building your tiny house on a rural piece of land with no existing water services, you'll need to find a solution. The most common solutions are wells, rain catchment, and water delivery services.

Making a choice between the three is largely a function of how long you intend on living on the land and the size of your budget. The most expensive solution is typically a well. If you don't plan on living in the same place for more than five or so years, you might want to consider the other two options.

Well

A well is typically the safest and most reliable water source on rural land. Unfortunately, wells can be very expensive ($3,000 to $15,000 or more) and represent a major investment in a tiny house budget. The well on our property cost $8,000 and ended up being 280 feet deep.

When looking for land, always speak with neighbors and look at well records. Not every place has water that can be reached by drilling a well. For example, there are some areas in New Mexico where even 800-foot-deep exploratory holes yielded no water.

Despite modern-day technologies, it can actually be very challenging to pinpoint the best location for drilling a well. The best well-drilling companies can do is survey geologic maps, look at well records for the area, and analyze other pieces of data. Many companies utilize a technique known as "water witching," which, despite the name, is a reliable and commonplace practice to locate groundwater. We hired a water witcher to locate the site for our well and were quite impressed by the speed and accuracy of the process. Ultimately though, there's no guarantee that they'll find water, and whether they do or not, you're the one stuck with the bill.

After your well is drilled and cased, you'll need to get the water from the bottom of the well to your house. For this, you'll need a pump and pipe attached to a rope, which is lowered into the water column. You'll also most likely need a pressure tank. This tank stores water under pressure and supplies flow to each point of use as needed. Pressure tanks are too large to be installed inside a tiny house, so they must be placed either in a pump house or some other structure.

A great alternative to a pressure tank is a gravity-fed system. If you have a hill on your property and plan on building below it, you can set up such a system. Place a 500-gallon storage tank about 100 feet above your tiny house. Plumb your system so that a buried water line carries water from your well to the holding tank, and another travels from the tank to your tiny house water shut-off valve.

A gravity-fed system spares the off-grid homeowner the expenditure of a larger solar system needed to power a pressure tank. This is the setup we have here at hOMe and it works perfectly. We manually kick on our well pump once every four to six weeks on a day we know we'll get about four hours of direct sunshine on our panels. This is about how long it takes to fill our 1,500-gallon storage tank. The rest of the time, gravity does the work for us and provides adequate pressure for comfortable showers and for our water heater.

Trucked-In Water Systems

If a well is out of your budget or you don't plan on living on the same piece of property for more than a few years, you can always install a storage tank and have water trucked in. A 1,500-gallon tank holds enough water for full-time use by four adults for about four to six weeks. A tiny house with only one or two occupants could likely get away with just a 500-gallon tank. It all depends on how often you want to get it filled and how much space you have on your land to store a tank.

Storage tanks aren't terribly expensive and can even be found used. You'll need to install a pump (unless gravity fed) inside to deliver the water to your tiny house. These systems are quite simple and are certainly within the grasp of the DIY builder.

Rainwater Catchment

You are lucky if you live in a region with year-round rainfall potential because you might be able to harvest your own water in a rain catchment system. A 1-inch rainfall on a 200-square-foot roof can gift you with 150 gallons of beautiful fresh water at no cost to you (besides the cistern).

Rainwater catchment systems divert water from the roof via a gutter and into a storage tank or cistern. Cisterns can be stored above or below ground and can be made of plastic, concrete, steel, or fiberglass. A pump placed at the bottom of the cistern makes easy work of delivering water to your tiny house.

If you plan on drinking this water, use a metal roof on your tiny house because some other materials can contribute a lot of toxins. Install a high-quality filtration system to ensure your drinking water is free of any contaminants.

If your area only receives seasonal rainfall, you might want to consider installing more storage tanks or creating a hybrid rain catchment/water-delivery system. This allows you to take advantage of free and local water when the getting's good, but not run out during dry months.

Believe it or not, some states *own* the rights to rainfall and make rainwater harvest illegal. However, most have no restrictions whatsoever, and some states even have special incentives in place to try and abate the burden on municipal water systems. Check in with your local regulators to be sure you won't have any issues and to determine if there is an incentive program in place.

To Summarize

The term *off-grid* means different things to different people; regardless of other's perceptions, you should pursue the lifestyle that is the best fit for you. Gauging alternative energy needs is a big step in moving toward power independence. When you know roughly how much energy you use on a daily basis, you can begin weighing alternative energy generation options. Solar systems have become less and less expensive through government rebates and incentives in recent years, making this a great time to go solar. Water solutions such as rain-catchment systems exist for off-grid applications even if you don't want to drill a well.

Glossary

365-day rule A system for thinning out material possessions in which any item that hasn't been used within a year gets placed into a pile for potential discard/giveaway.

accent wall An area within a larger wall finished differently with intention of creating a visual point of interest.

Accessory Dwelling Unit (ADU) A secondary dwelling built on a lot with a primary residence. ADUs can be created within the primary residence, as an addition to an existing house, or can be a totally separate dwelling.

acrylonitrile-butadiene-styrene (ABS) A plastic material used in plumbing applications.

actual cash value (ACV) coverage An insurance valuation term referring to a property's worth at current market prices.

adjustable rate mortgage (ARM) A mortgage loan with a periodically adjusted interest rate.

air admittance valves (AAVs) Code-approved, under-the-sink venting solutions.

alternating tread devices (ATDs)   Stairs in which each tread staggers from the next one, allowing for a steeper angle, and thus, less floor space to be taken up in a tiny house.

American National Standards Institute (ANSI)   A code development agency that regulates construction standards for RVIA-certified vehicles including Tiny Houses On Wheels.

anchor bolts   Bolts that are threaded, rod-welded, or otherwise attached to a trailer that are integral to the safe attachment of wall systems to a frame.

angel investor   An individual who provides capital for an investment typically in exchange for ownership equity.

arc fault circuit interrupter (AFCI)   An electrical receptacle that breaks a circuit when it detects an electrical arc.

architectural scale   A triangular-shaped ruler used to create various scale options on a set of architectural plans.

bottom plate   A horizontal framing member placed atop floor sheathing and to which studs are connected.

British thermal unit (BTU)   The amount of energy needed to raise the temperature of 1 pound of water by 1 degree Fahrenheit.

builder's risk insurance   This type of insurance provides coverage during the construction process in the case of loss, theft, or damage; it does not include liability coverage.

building codes   A set of enforceable standards used to specify safe construction practices.

bump-out   A bump-out in a residential structure is an extension in a room that creates a projection in a wall plane. In an RV, it's a wall that slides out to create additional interior space.

bumper pull trailer   The most common form of trailer on the market. The trailer's tongue attaches to a ball hitch that juts straight out from the towing vehicle's frame.

butt joint   A joint in which two pieces of material meet flush to each other, forming a 90-degree angle to the material in question.

capsule wardrobe   A collection of only essential clothing items.

ceiling joist   A horizontal framing member connected to the double top plate.

certificate of occupancy (COO)   A certificate that gives a homeowner the green light to live in their new residence full-time.

closed-cell spray foam   Dense spray foam insulation material.

collar tie   A horizontal framing member connecting two rafters on a gable roof.

concrete pad and pier foundation   A foundation system in which load paths are concentrated over individual columns and footers.

concrete slab on grade   A foundation system in which the concrete serves as the foundation and also the flooring base.

contingency fund   An emergency fund often built into a loan in case of unexpected expenses during the construction process.

corner stud assembly   A vertical framing member placed at corner locations.

cripple stud   A vertical framing member installed above and/or below doors, windows, and headers; it never touches the bottom and top plates at the same time.

Department of Transportation (DOT)   A federal cabinet department concerned with transportation. The DOT can certify a tiny house as a *load on a trailer*.

detail section flags   Identification flags that give the location and direction of the building detail to which they refer; there are a variety of types, including building section flags, detail flags, and exterior elevation flags.

direct vent heater   A heater with a ventilation channel that vents directly to the home's exterior.

door schedule   On architectural plans, a door schedule details the structure's door information.

dormer   A window that projects vertically from a roof, creating a bump-out.

dried-in   When the exterior envelope (siding, roofing, windows, and doors) are installed in a house.

drop axle trailer   A trailer that allows for about 4 inches of added headroom in a THOW.

emergency egress   Doors, windows, and emergency access loft windows that provide escape routes for building inhabitants.

energy recovery ventilator (ERV)   A mechanical system that provides conditioned fresh air to a home by means of exchange.

expanded polystyrene (EPS)   A rigid foam insulation product.

extruded polystyrene (XPS)   A rigid foam insulation product.

fifth-wheel trailer   A system in which the trailer connects to a pickup truck with a hinged plate.

floor plan   An architectural representation of a structure or room from a bird's eye point-of-view.

foundation plans   Details on a set of architectural plans that highlight how to construct the foundation.

full-timer's RV insurance   A policy extended by certain insurance companies to people living full-time in their RVs.

gable roof   A roof design in which both roof sides angle up to a gable peak.

gooseneck trailer   A system in which the trailer slides over a ball hitch in a pickup truck bed.

Gross Trailer Weight Rating (GTWR)   The total weight of a trailer when loaded to capacity, including the trailer itself and any loads.

Gross Vehicle Weight Rating (GVWR)   The total weight of a vehicle when loaded to capacity, including the vehicle itself and any loads plus people.

ground fault circuit interrupter (GFCI) plugs   Plugs designed to shut off an electric circuit when a current is flowing along an undesired path (such as through water or a person).

header   A horizontal framing member placed above a door, window, or other opening.

heat recover ventilator (HRV)   A mechanical system that provides conditioned fresh air to a home by means of exchange.

homeowner's insurance policy   A standard policy that protects a house, its contents, and the property the home sits on; liability coverage is included, too.

homeowners association (HOA)   An association that governs a planned development, such as a condo, townhouse, or neighborhood, to which homeowners pay maintenance dues.

Housing and Urban Development (HUD)   A federal organization tasked with developing affordable housing in the United States. It regulates construction standards of manufactured housing as well as other tasks.

HTT4   Heavy-duty metal brackets used when connecting wall framing systems to a trailer frame.

hurricane clips   Metal clips used to anchor roofing systems to the wall systems to withstand high-wind events.

HVAC system   Heating, ventilation, and air condition systems involved in climate control.

in-line vents   An integral part of the plumbing system designed to enable P-traps to retain water.

inland marine insurance policy   Insurance for property in transit over land.

insurance endorsement   A document attached to an insurance policy that amends the policy in some way.

insurance rider   An insurance add-on that provides additional coverage benefits.

International Code Council (ICC)   An organization that develops construction standards and codes for the construction industries.

International Residential Code (IRC)   Construction code used for one- and two-family dwelling unit construction in the United States and its territories.

item priority circle drawing   An architectural drawing technique that creates bubble representations of various rooms in a floor plan.

jack stand   A vertical support member designed to carry trailer loads.

king stud   A vertical framing member placed on either side of a door or window, running from bottom plate to top plate.

live load   Any consistent load exerted on a structure.

load on a trailer   Any item carried on a trailer. A permit can sometimes be issued by the DOT in which a tiny house is considered a load on a trailer.

load path   The path through which loads pass from the highest point in a structure through the wall systems, floor, foundation, and eventually to the ground.

maximum vehicle height   The tallest that a trailer may be in order to be road legal without the use of special permits. In most states, it's 13'6", while in some it's 14'6".

maximum width limit   The widest that a trailer may be to be road legal without the use of special permits. In most states, it's 8'6".

metal strapping   Continuous banding made of differing gauges of galvanized steel used to secure structures to the ground.

mini-split   A small-space conditioning system that sometimes includes both heating and cooling in the same device.

miter joint   A joint in which two opposing angles are cut to equal the total angle of the joint.

moisture barrier   Membrane installed on exterior face of a wall to eliminate movement of moisture into a house.

municipality   Any city or town with corporate status and a local governing body.

National Electric Code (NEC)   Standards used for code enforcement of electrical installations in the United States.

open-cell spray foam   A spray foam insulation product that is less dense than closed-cell foam.

Pacific West Associates, Inc. (PWA)   A fee-based, third-party inspection program designed for tiny houses.

perimeter concrete foundation   A continuous concrete wall atop concrete footers designed to support structural loads above it.

permanent foundation   A foundation permanently attached to the ground.

permanent wood foundation   A continuous foundation wall built from pressure treated wood in combination with drainage rock.

PEX   A flexible plastic material often used in plumbing applications.

pigtail   A small length of wire attached to the main electrical wires inside an electrical box.

pintle hitch   A hook and loop trailer hitch designed to carry heavy loads.

plat   A scaled map showing divisions of a piece of land.

polyiso (ISO)   A rigid foam insulation product.

PVC A plastic composite material used in plumbing applications.

R-value The insulation potential of a material.

rafter A framing member that supports the roof sheathing.

rainscreen A construction system designed to provide ventilation behind siding in order to improve durability and eliminate excess moisture in a wall system.

Recreational Vehicle Industry Association (RVIA) An organization tasked with promoting the RV industry. It's also in charge of adopting and enforcing construction safety standards.

renter's insurance policy An insurance policy providing coverage for the contents in a rental property; the structure itself, however, is not covered.

replacement cost coverage (RCC) An insurance option that replaces contents at current market value without taking depreciation into consideration.

ridge beam A horizontal framing member that supports the end rafter at the ridge.

riser The vertical portion of each step on a set of stairs.

Romex The most common type of electrical wiring on the residential construction market.

roof dormer A vertical opening in a gabled roof line that increases the amount of usable space in a loft.

room-relationship bubble sketch A series of simple hand-drawn circles that represents the rooms in a house.

rough opening (R.O.) The space left open in a framed wall assembly to accommodate the future placement of a door or window.

rough sill A horizontal framing member placed below a rough window opening; it is attached to the cripple stud below the R.O., and the trimmer and king studs on the side.

rule of thirds A composition concept used in photography to visually add interest to the subject.

RVIA certification The seal of approval given to a participating builder that has met RVIA standards.

RVIA manufacturer   A construction company that has passed the RVIA certification process.

scale   When proportions between all objects and lines remain the same no matter how large or small a structure is represented.

section   A perspective view on a detail on a set of architectural plans.

septic tank   An underground tank where sewage is collected and permitted to decompose before being carried to a leach field.

shear strength   A structure's ability to resist forces imposed in-line with the plane of the wall.

shed roof   A single sloped roof. In tiny house construction, it's often the roof style that allows for the greatest usable head room in a loft.

ships ladder   A hybrid between stairs and a ladder.

sill plate   A horizontal framing member fastened directly to top of foundation (or trailer).

stair riser   The vertical portion of each step on a set of stairs. It's the part of each step that actually rises the stairs from one tread to the next.

stair tread   The horizontal step on a set of stairs. This is the weight-bearing portion of the stairs.

structural insulated panels (SIPs)   A custom factory-built structural system with embedded high-insulation foam.

structural screws   Specialty screws rated to withstand shear forces.

sway bars   An aftermarket add-on that helps spread loads from the trailer to the tow vehicle's rear axle.

thermal bridging   The process in which heat moves to colder areas.

tiny house   A dwelling that's 400 square feet or less, excluding lofts.

tiny house movement   A collective of people interested in the tiny house lifestyle.

tiny house on foundation (THOF)   A tiny house built on a permanent foundation.

tiny house on skids (THOS)   A tiny house built on a skid system that can be hauled on a trailer or attached to a permanent foundation.

tiny house on wheels (THOW)   A mobile tiny house built on a trailer with wheels.

tiny house shell   A prebuilt tiny house typically completed to the point of being dried-in.

title page   The first page on a set of architectural plans that contains important details about the plans.

tongue weight   Downward force exerted from the trailer tongue to the tow vehicle's hitch.

top plate   A horizontal framing member fastened to the top of wall studs.

trailer brakes   Brakes installed on the trailer and connected electronically to the tow vehicle.

tread   The horizontal step on a set of stairs.

trimmer stud   A vertical framing member placed on the inside of a king stud.

vapor barrier   A protective membrane installed into a structure to seal out moisture.

variance   An official request to deviate from the standards of current zoning requirements.

ventilation   Mechanical systems that exhaust stale air and/or provide fresh air to a home.

virtual private network (VPN)   A security measure added to a web network that encrypts personal information and data.

wall stud   A vertical framing member in a wall system.

wide load permit   A special permit issued to an applicant allowing for the legal transport of a trailer that exceeds normal width limits.

window schedule   On architectural plans, it describes the window information for a structure.

zoning department   This organization is charged with regulating the use of land in a municipality, including where a THOW may be parked.

Resources

General Tiny House Resources

Tiny Home Builders
Jay Shafer
tinyhomebuilders.com

Humble Homes
humble-homes.com

Tiny House Blog
Kent Griswold
tinyhouseblog.com

Tiny House Build
Alexis DeHart Stephens and Christian Parsons
tinyhousebuild.com

The Tiny Life
Ryan Mitchell
thetinylife.com

The Tiny Project
Alek Lisefski
tiny-project.com

Tumbleweed Tiny House Company
Steve Weissmann
tumbleweedhouses.com

Tiny House Workshops

Tiny House Build
Alexis DeHart Stephens and Christian Parsons
tinyhousebuild.com/workshops

Tiny Home Builders
Dan Louche
tinyhomebuilders.com/tiny-house-workshops/hands-on

Daniel Bell Construction
Daniel Bell
danielbellconstruction.com/tiny-house-workshops

Relaxshacks
Derek "Deek" Diedricksen
relaxshacks.blogspot.com

Wild Abundance
Natalie Bogwalker
wildabundance.net/in-person-classes/tiny-house-workshop/

Tiny House Instructional Videos

Tiny House Build
Alexis DeHart Stephens and Christian Parsons
tinyhousebuild.com/how-to-videos

Tiny Home Builders
Dan Louche
tinyhomebuilders.com/tiny-house-videos

Tiny House E-Courses

Tiny House Build
Alexis DeHart Stephens and Christian Parsons
tinyhousebuild.com/free-7-day-ecourse

Tiny Home Builders
Dan Louche
tinyhomebuilders.com

Wild Abundance
Natalie Bogwalker
wildabundance.net/online-classes/online-tiny-house-building-class

Tiny House Construction Plans

Tiny House Build
Alexis DeHart Stephens and Christian Parsons
tinyhousebuild.com/home-plans

Tiny Home Builders
Dan Louche
tinyhomebuilders.com/tiny-house-plans

Portland Alternative Dwellings
Dee Williams
padtinyhouses.com/books-plans

The Tiny Project
Alek Lisefski
tiny-project.com/shop

Sol Haus Design
Vina Lustado
vinastinyhouse.com

Tiny House Communities

Orlando Lakefront
Orlando, Florida
orlandolakefrontth.com

Spur, Texas
spurfreedom.org

Tiny House Community Listings
General Listings
thespruce.com/livable-tiny-house-communities-3984833

Short-Term Tiny House Rentals

Airbnb
airbnb.com

Caravan—The Tiny House Hotel
Portland, OR
facebook.com/caravanthetinyhousehotel

Mount Hood Tiny House Village
Mount Hood, Oregon
mthoodtinyhouse.com

Tiny House Vacations
tinyhousevacations.com

VRBO—Home Away Family
vrbo.com

Wee Casa Tiny House Hotel
Lyons, Colorado
weecasa.com

Tiny House Communities for the Houseless

Community First
Austin, Texas
mlf.org/ptwh

Dignity Village
Portland, Oregon
dignityvillage.org

OM Village
Madison, Wisconsin
occupymadisoninc.com

Opportunity Village and Emerald Village
Eugene, Oregon
squareonevillages.org

Quixote Village
Olympia, Washington
quixotecommunities.org/olympia-quixote-village.html

Second Wind Cottages
Ithaca, New York
secondwindcottages.org

Tiny House Books

Caldwell, Rex. *Wiring a House: Fifth Edition (For Pros By Pros)*. Newtown, CT: Taunton Press, 2014.

Kahn, Lloyd. *Shelter*. Bolinas, CA: Shelter Publications, 2000.

Kondo, Marie. *The Life Changing Magic of Tidying Up*. Berkeley, CA: Ten Speed Press, 2014.

Lidz, Jane. *Rolling Homes: Handmade Houses on Wheels*. New York, NY: A & W Publishers, 1979.

Susanka, Sarah. *The Not So Big House: A Blueprint for the Way We Really Live*. Newtown, CT: Taunton Press, 2009.

Walker, Lester. *Tiny Houses: Or How to Get Away from It All*. New York, NY: Overlook Books, 1987.

Tiny House TV Shows

Tiny House Nation, FYI Network

Tiny House Hunters, HGTV

Tiny House Builders, HGTV

Tiny House: Big Living, HGTV

Tiny House Gatherings

Florida and Georgia Tiny House Festivals
unitedtinyhouse.com

Tiny House Conference
tinyhouseconference.com

Tiny House Jamboree
Colorado Springs, Colorado
tinyhousejamboree.com

Tiny House Funding

Bankrate
bankrate.com/loans/home-improvement/tiny-home-financing

LightStream: A Division of Sun Trust Bank
lightstream.com

Project Lending at The Home Depot
homedepot.com/c/project_loan

Tiny House Insurance

Strategic Insurance Agency (division of Burlingame Insurance)
tinyhome.insure

Titan Tiny Homes
titantinyhomes.com/tiny-house-insurance

Tiny House Builders

Tiny House Listings
Comprehensive List of Tiny House Builders
tinyhouselistings.com

Mitchcraft Tiny Homes
mitchcrafttinyhomes.com

New Frontier Tiny Homes
David Latimer
newfrontiertinyhomes.com

Shelter Wise
shelterwise.com

Tiny Heirloom
tinyheirloom.com

Tiny House Building Company
Kristopher Angstadt
tinyhousebuildingcompany.com

Tiny House Chattanooga
tinyhousechattanooga.com

Tumbleweed Tiny House Company
tumbleweedhouses.com

Wind River Tiny Homes
Jeremy Weaver
windrivertinyhomes.com

Zyl Vardos
zylvardos.com

Tiny House Haulers

Heavy Haul Trucking
heavyhaul.net

Tiny Home Transport
tinyhometransport.com

Tiny House Trailer Manufacturers

Iron Eagle Trailers
ironeagletinyhousetrailer.com/tinyhomes

PJ Trailers
pjtrailers.com/uses/tiny-house-trailers/

Tiny Home Builders
tinyhomebuilders.com/tiny-house-trailers

Tiny House Basics (trailers and shells)
tinyhousebasics.com

Tumbleweed Tiny House Company
tumbleweedhouses.com/diy/tumbleweed-tiny-house-trailers

Tiny House Architects and Designers

Chris Keefe
organicformsdesign.com

Deborah Buelow
cedararch.com

James Herndon and Macy Miller
minimotives.com

Sean David Burke
unboxedhouse.com

Vina Lustado
solhausdesign.com

Index

Numbers

A

B

C

Z